JU

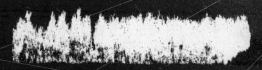

TOKYOPOP Presents
Juline 2 by Narumi Kakinouchi
TOKYOPOP is a registered trademark
of Mixx Entertainment, Inc.
ISBN: 1-892213-85-0
First Printing August 2001

10   9   8   7   6   5   4   3   2

This volume contains the Juline installments from Smile Magazine
issue 3-2 through 3-7 in their entirety.

Translator – Dan Papia. Retouch Artist – Jinky De Leon.
Graphic Designer – Akemi Imafuku. Graphic Assistant – Dao Sirivisal.
Senior Editor - Jake Forbes. Editor - Michael Schuster.
Associate Editor - Katherine Kim. Production Manager – Fred Lui.

Email: editor@press.TOKYOPOP.com
Come visit us at www.TOKYOPOP.com

TOKYOPOP
Los Angeles - Tokyo

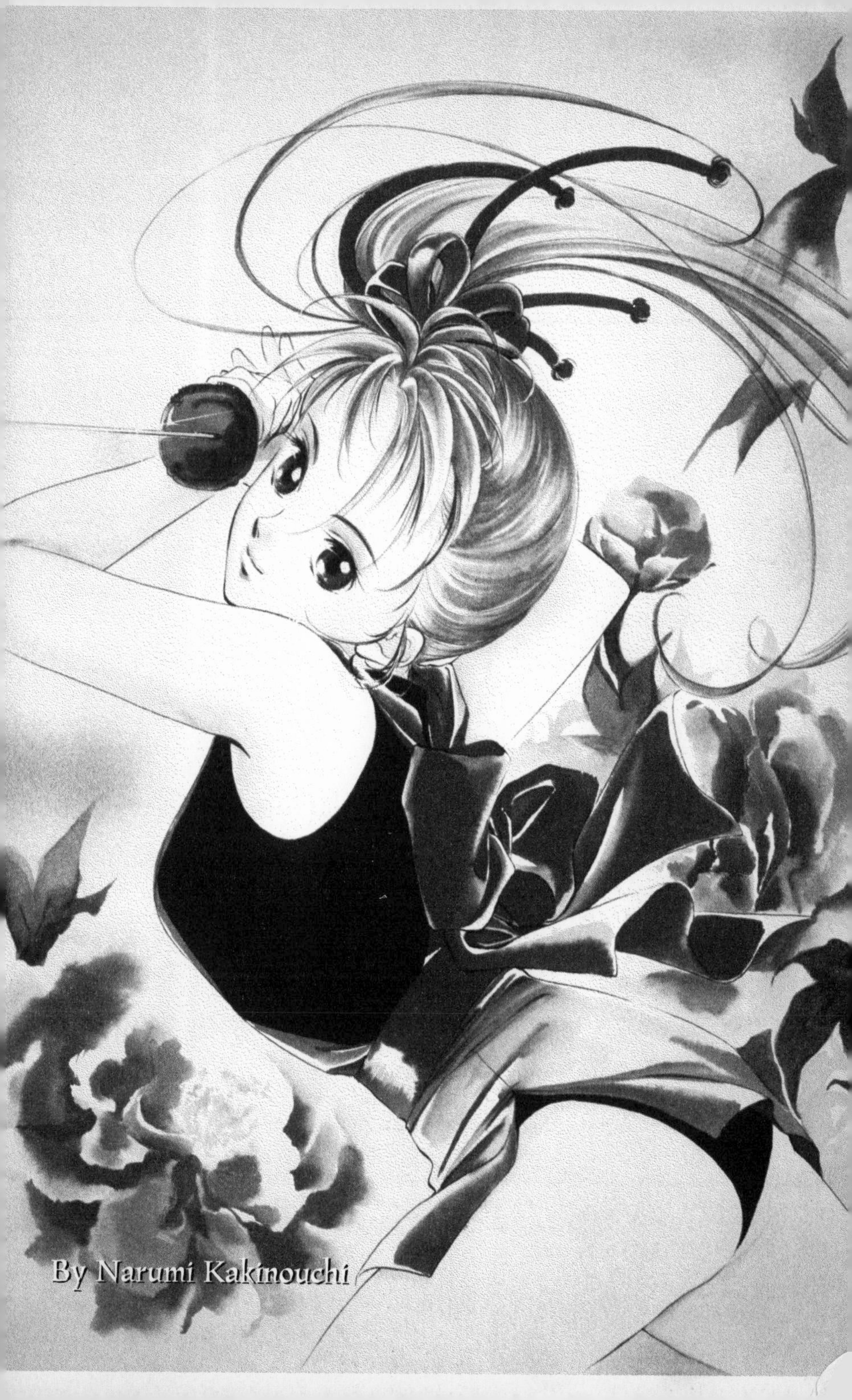

By Narumi Kakinouchi

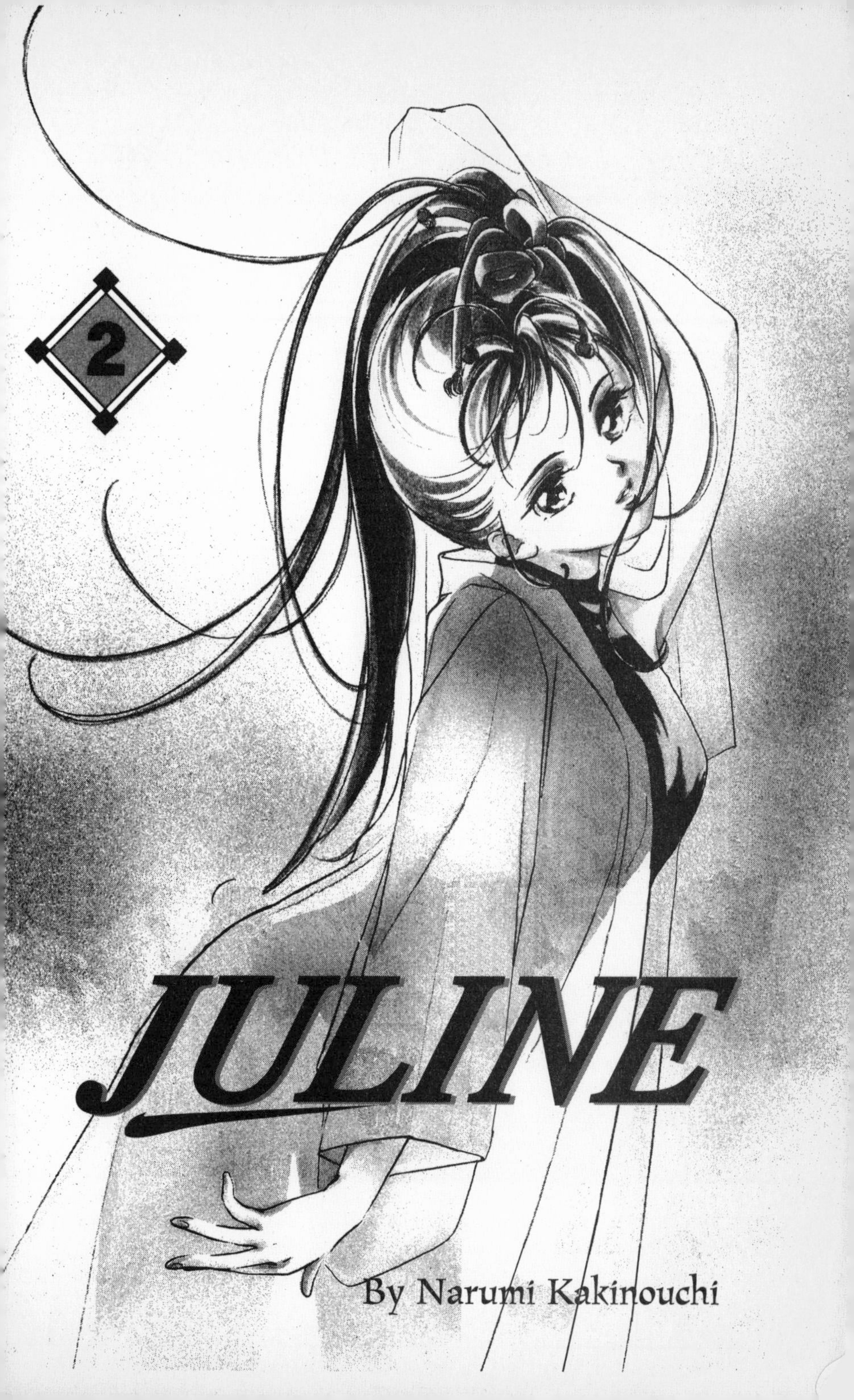
2
JULINE
By Narumi Kakinouchi

Juline • Character Guide

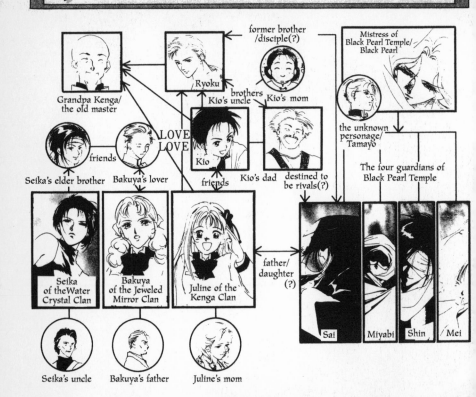

former brother /disciple(?)

Mistress of Black Pearl Temple/ Black Pearl

Ryoku

Kio's uncle — brothers — Kio's mom

Grandpa Kenga/ the old master

the unknown personage/ Tamayo

LOVE LOVE

Kio

The four guardians of Black Pearl Temple

friends

Seika's elder brother   Bakuya's lover   friends   Kio's dad   destined to be rivals(?)

Seika of the Water Crystal Clan

Bakuya of the Jeweled Mirror Clan

Juline of the Kenga Clan

father/ daughter (?)

Sai   Miyabi   Shin   Mei

Seika's uncle   Bakuya's father   Juline's mom

BACKSTORY

A new kung-fu temple has appeared in Juline's neighborhood, the House of the Black Pearls. Fighters from the local dojos are disappearing and defecting to the new dark house ruled by the mysterious Black Pearl (Is she a woman? Is he a man?). Black Pearl has assembled the three special things she believes she needs to rule the world--the jeweled mirror of the Houkyo clan, the water crystal of the Suisho clan, and the ivory sword of Kenga, and yet something still seems to be missing. Perhaps the Kenga princess Juline holds the secret and that's why the strange new student Tamayo Black suddenly appeared at Juline's school (Is she a girl? Is he a boy?). Juline and friends Bakuya, Seika and Kio have stolen onto the secluded grounds of Black Pearl temple and made it away unharmed. But now the Four Guardians of this dark and eerie place have come looking for them...

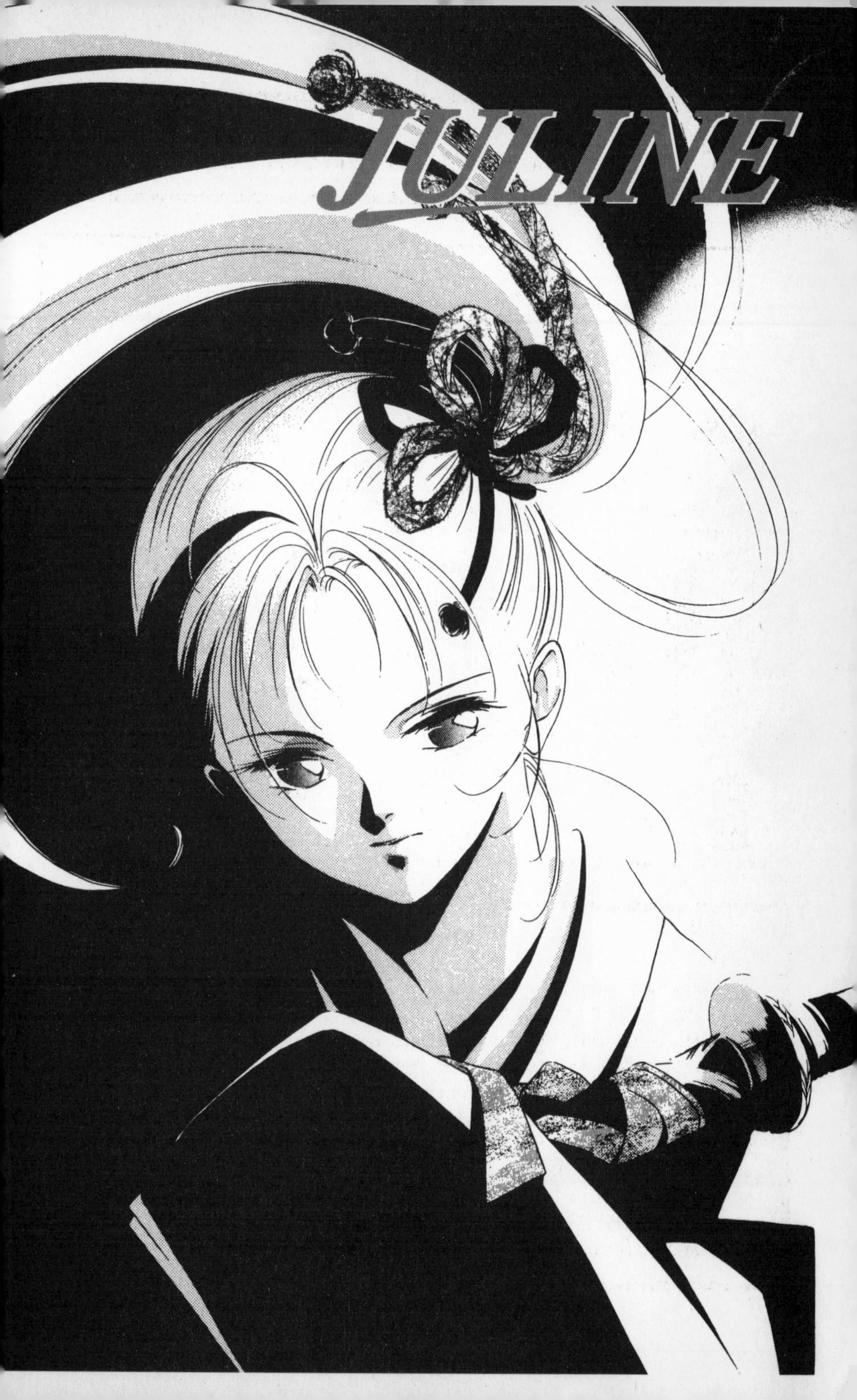
JULINE

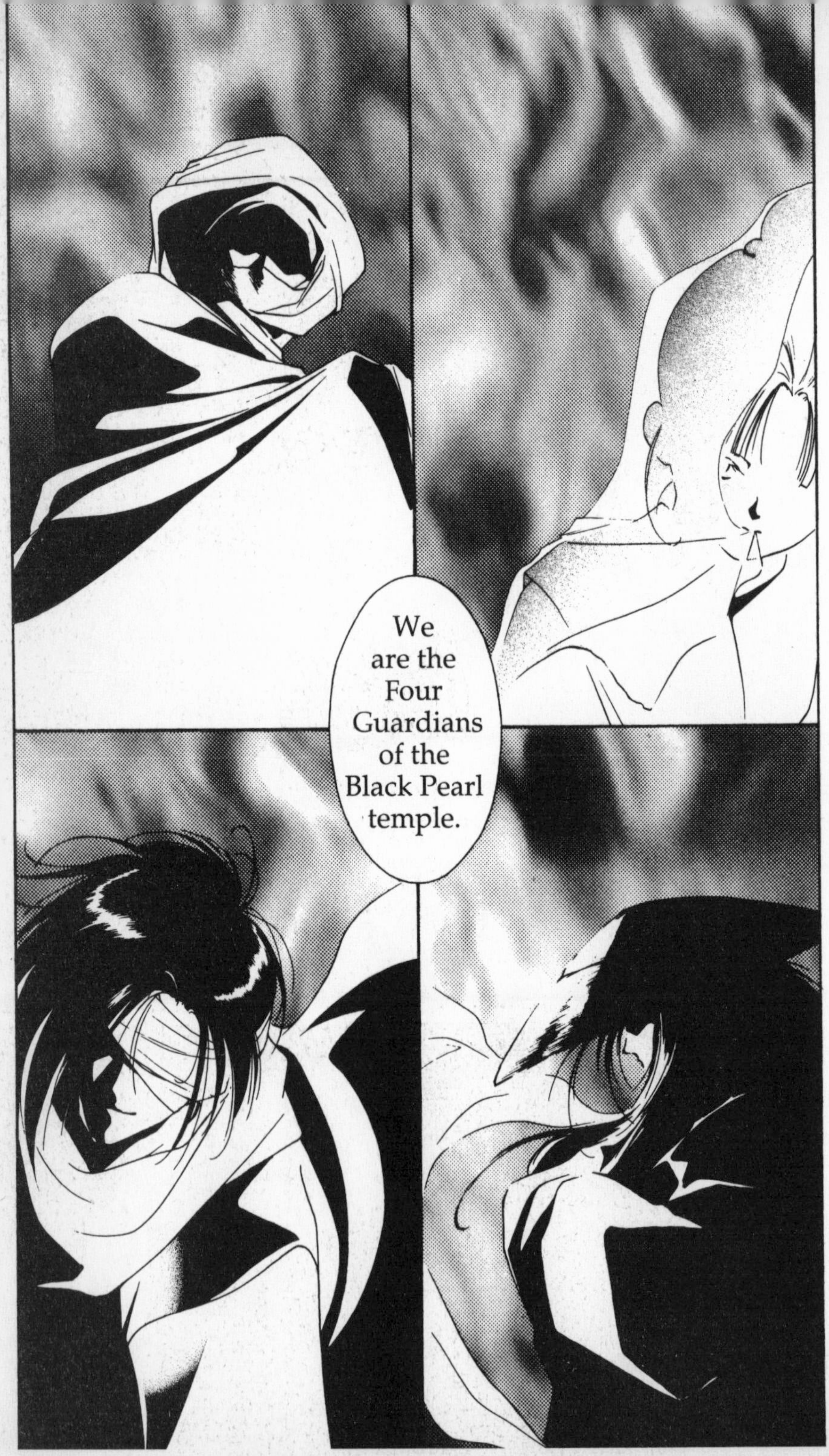
We are the Four Guardians of the Black Pearl temple.

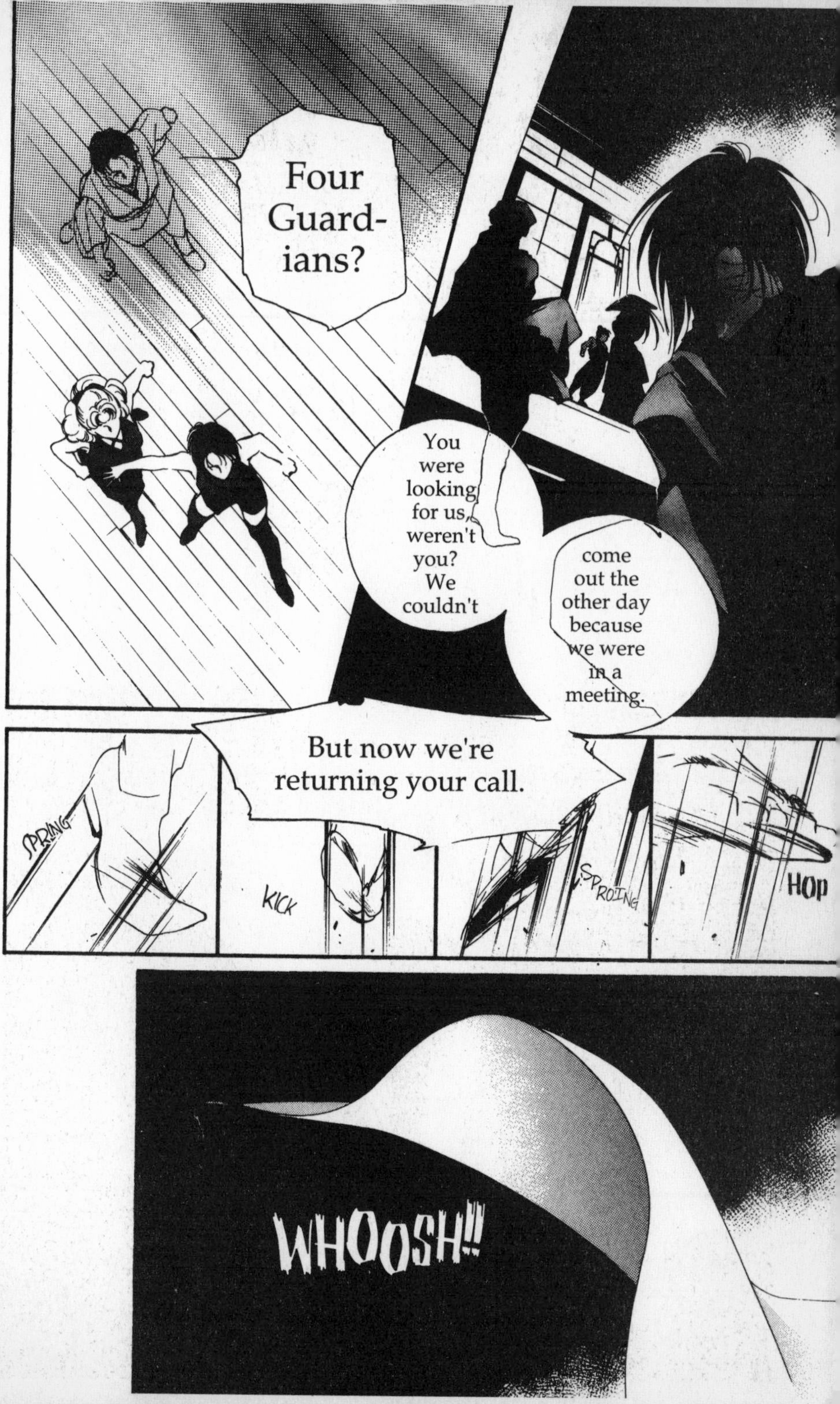

Four Guard-ians?
You were looking for us, weren't you? We couldn't
come out the other day because we were in a meeting.
But now we're returning your call.
SPRING
KICK
SPROING
HOp
WHOOSH!!

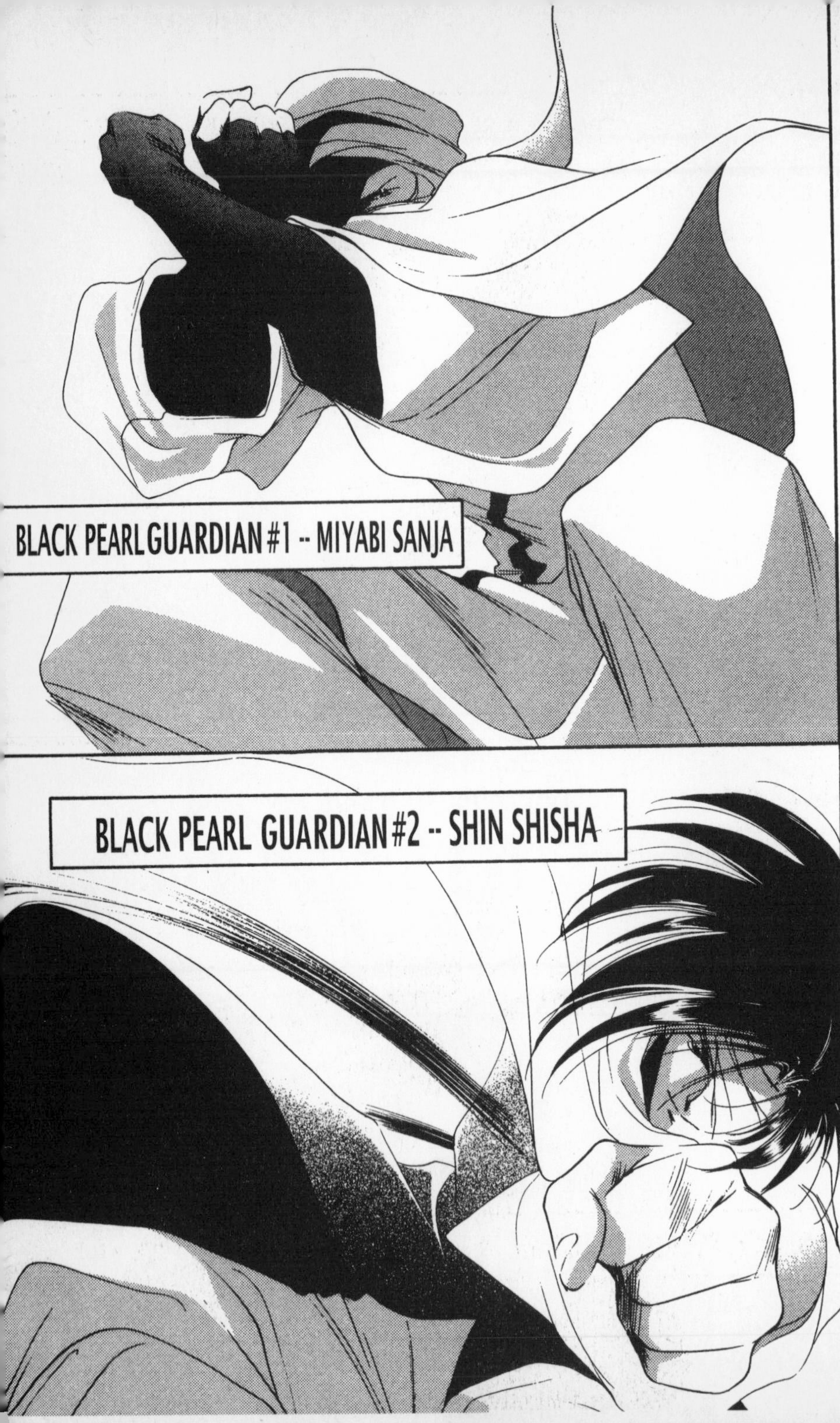
BLACK PEARL GUARDIAN #1 -- MIYABI SANJA
BLACK PEARL GUARDIAN #2 -- SHIN SHISHA

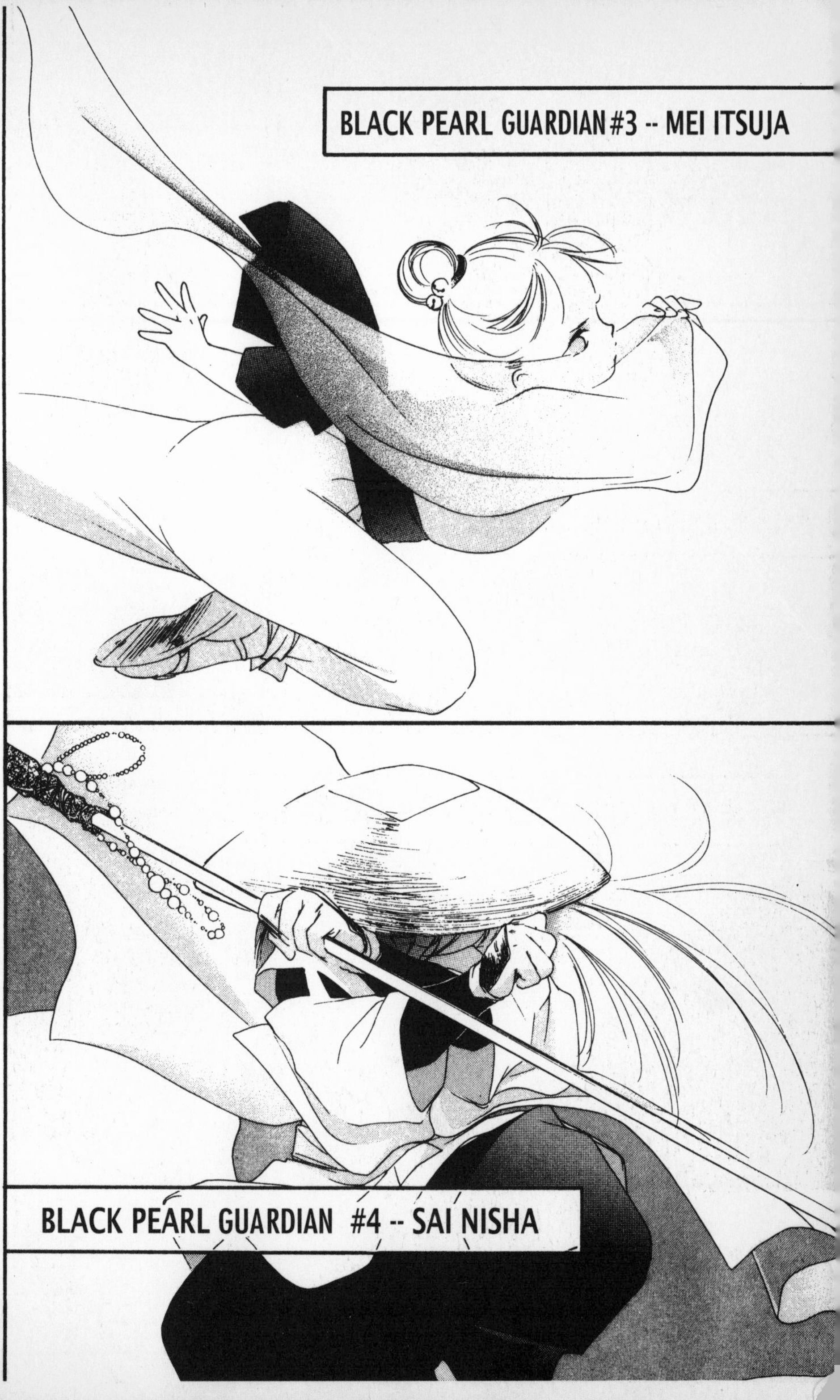
BLACK PEARL GUARDIAN #3 -- MEI ITSUJA
BLACK PEARL GUARDIAN #4 -- SAI NISHA

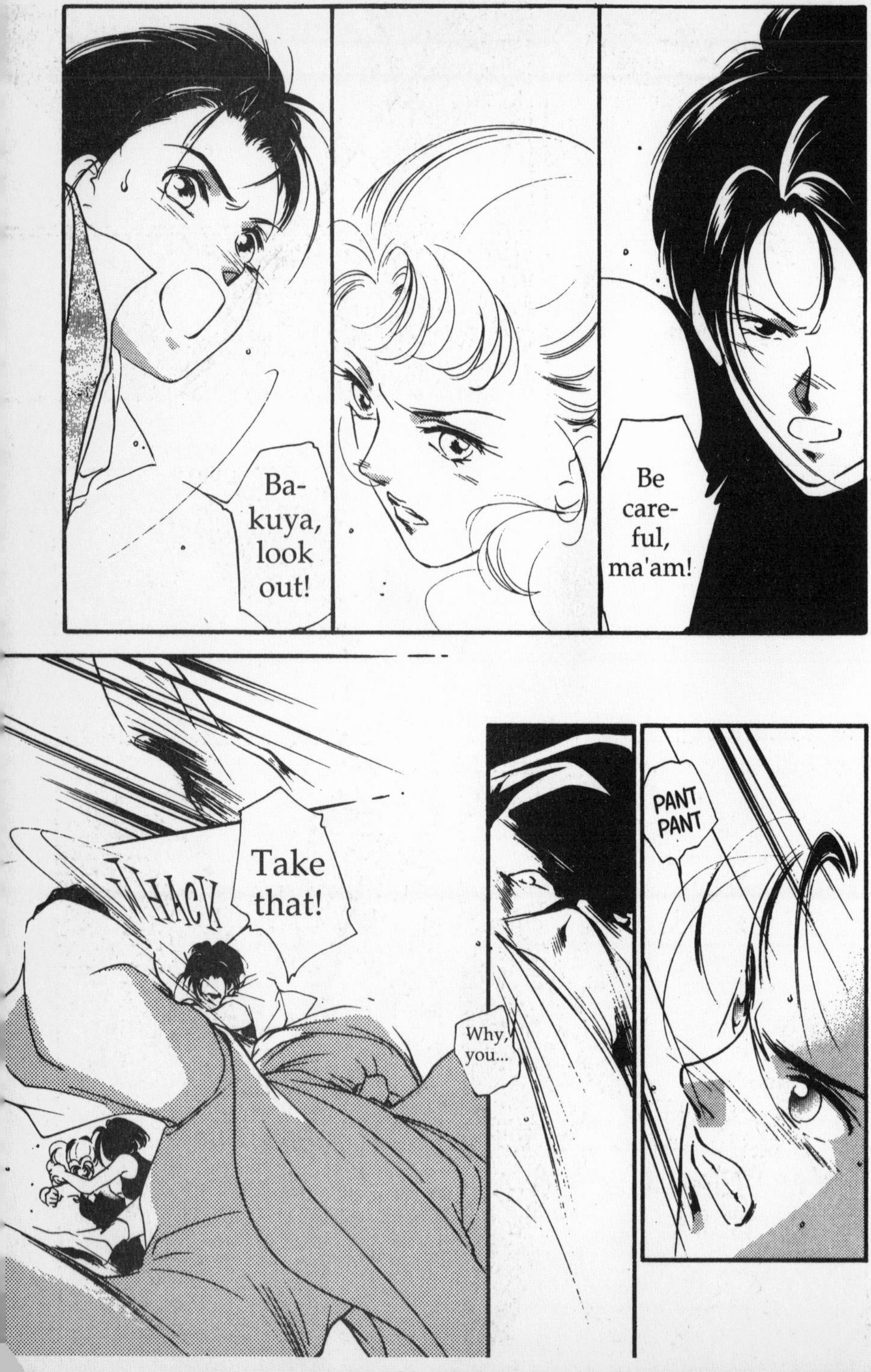
Ba-kuya, look out!
Be care-ful, ma'am!
WHACK
Take that!
Why, you...
PANT PANT

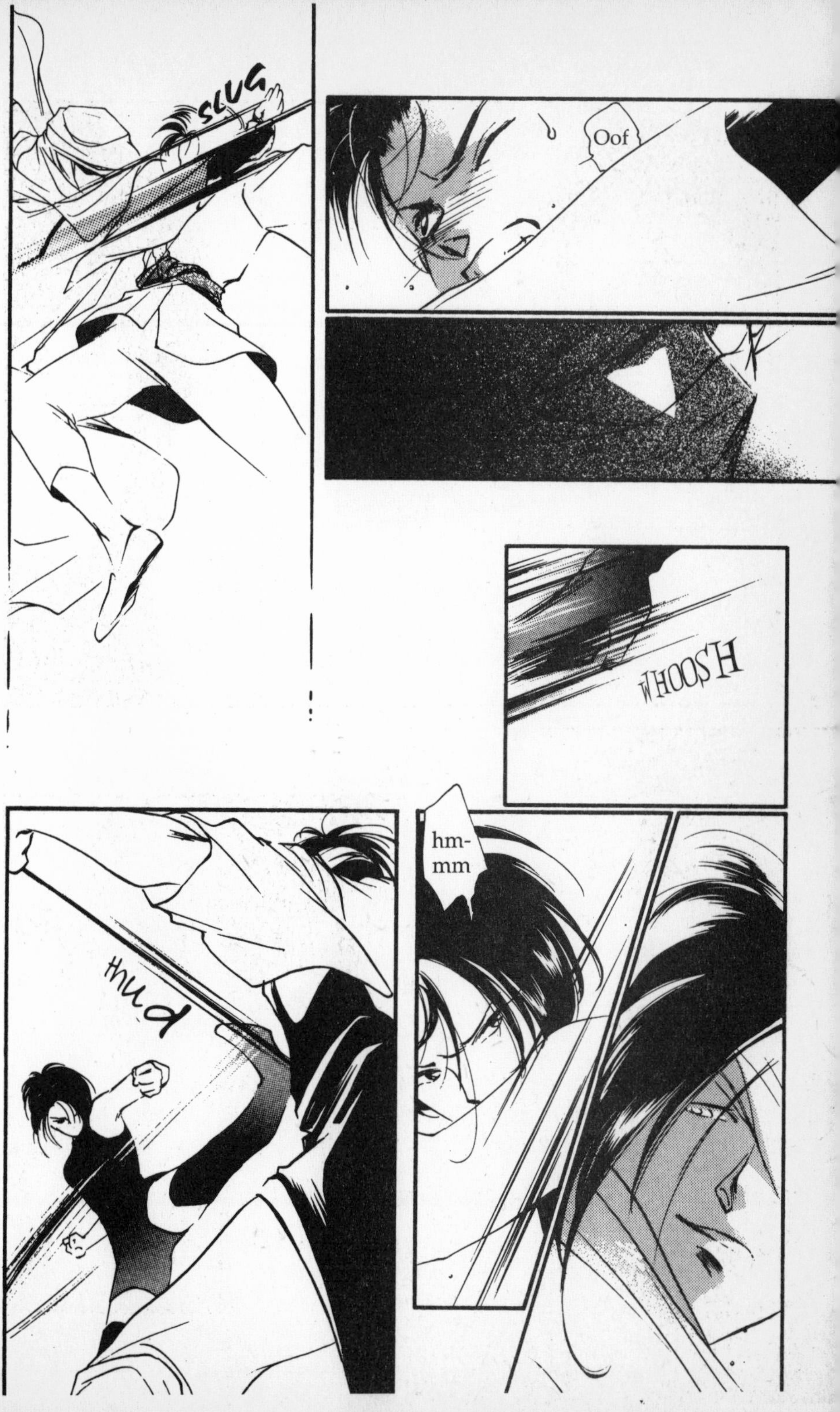
SLUG
Oof
WHOOSH
thud
hm-
mm

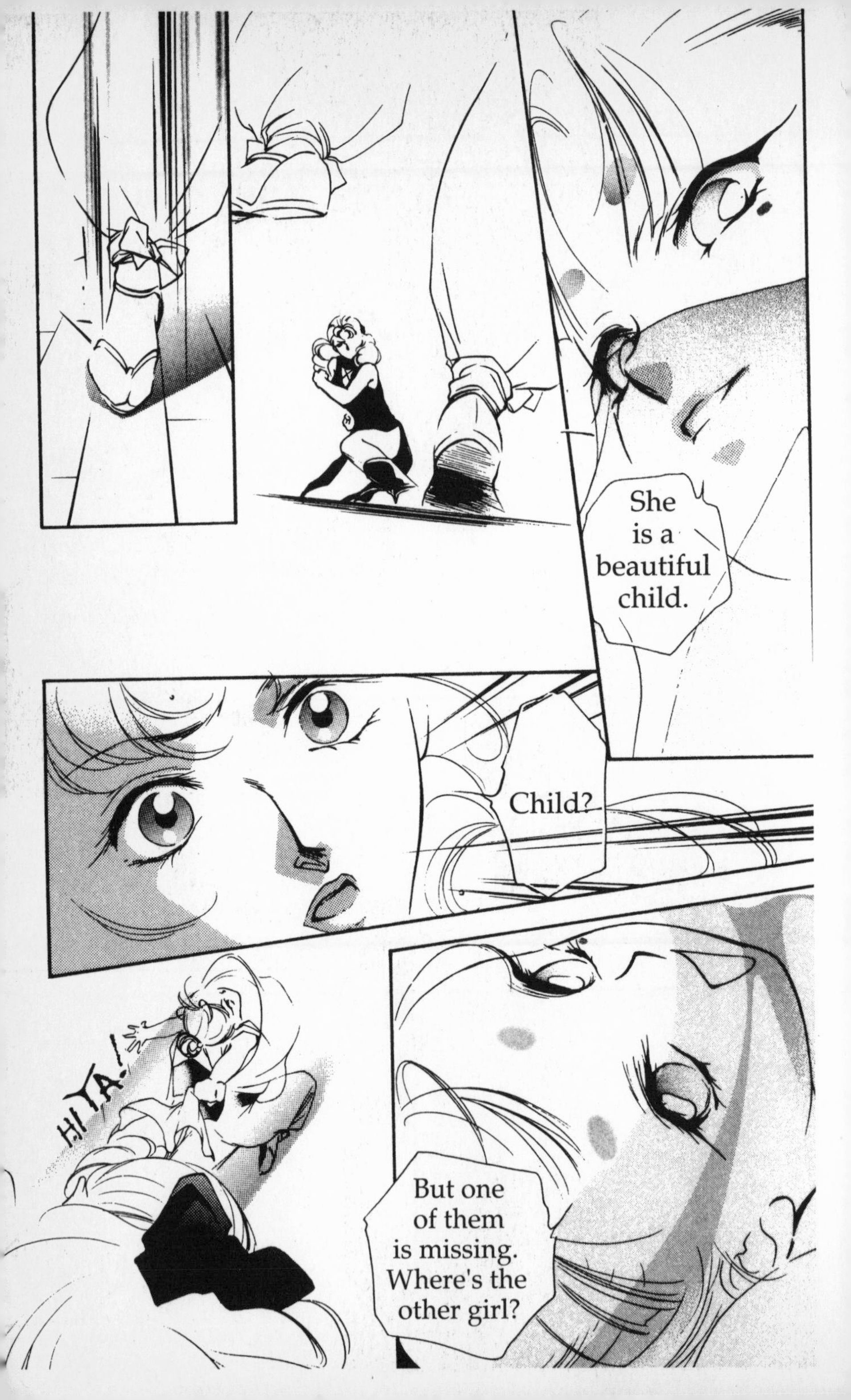
She is a beautiful child.
Child?
HIYA!!
But one of them is missing. Where's the other girl?

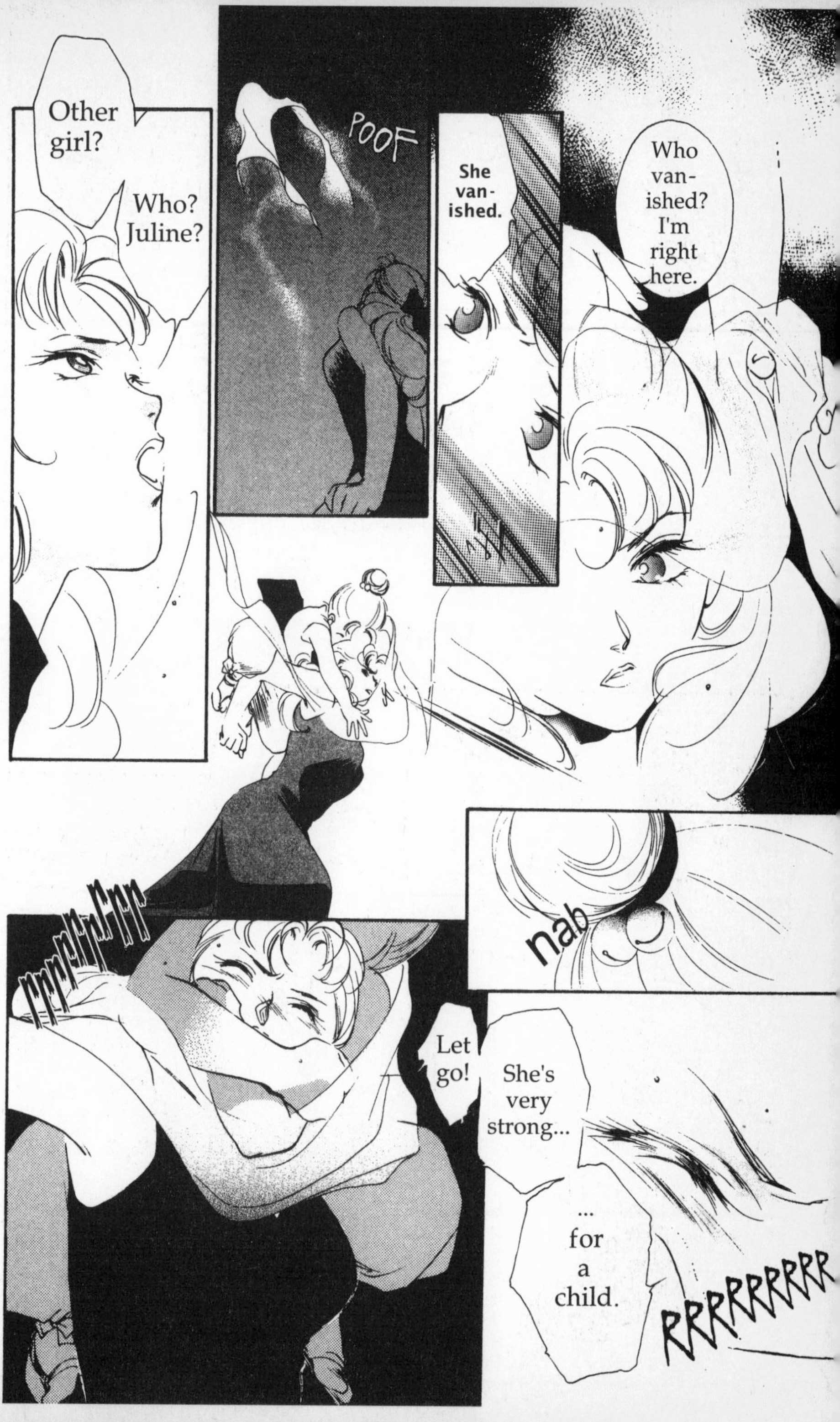

Other girl?
Who? Juline?
POOF
She vanished.
Who vanished? I'm right here.
nab
rrrrrrrrrrrr
Let go!
She's very strong...
... for a child.
RRRRRRRRR

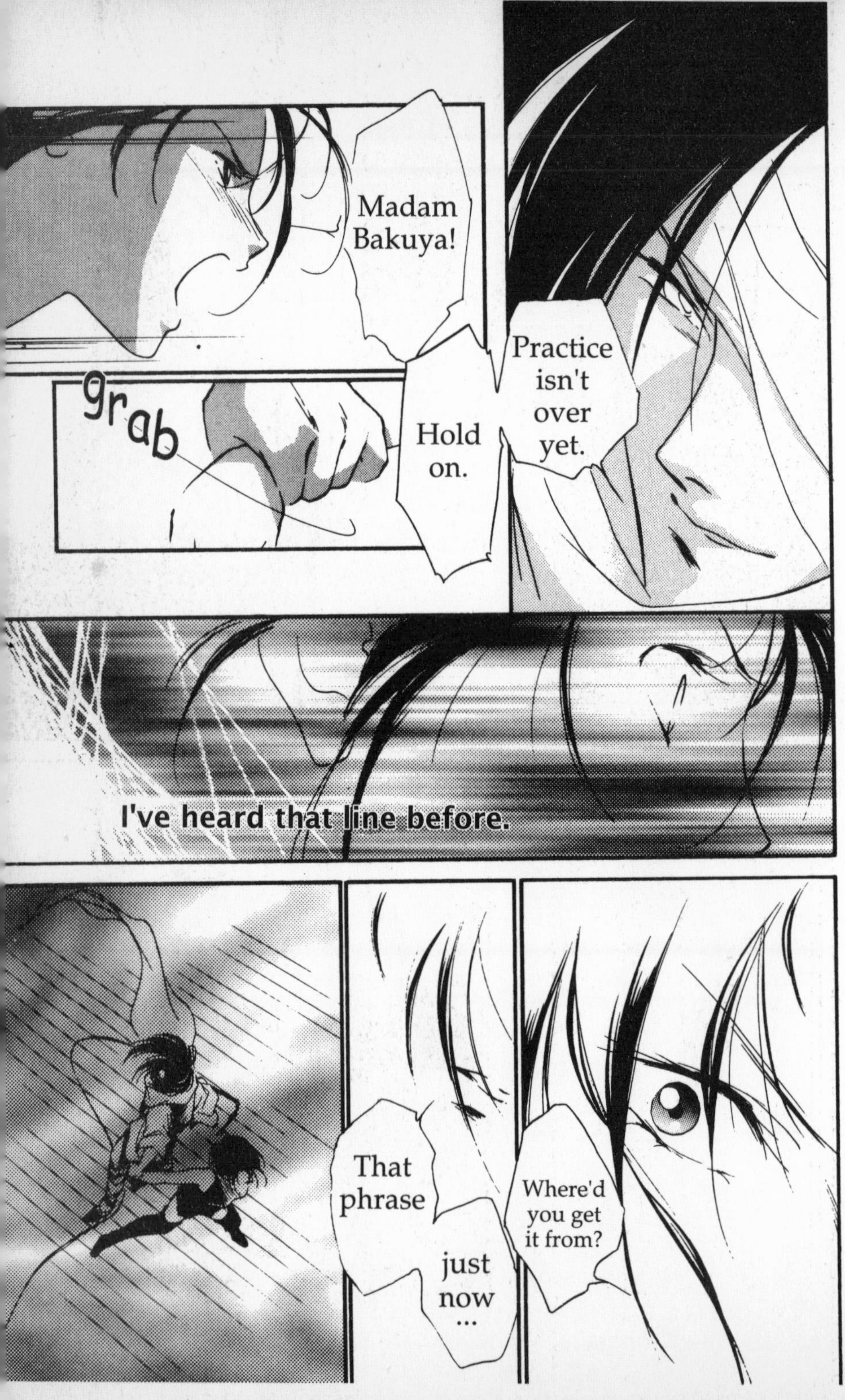
Madam Bakuya!
grab
Hold on.
Practice isn't over yet.
I've heard that line before.
That phrase just now...
Where'd you get it from?

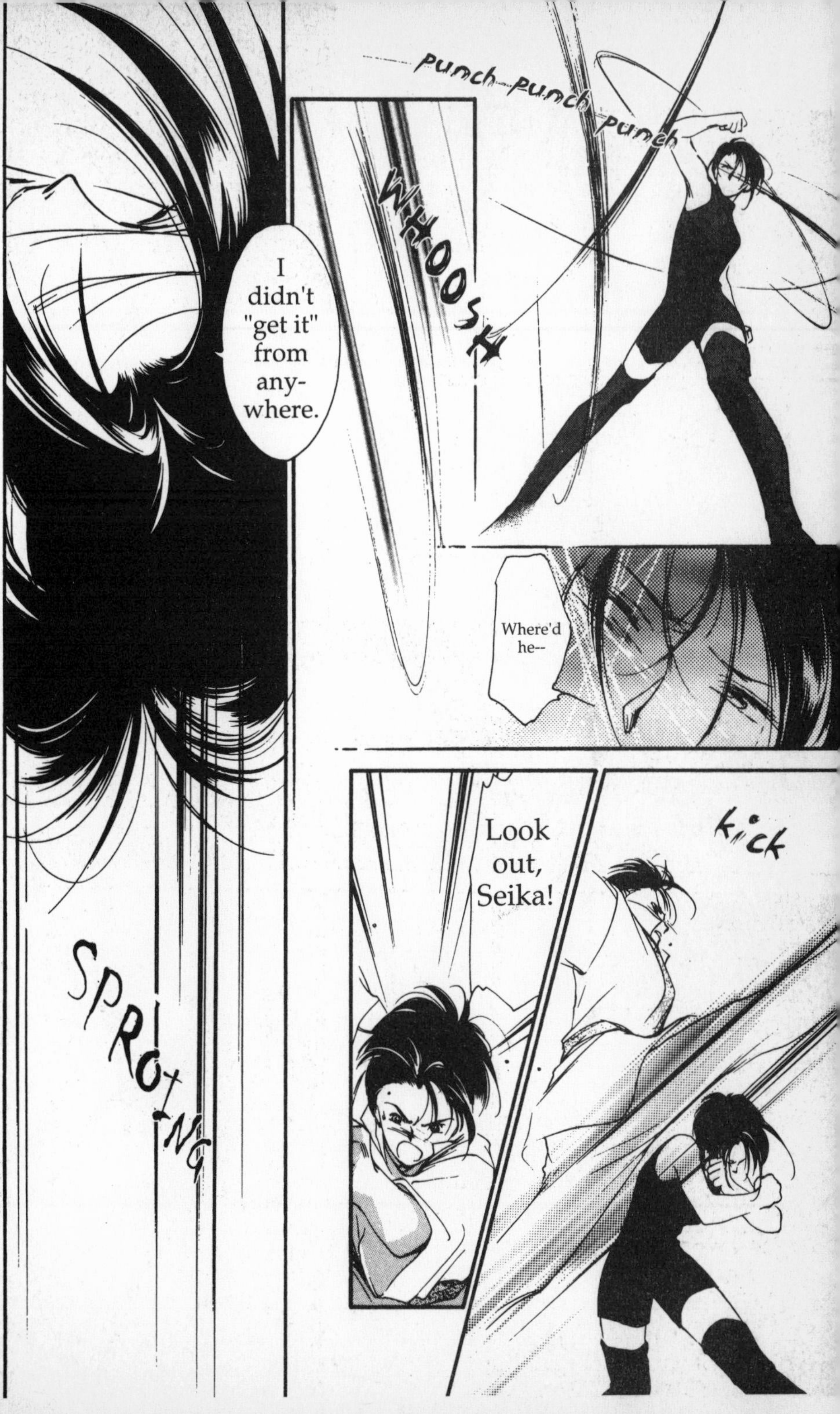
I didn't "get it" from any-where.
SPROING
WHOOSH
punch punch punch
Where'd he--
Look out, Seika!
kick

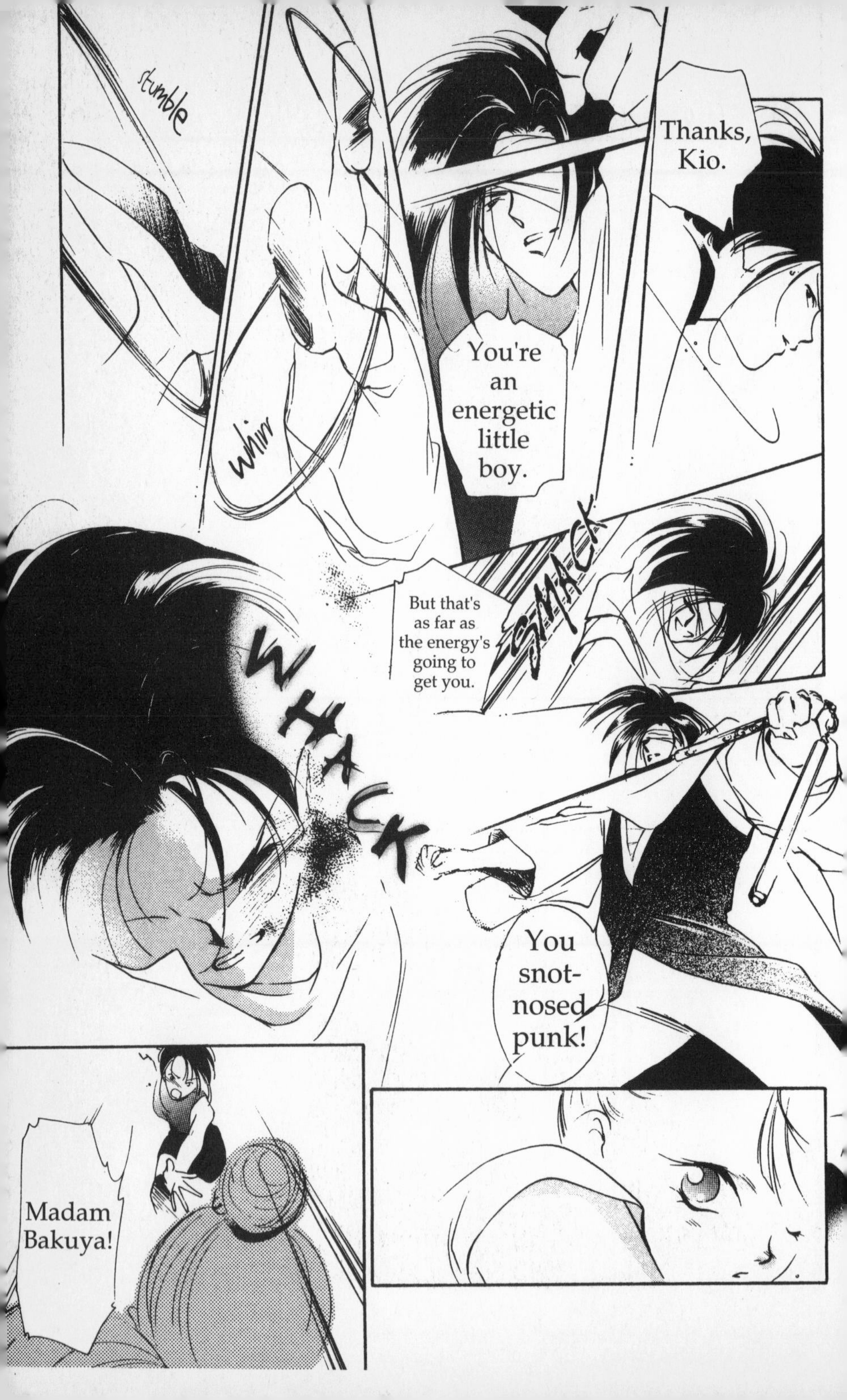
stumble
whirr
You're an energetic little boy.
Thanks, Kio.
But that's as far as the energy's going to get you.
SMACK
WHACK
You snot-nosed punk!
Madam Bakuya!

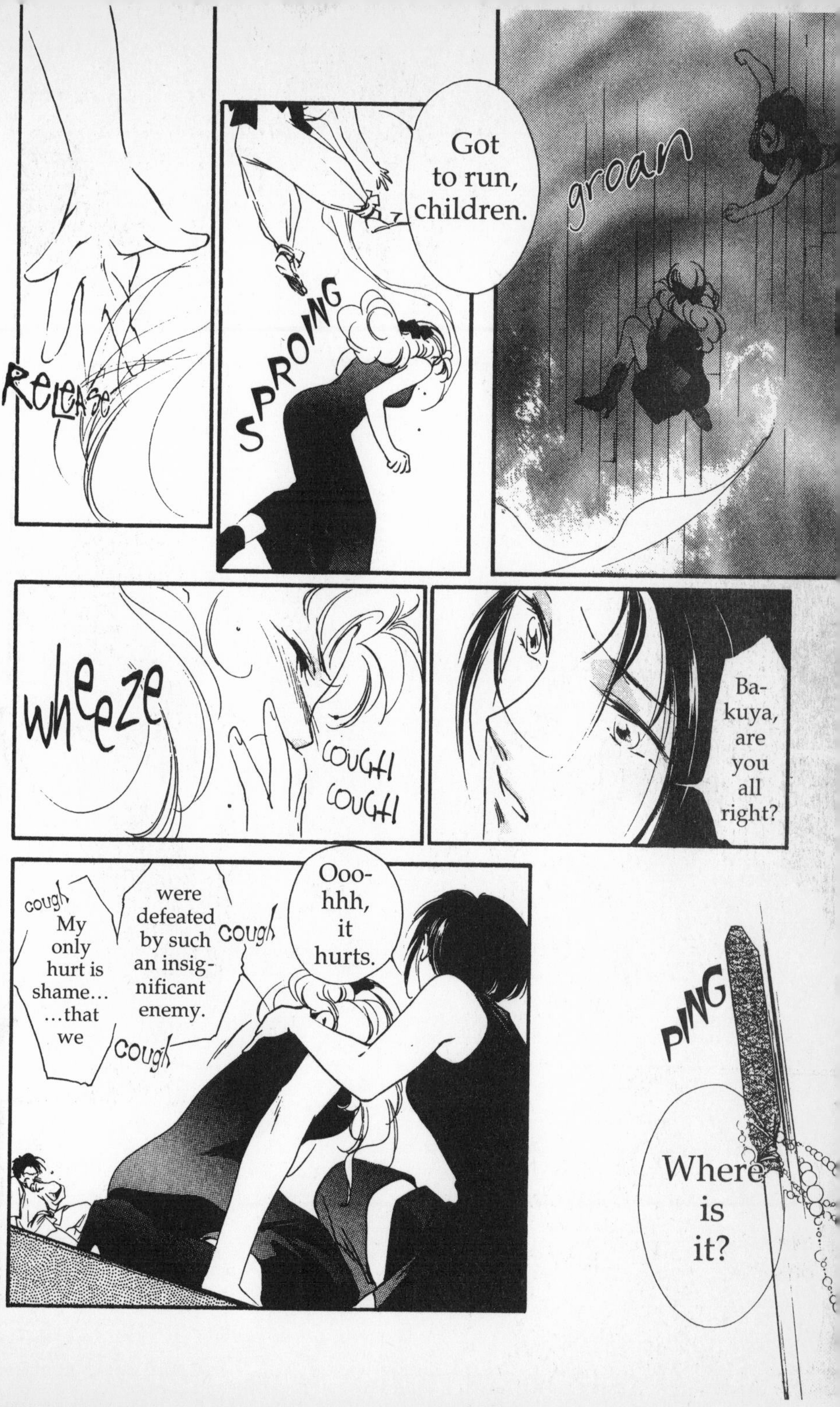
RELEASE
Got to run, children.
SPROING
groan
wheeze
COUGH! COUGH!
Ba-kuya, are you all right?
cough
My only hurt is shame… …that we
were defeated by such an insignificant enemy.
cough
cough
Ooo-hhh, it hurts.
PING
Where is it?

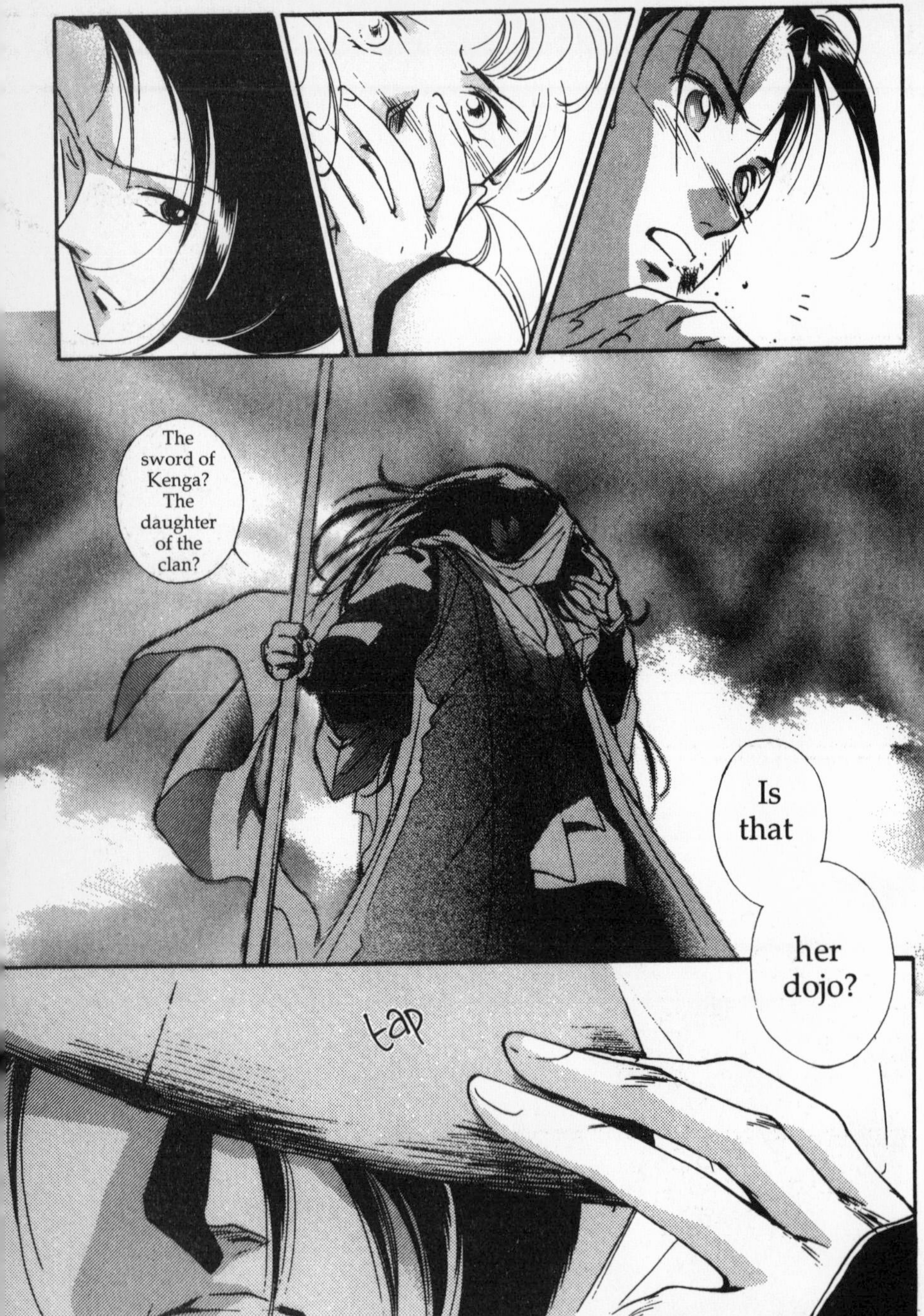
The sword of Kenga? The daughter of the clan?
Is that
her dojo?
tap

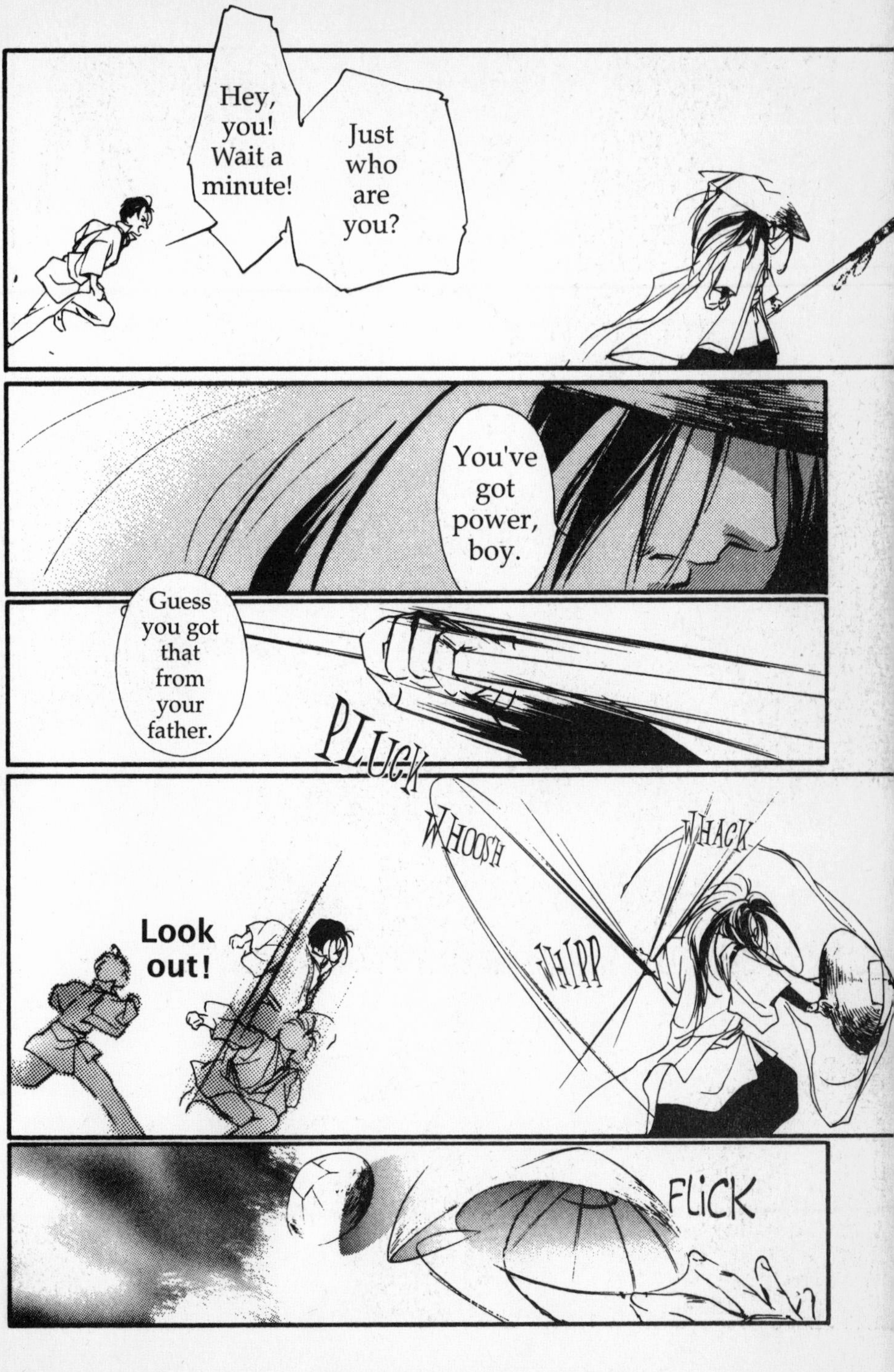
Hey, you! Wait a minute!
Just who are you?
You've got power, boy.
Guess you got that from your father.
PLUCK
WHOOSH
WHACK
Look out!
WHIPP
FLICK

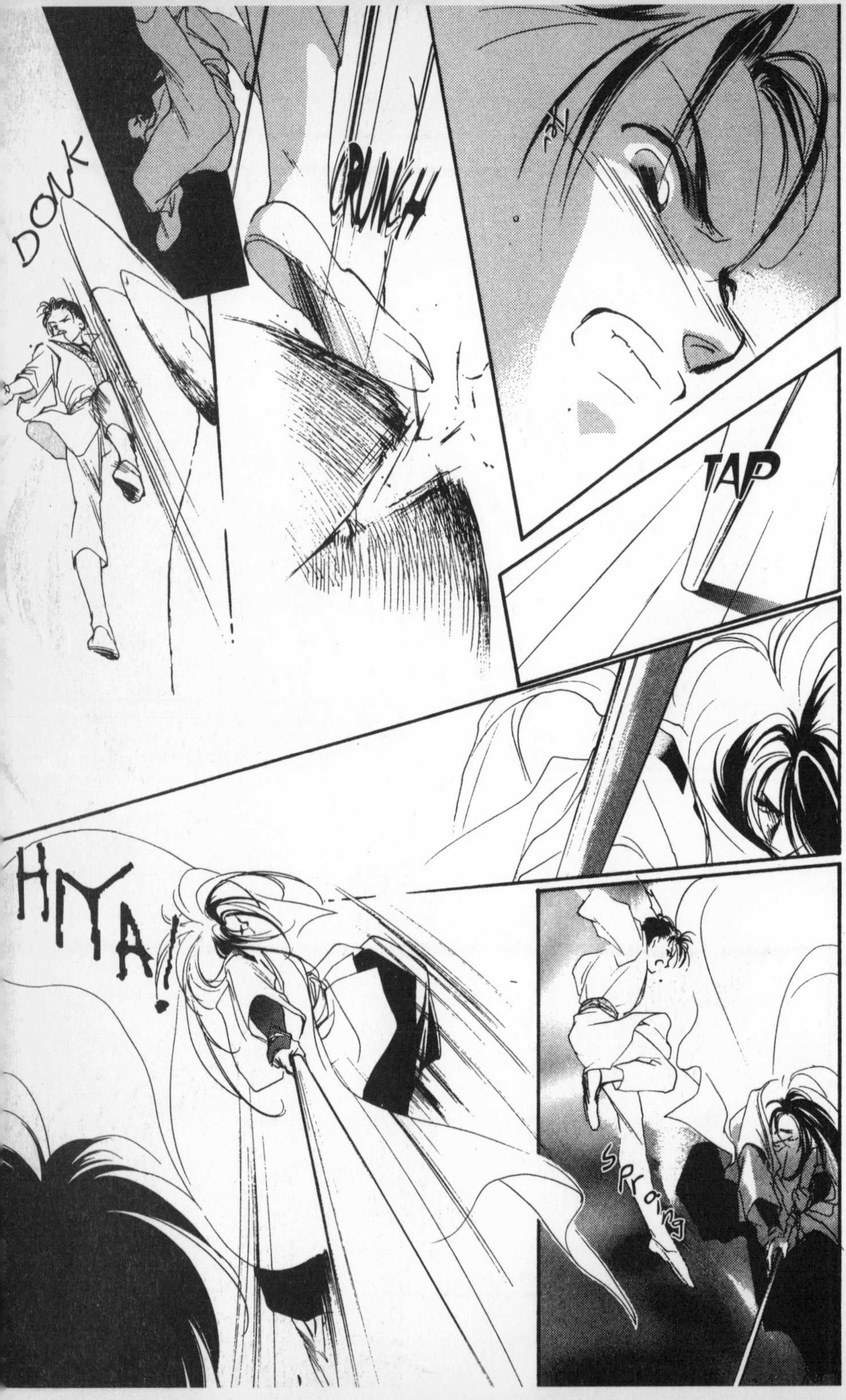
DONK
CRUNCH
TAP
HYA!
Sproing

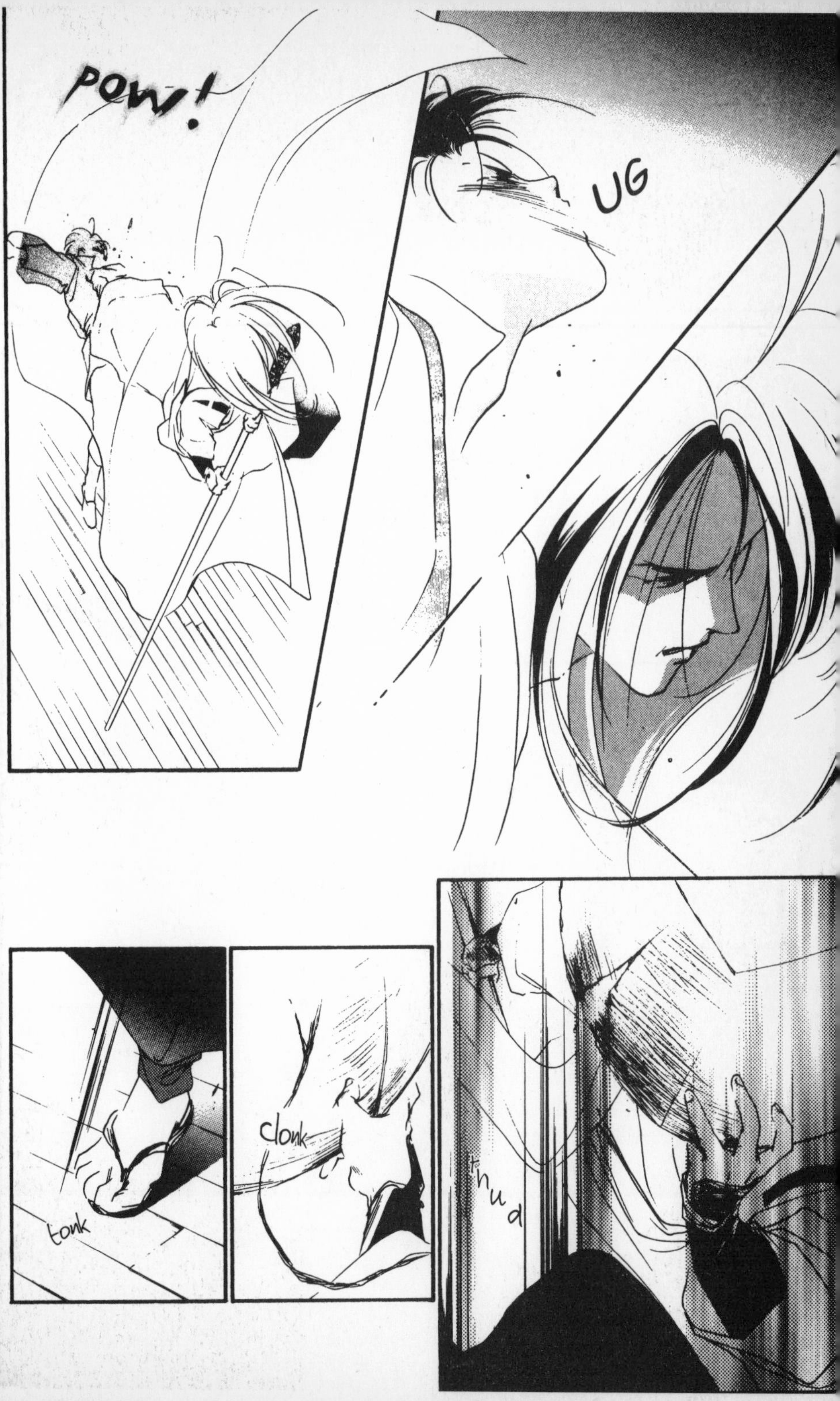
POW!
UG
tonk
clonk
thud

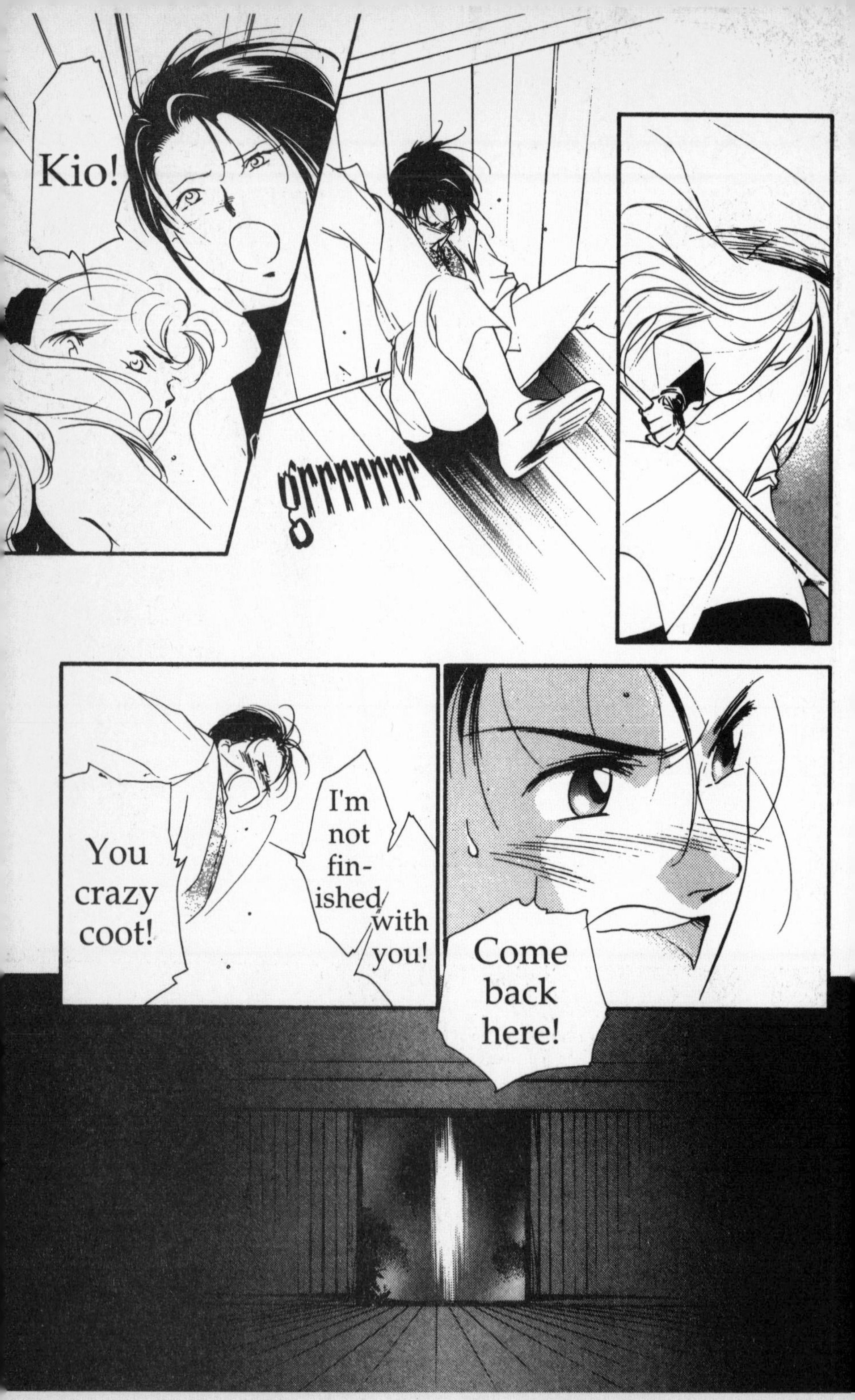
Kio!
grrrrrrr
You crazy coot!
I'm not fin-ished with you!
Come back here!

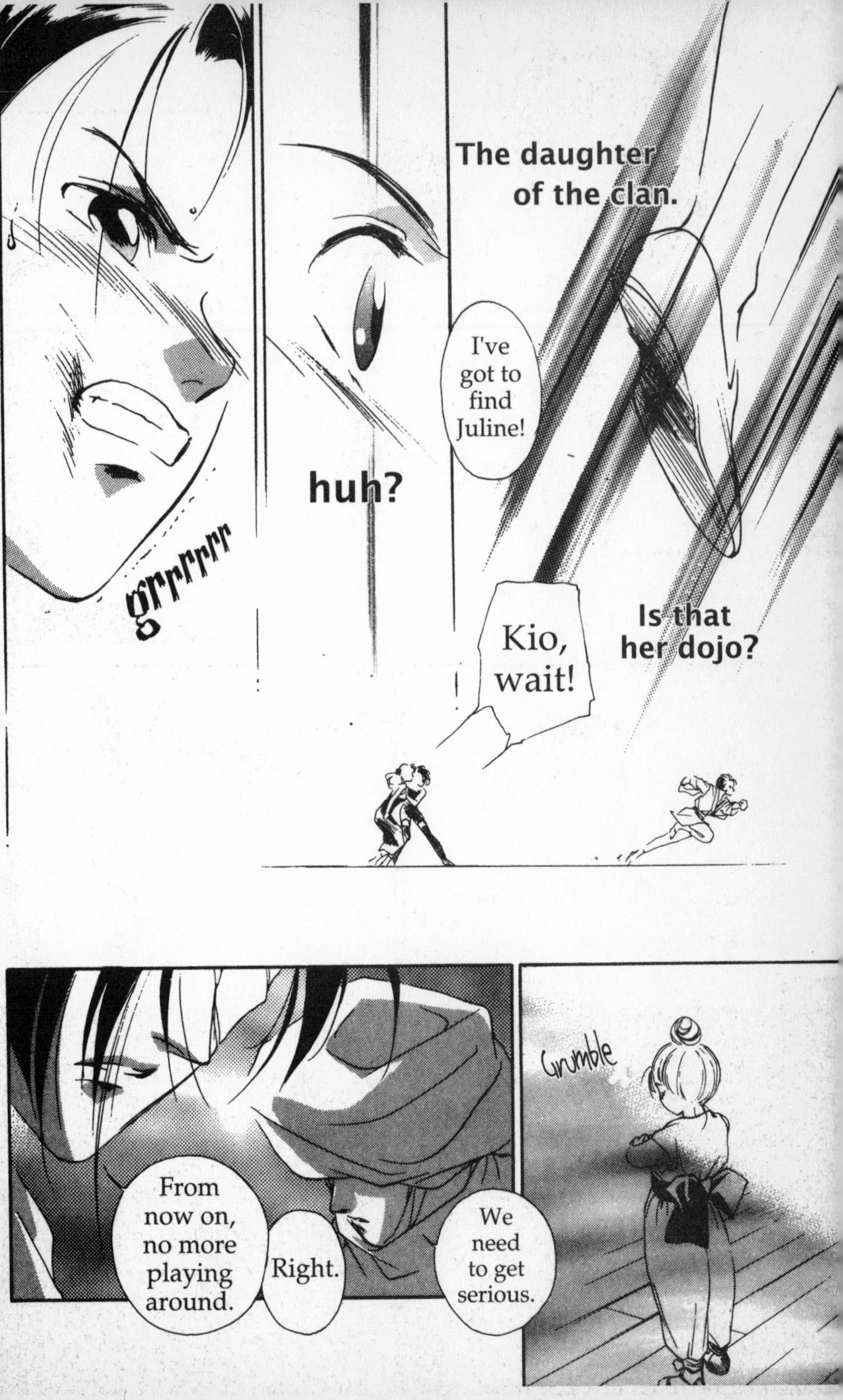
grrrrrr
huh?
The daughter of the clan.
I've got to find Juline!
Kio, wait!
Is that her dojo?
From now on, no more playing around.
Right.
We need to get serious.
Grumble

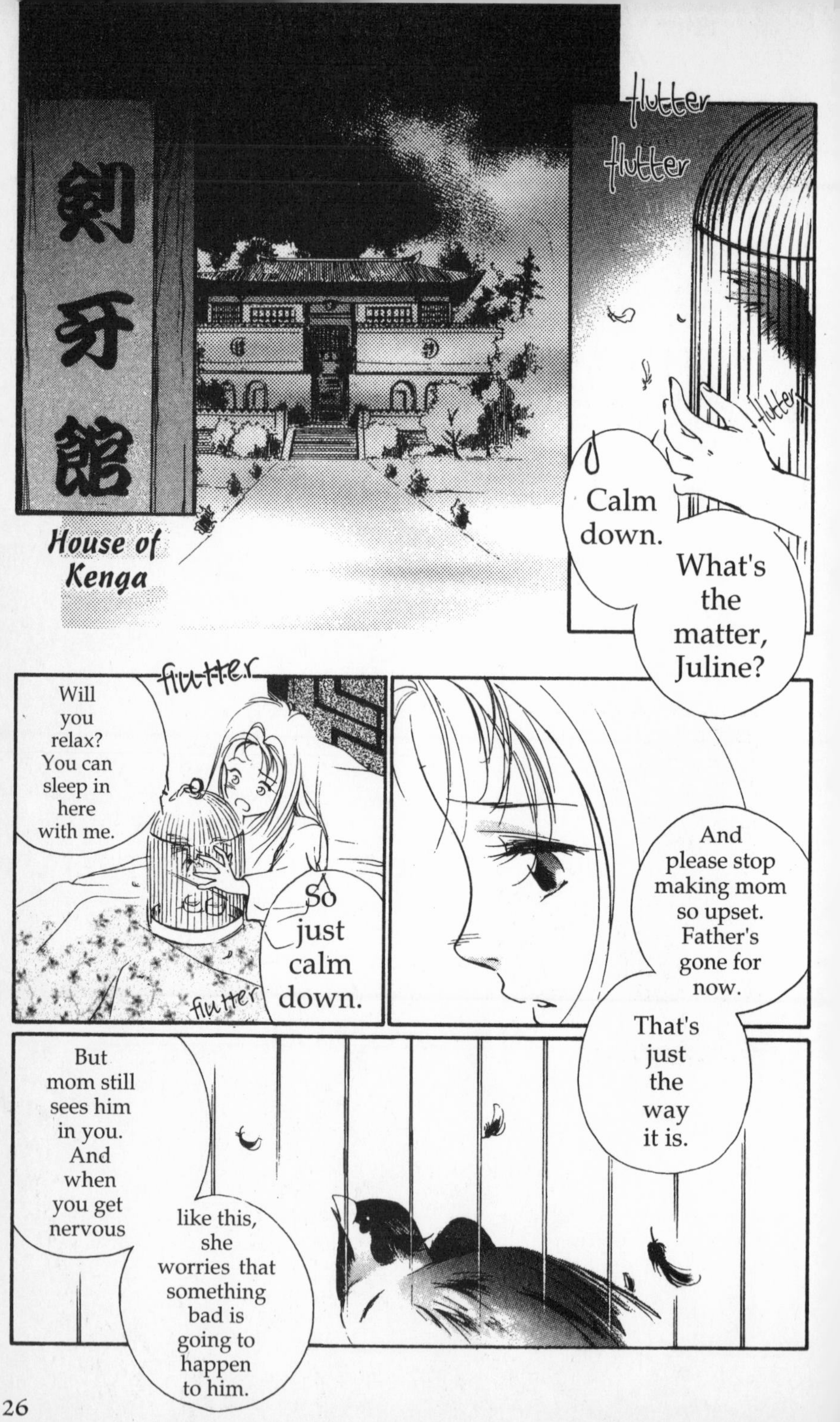
剣
牙
館
House of Kenga
flutter
flutter
flutter
Calm down.
What's the matter, Juline?
flutter
Will you relax? You can sleep in here with me.
So just calm down.
flutter
And please stop making mom so upset. Father's gone for now.
That's just the way it is.
But mom still sees him in you. And when you get nervous
like this, she worries that something bad is going to happen to him.

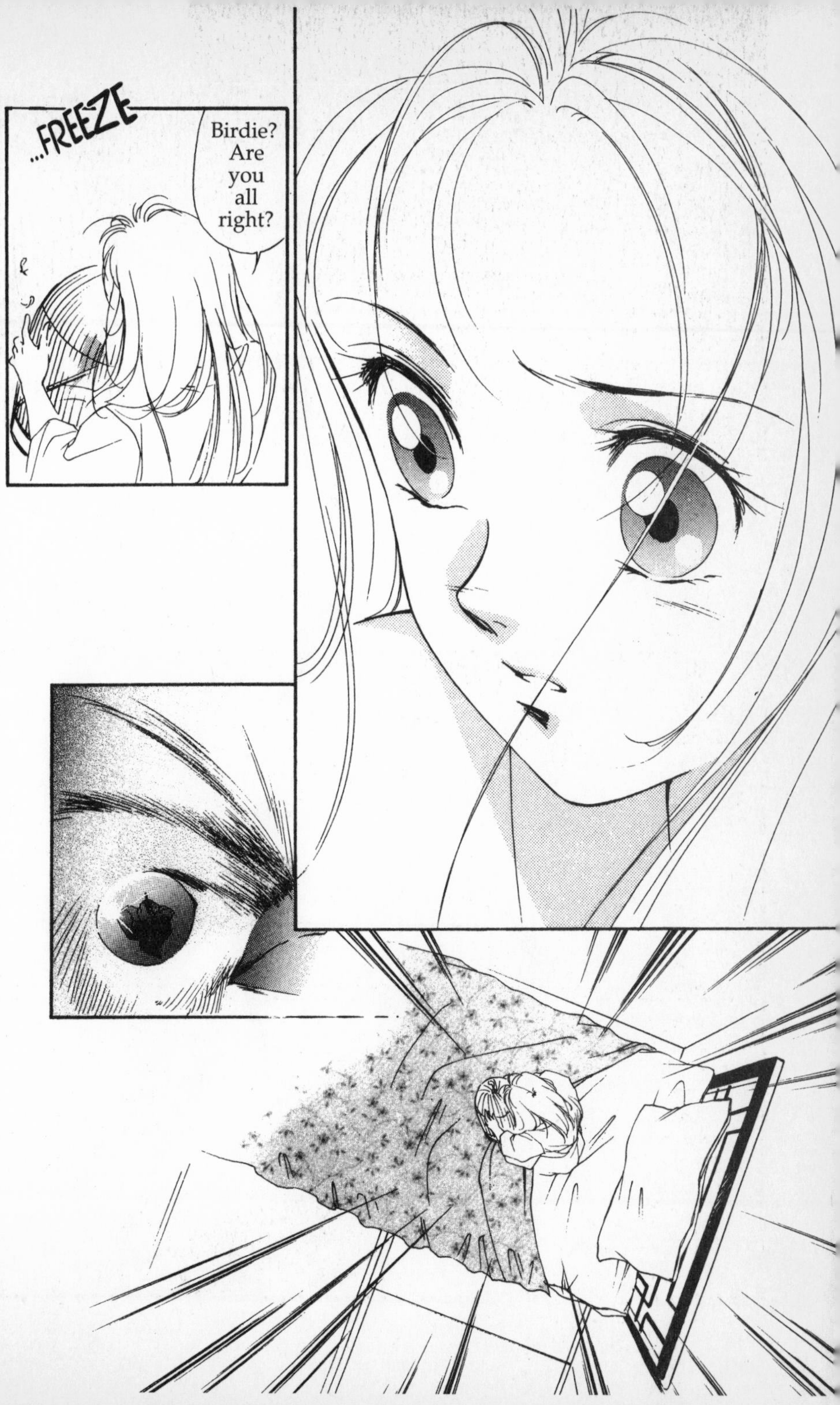
...FREEZE
Birdie? Are you all right?

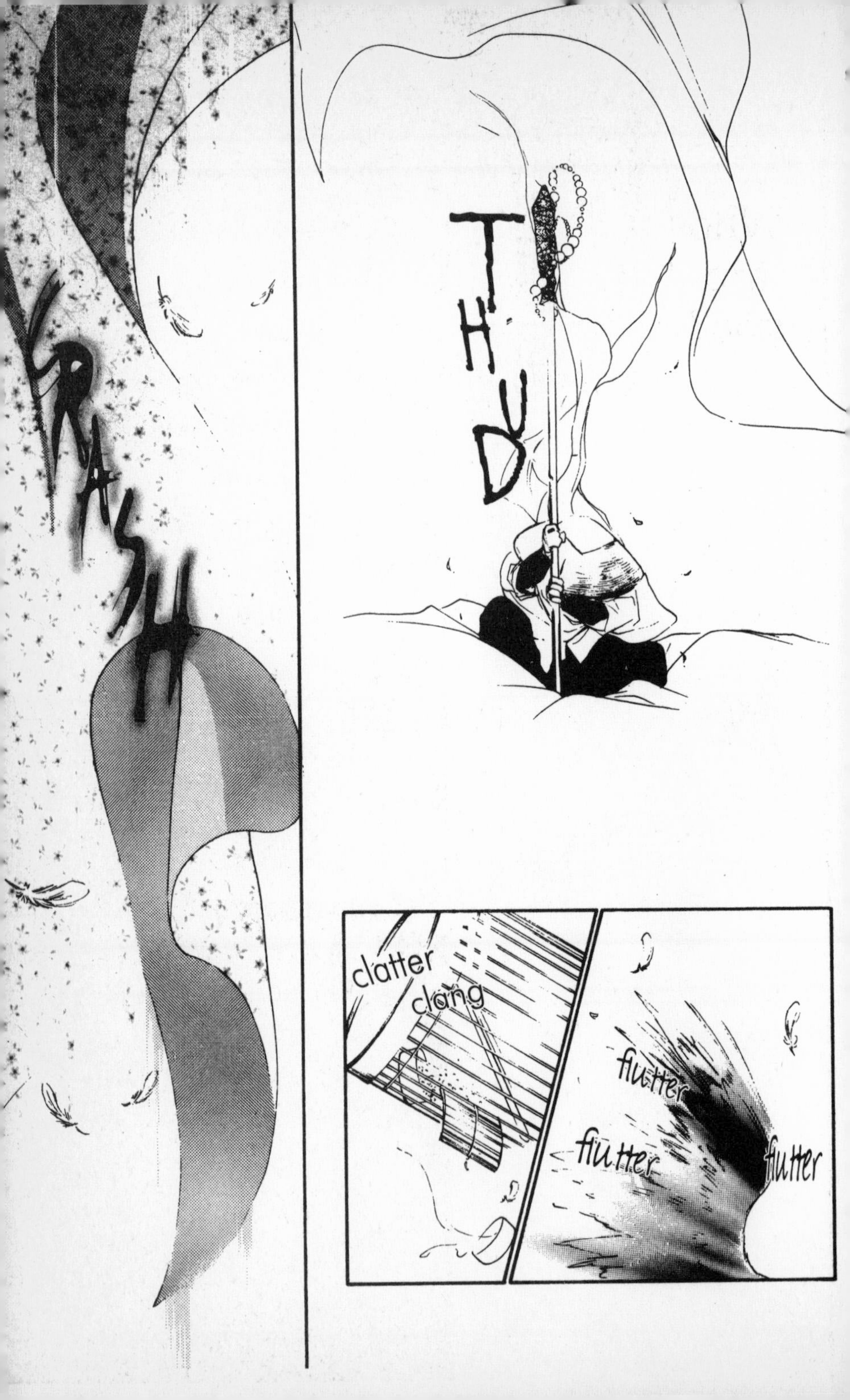
CRASH
THUD
clatter
clang
flutter
flutter
flutter

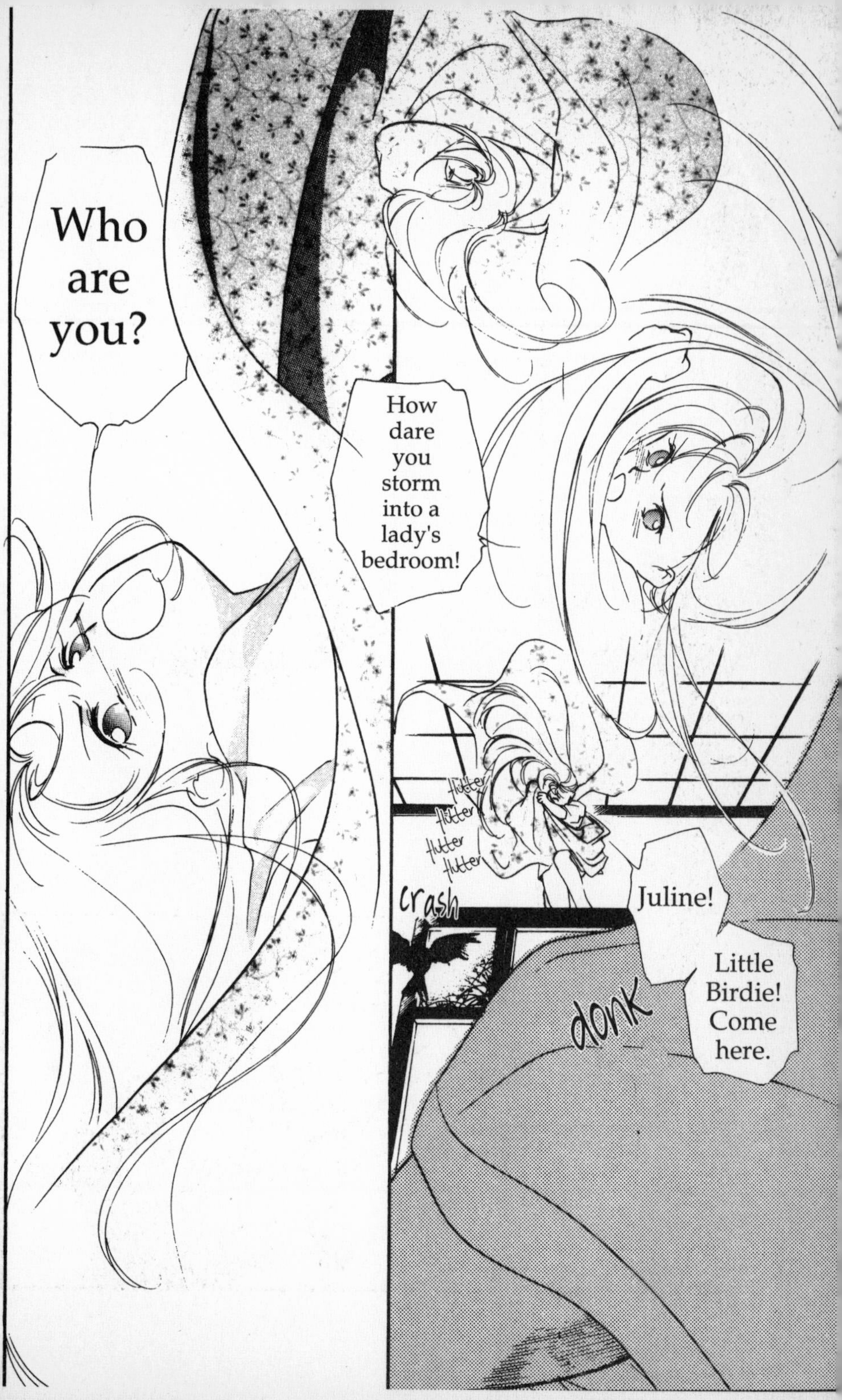
Who are you?
How dare you storm into a lady's bedroom!
flutter flutter flutter flutter
crash
Juline!
donk
Little Birdie! Come here.

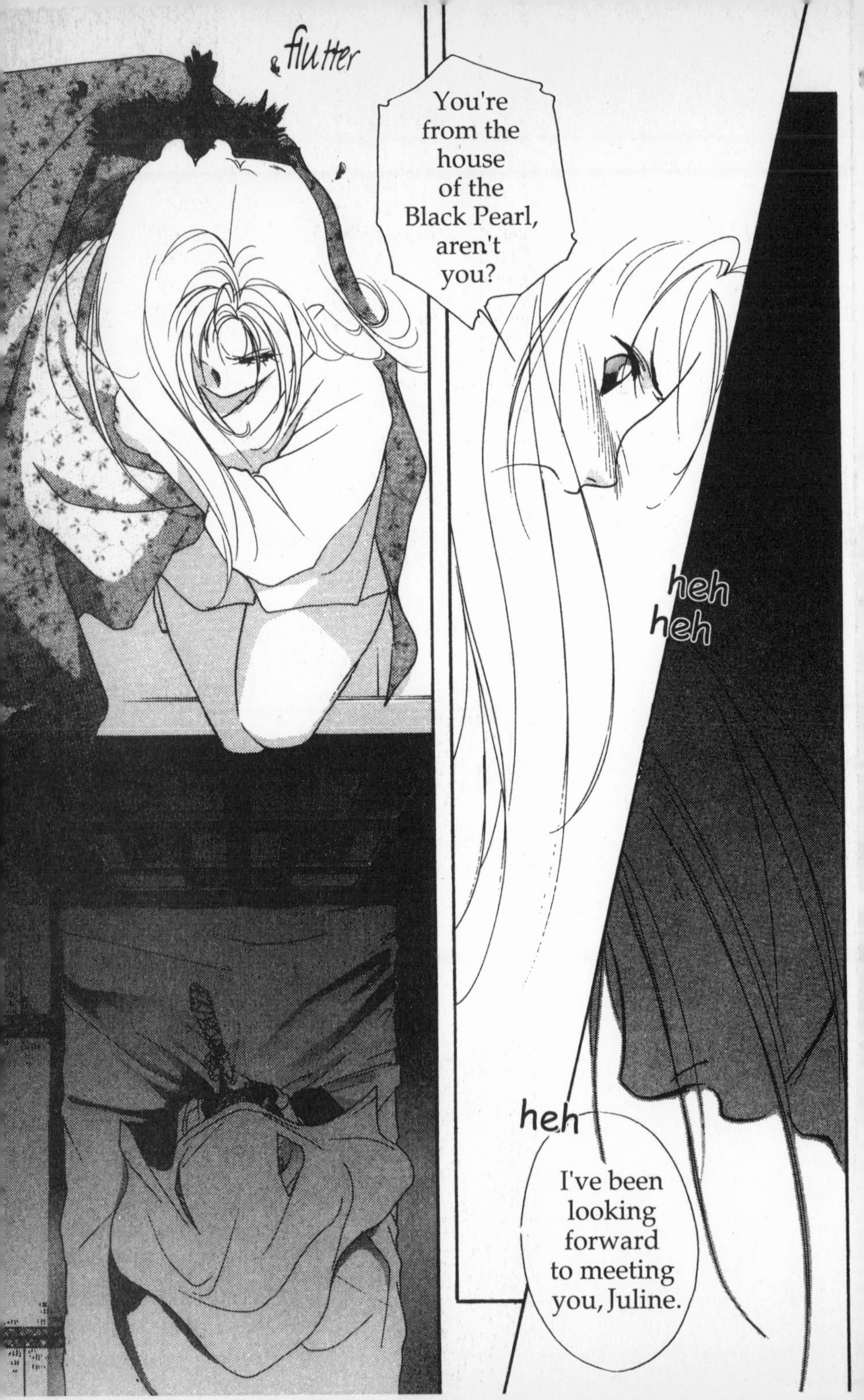
flutter
You're from the house of the Black Pearl, aren't you?
heh heh
heh
I've been looking forward to meeting you, Juline.

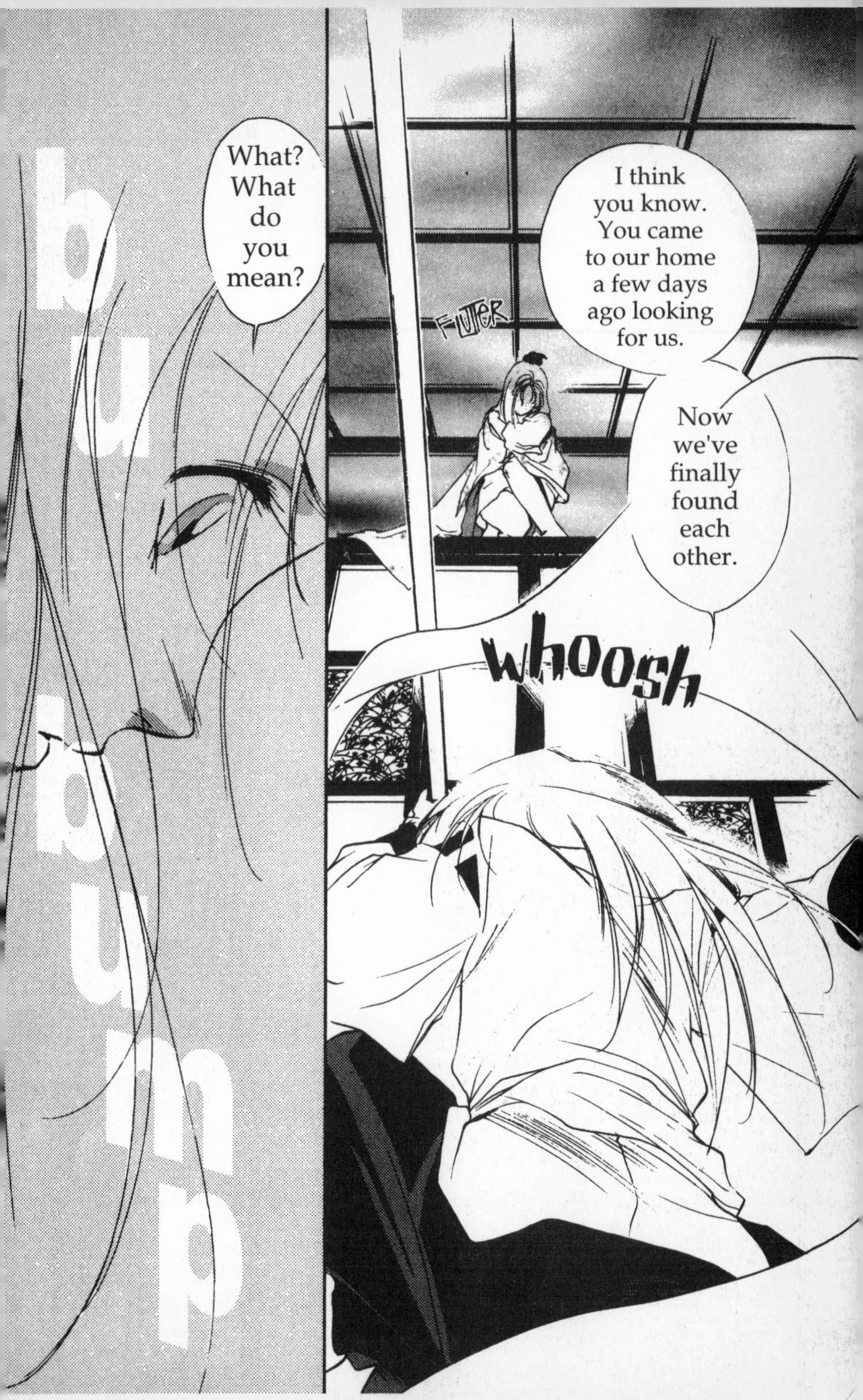
bump bump
What? What do you mean?
FLUTTER
I think you know. You came to our home a few days ago looking for us.
Now we've finally found each other.
whoosh

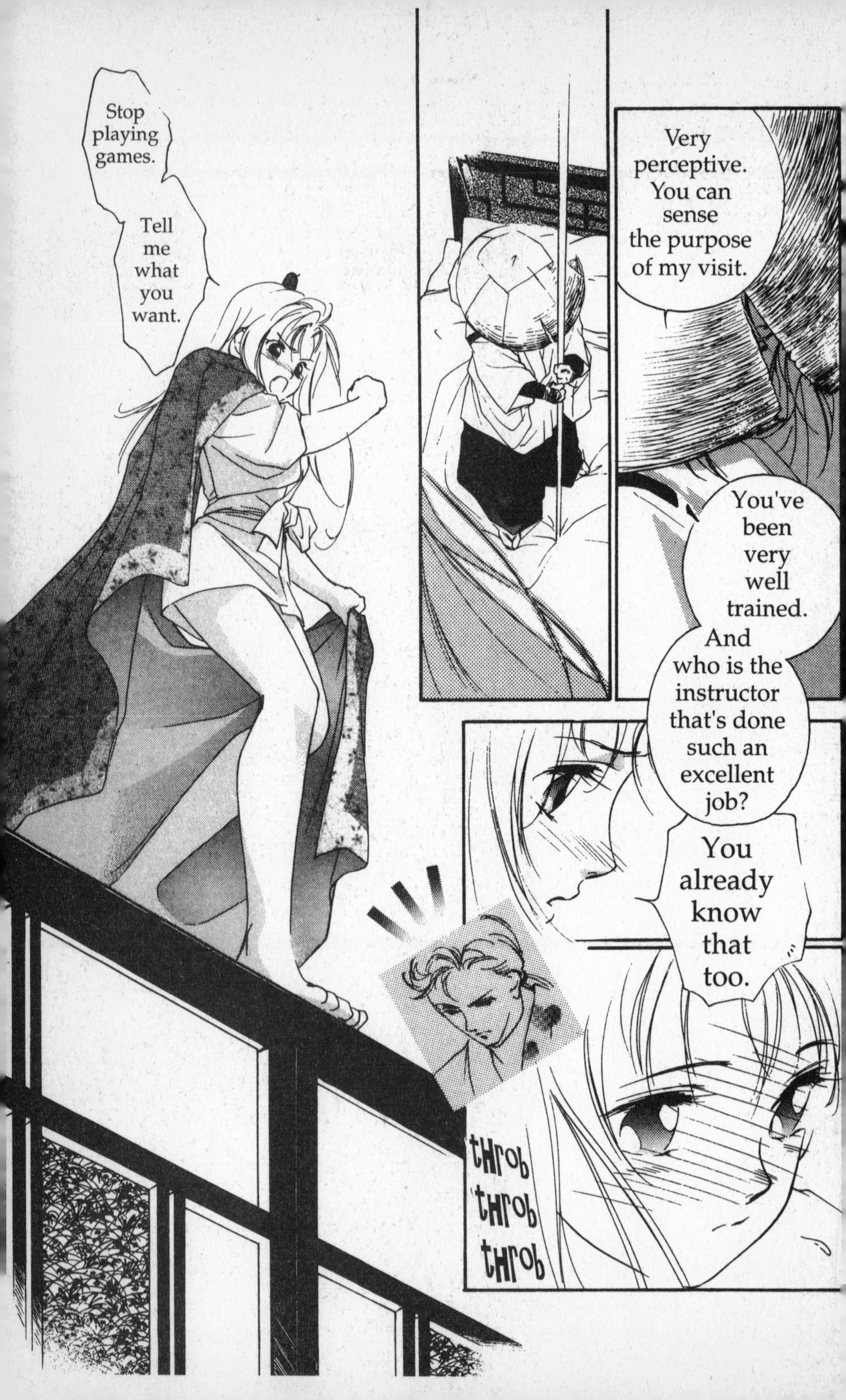
Stop playing games.
Tell me what you want.
Very perceptive. You can sense the purpose of my visit.
You've been very well trained.
And who is the instructor that's done such an excellent job?
You already know that too.
tHrob tHrob tHrob

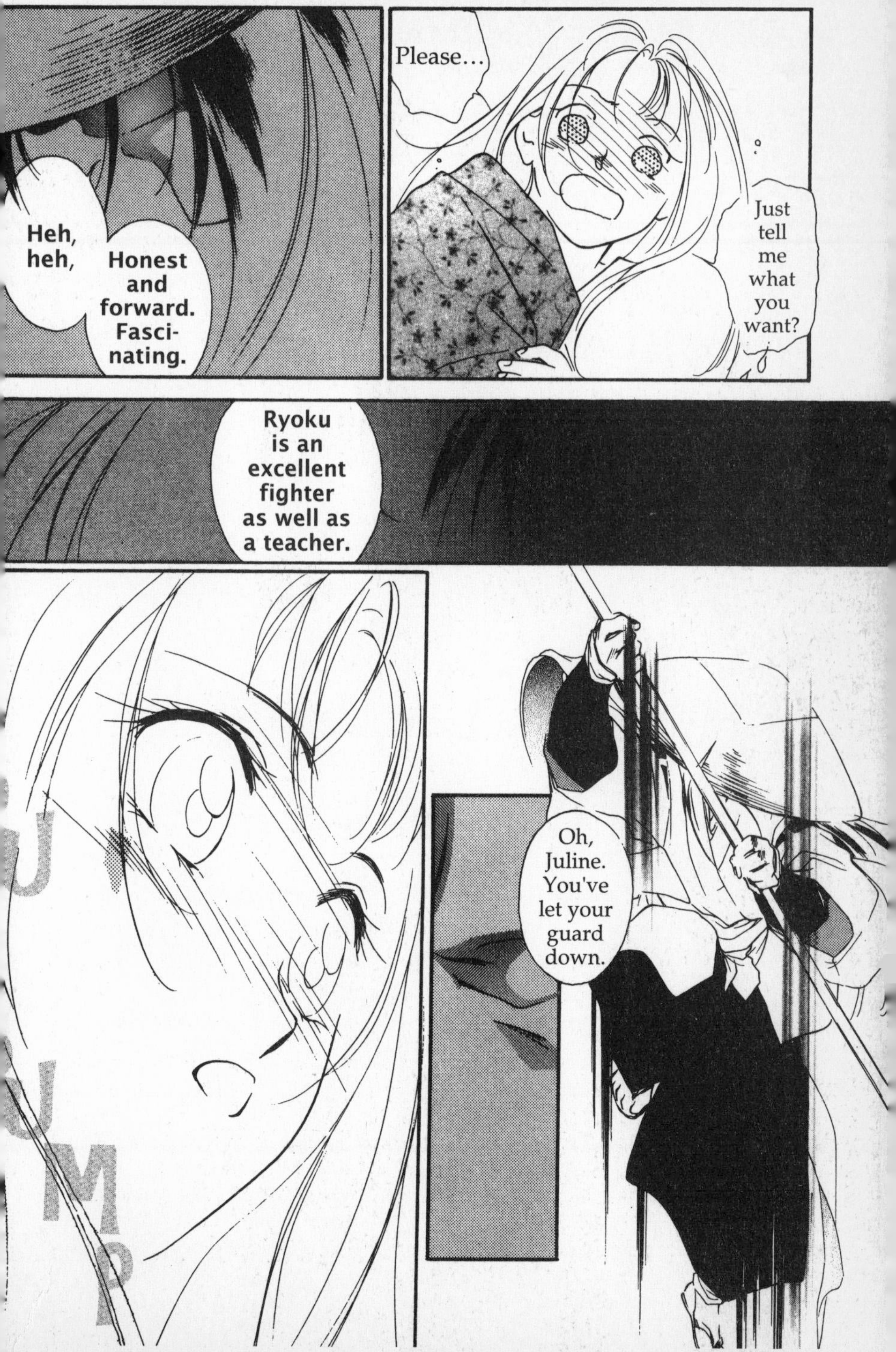
Heh, heh,
Honest and forward. Fasci-nating.
Please...
Just tell me what you want?
Ryoku is an excellent fighter as well as a teacher.
Oh, Juline. You've let your guard down.

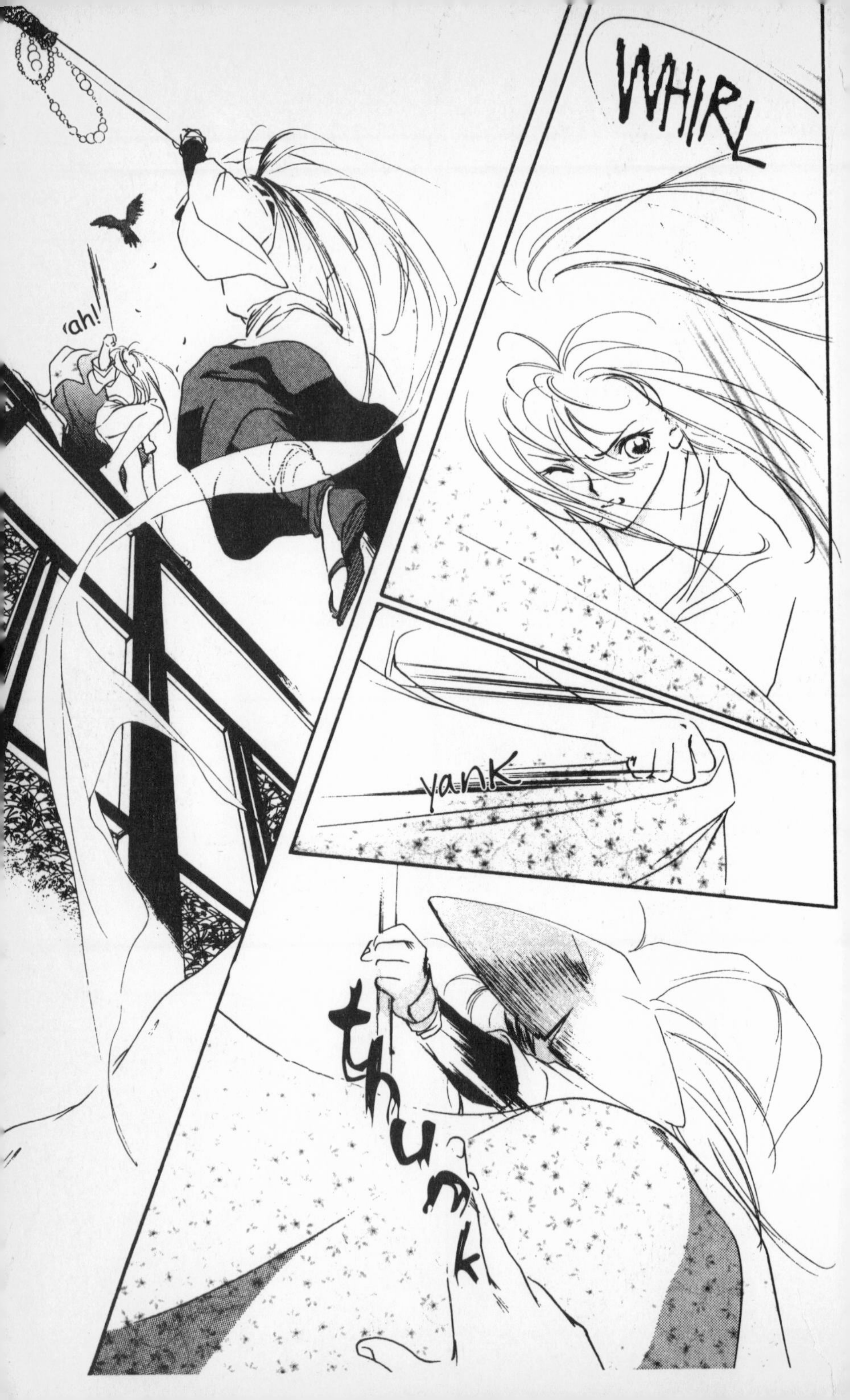
yah!
WHIRL
yank
thunk

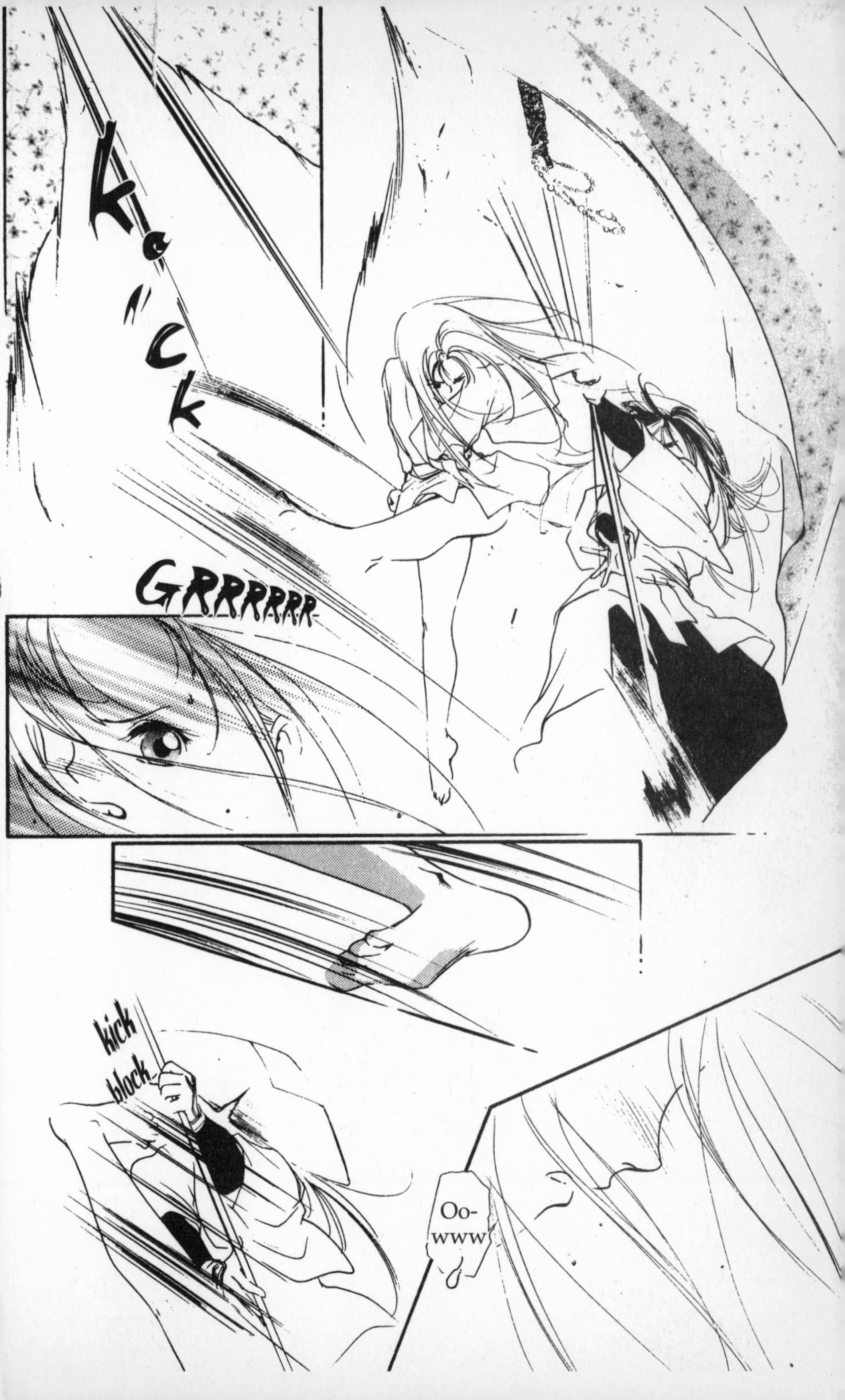
kick
GRRRRRRR
kick
block
Oo-
www

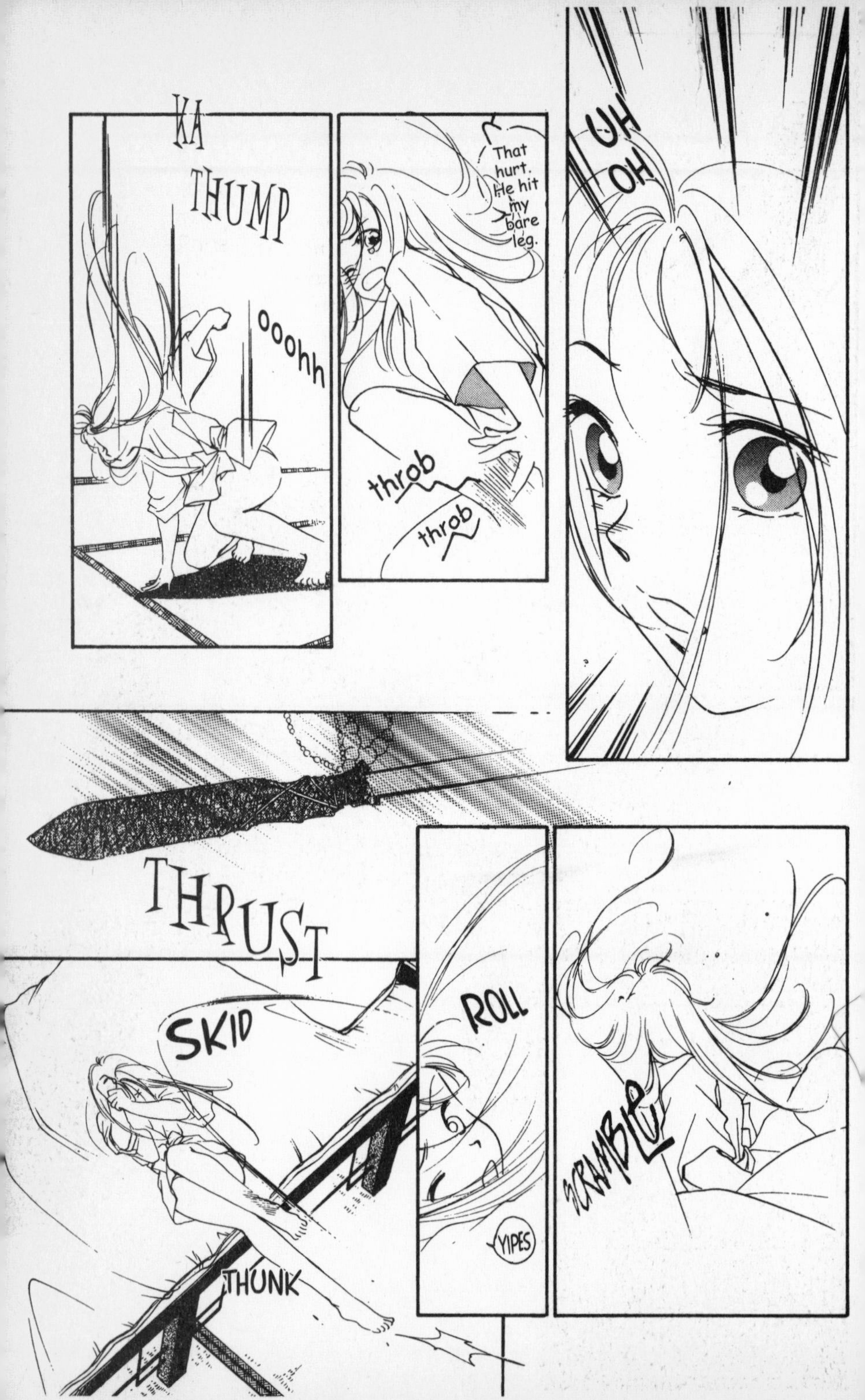
KA THUMP
ooohh
That hurt. He hit my bare leg.
throb
throb
UH OH
THRUST
SKID
THUNK
ROLL
YIPES
SCRAMBLE UP

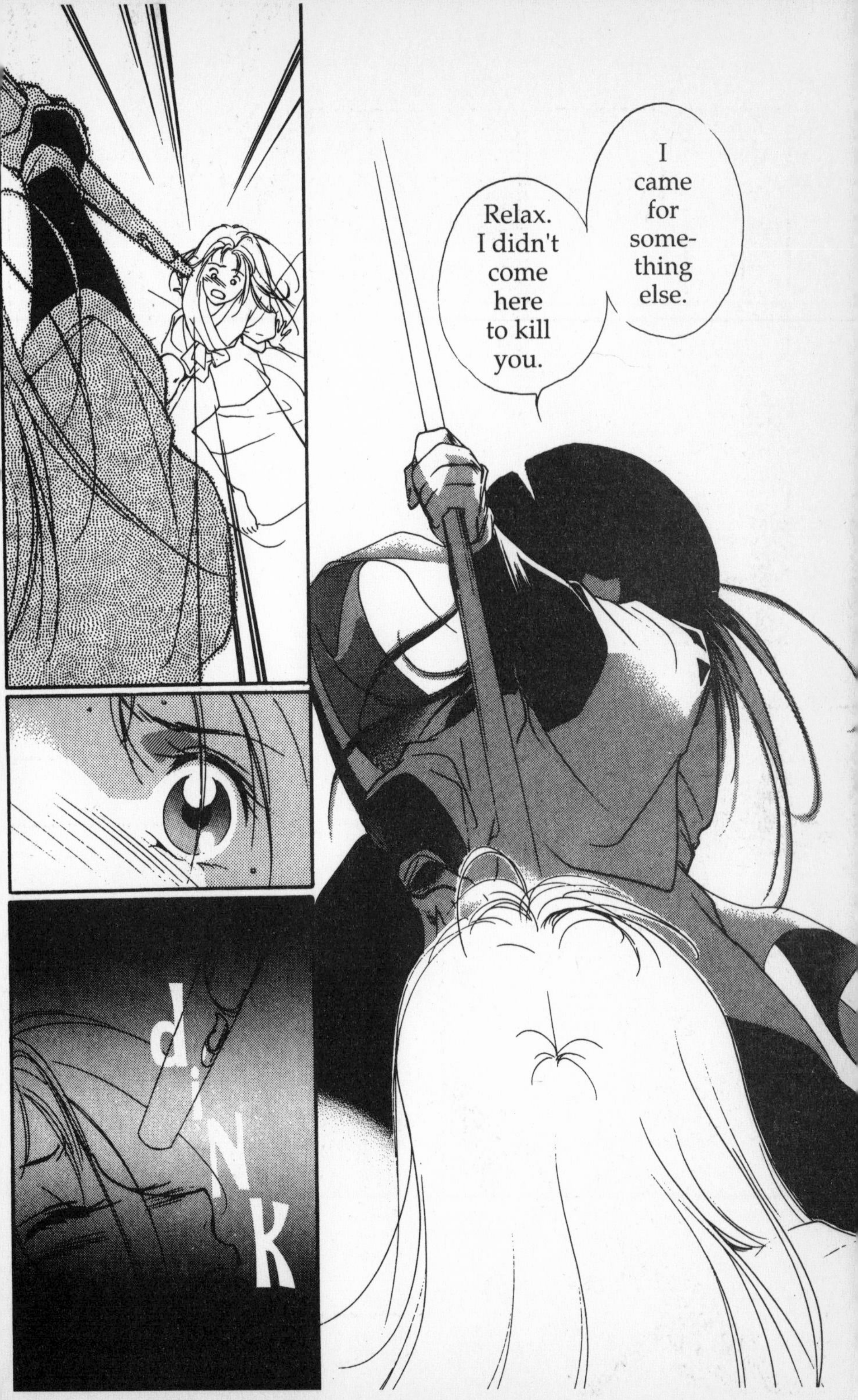
diNK
Relax. I didn't come here to kill you.
I came for some-thing else.

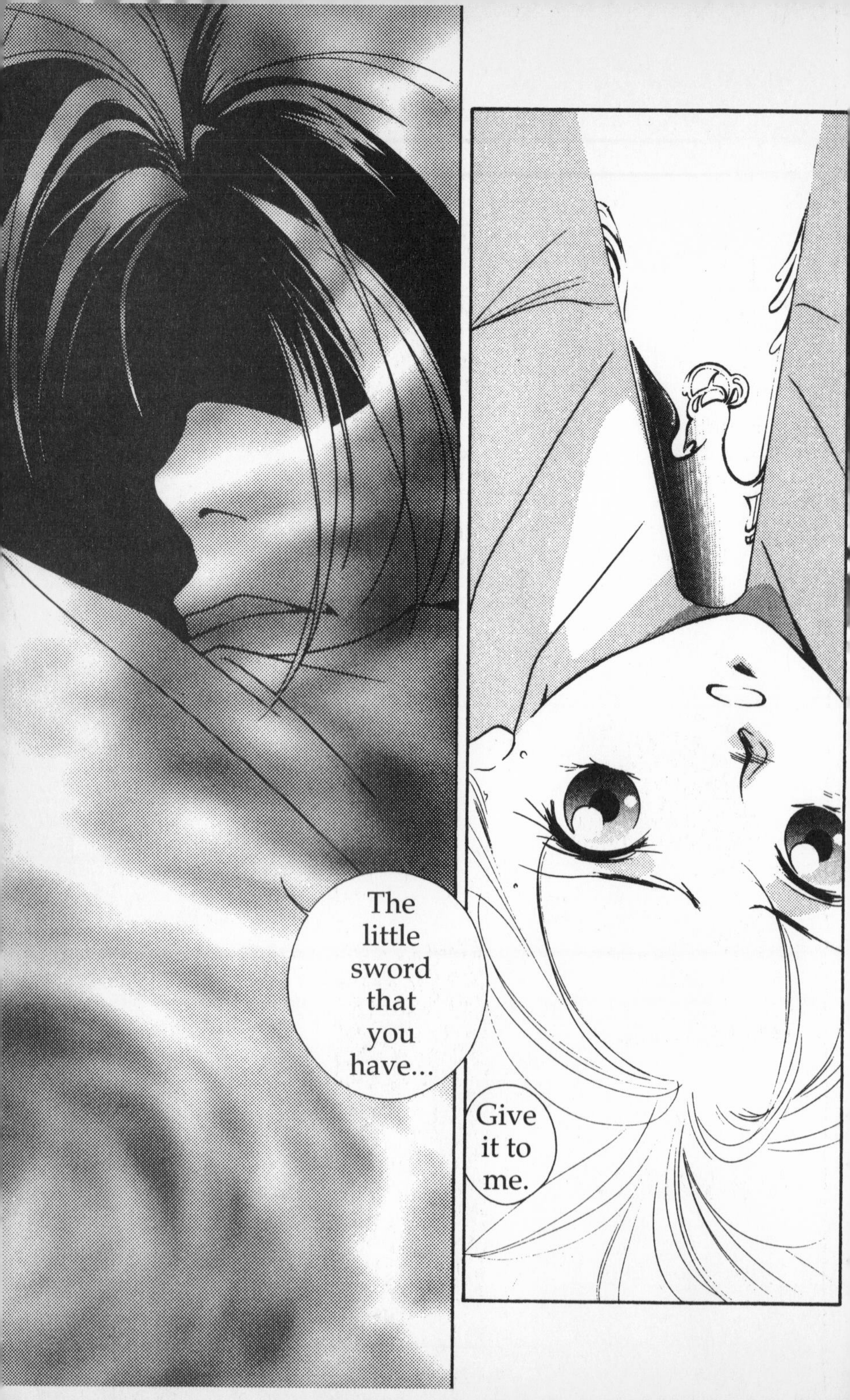
The little sword that you have...
Give it to me.

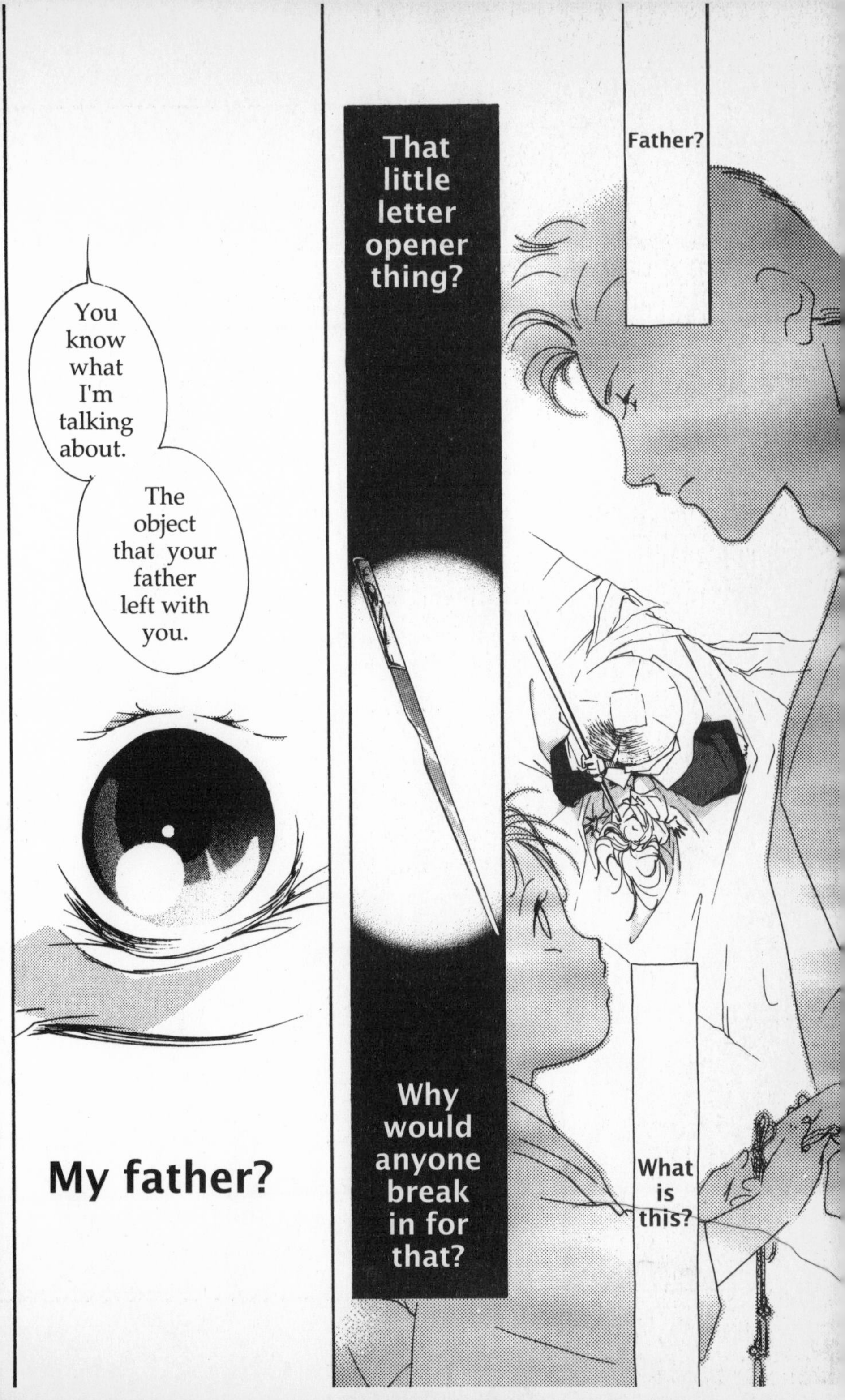

You know what I'm talking about.
The object that your father left with you.
My father?
That little letter opener thing?
Father?
Why would anyone break in for that?
What is this?

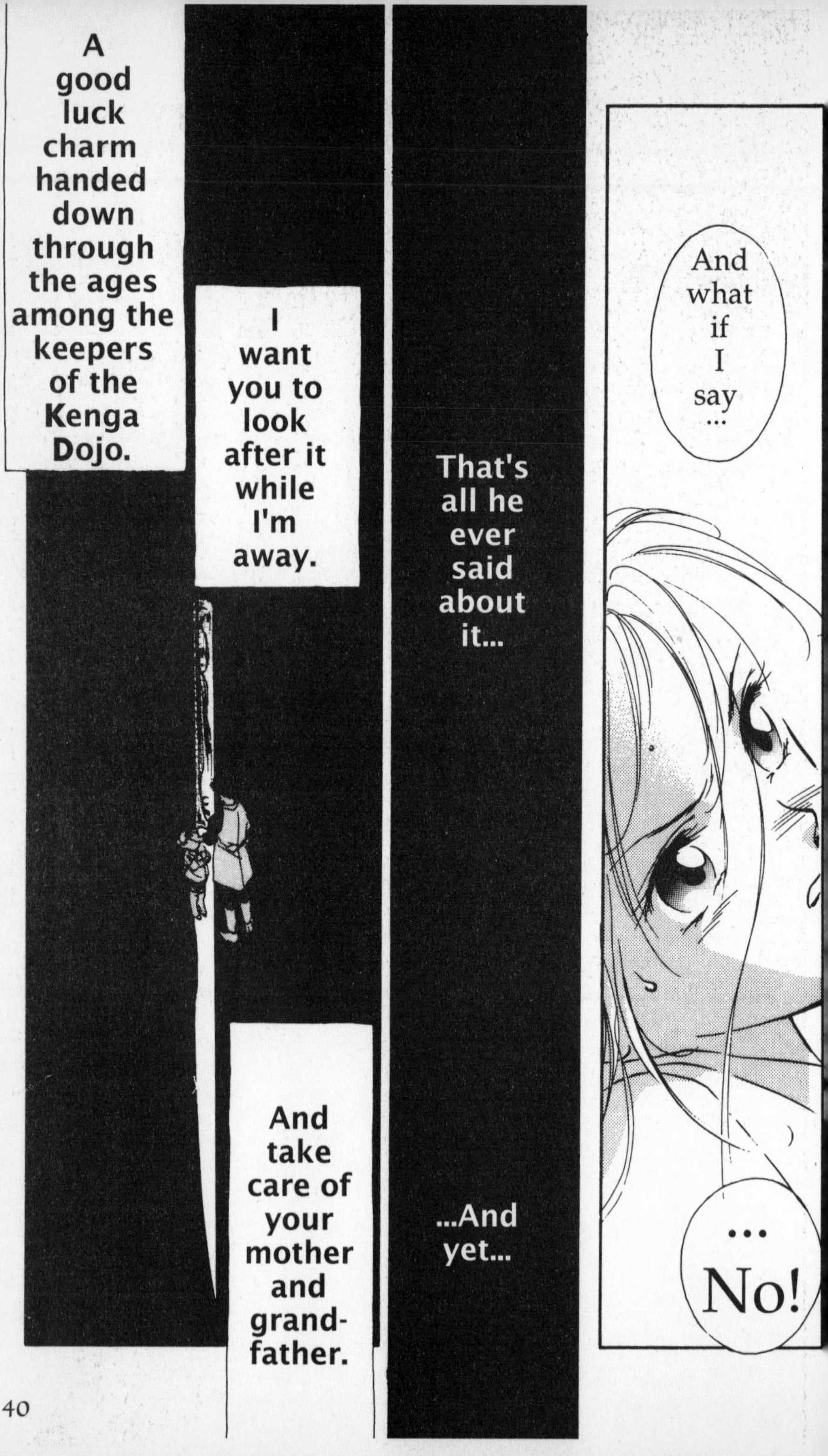
A good luck charm handed down through the ages among the keepers of the Kenga Dojo.
I want you to look after it while I'm away.
And take care of your mother and grandfather.
That's all he ever said about it...
...And yet...
And what if I say...
...No!

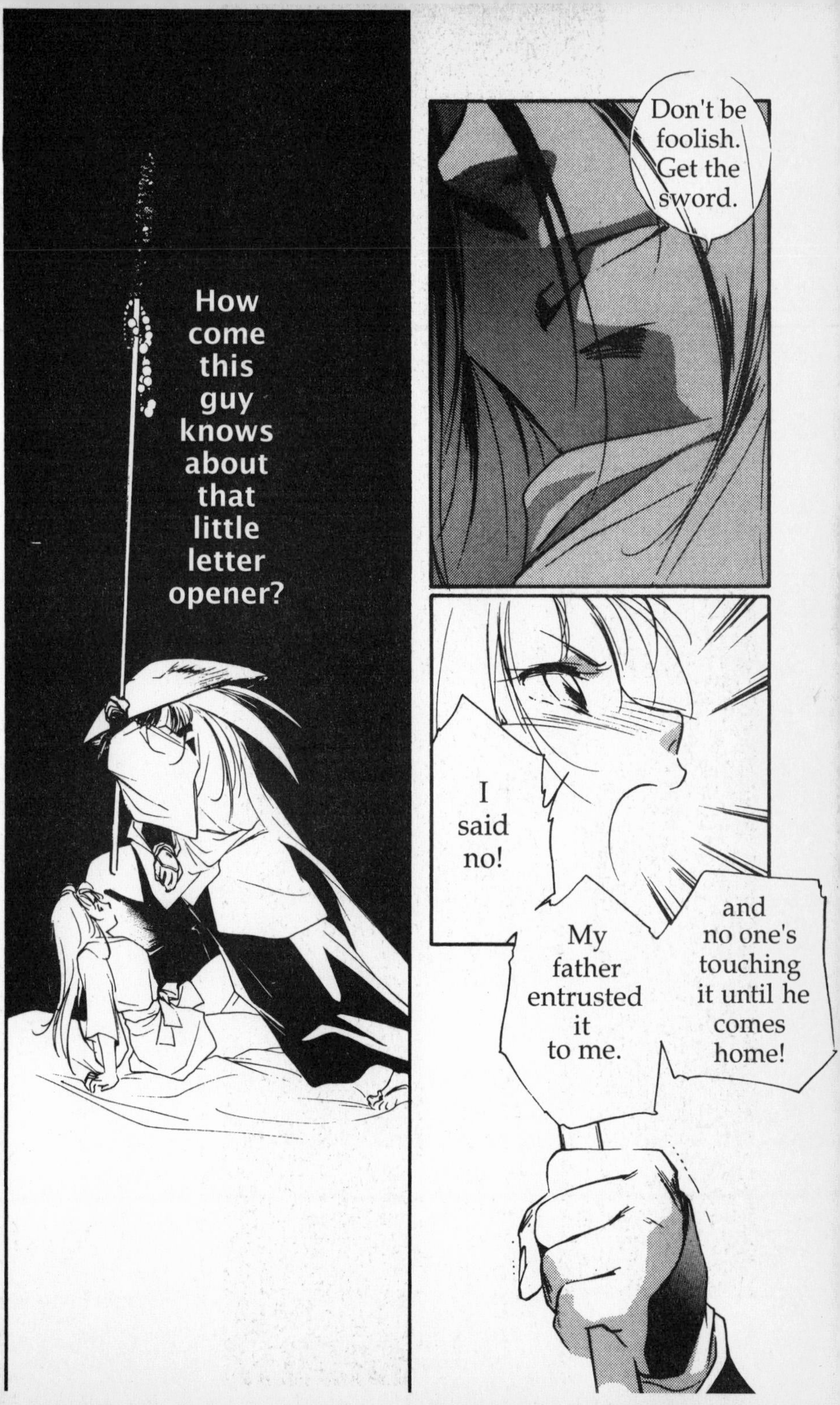
How come this guy knows about that little letter opener?
Don't be foolish. Get the sword.
I said no!
My father entrusted it to me.
and no one's touching it until he comes home!

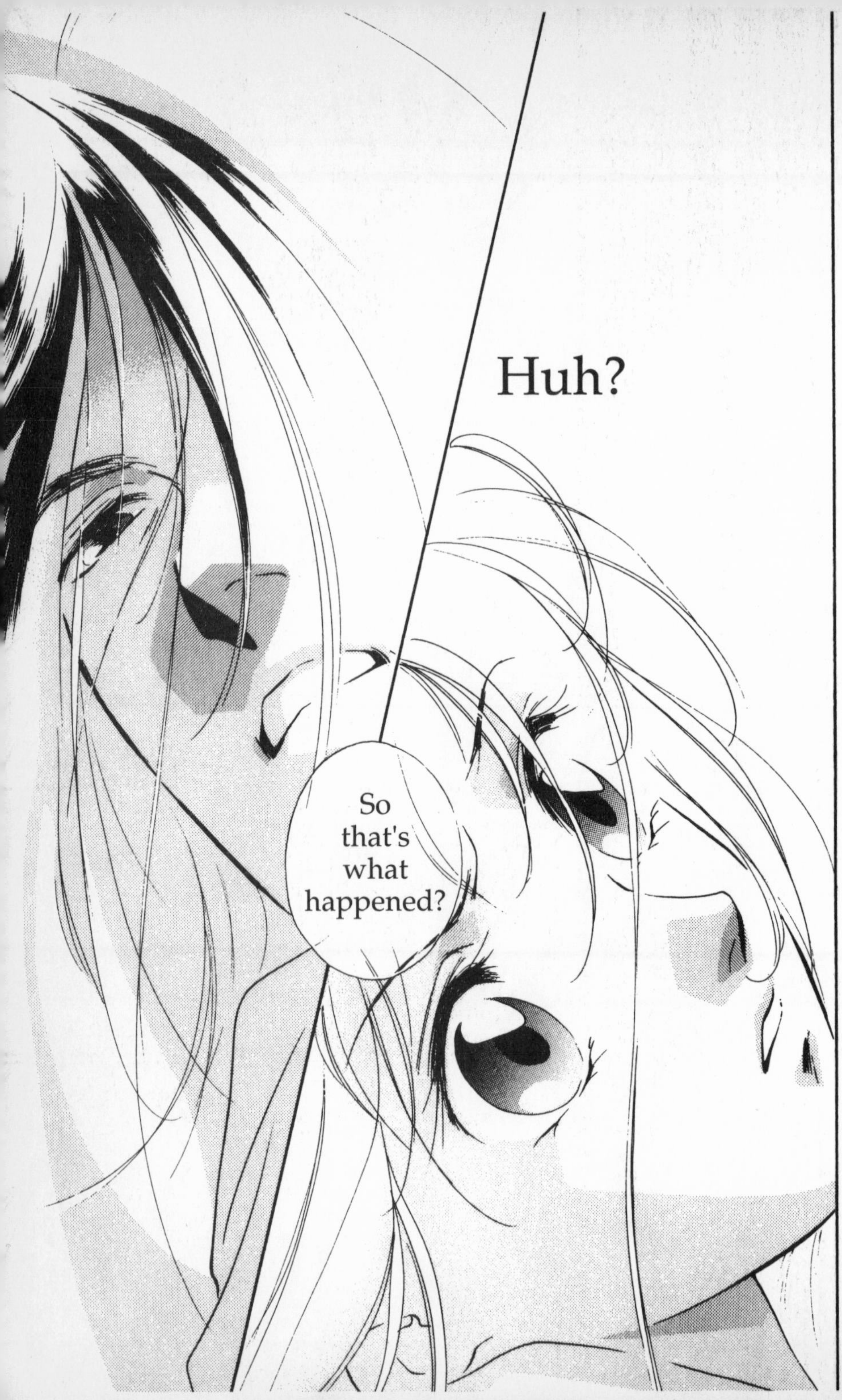
So that's what happened?
Huh?

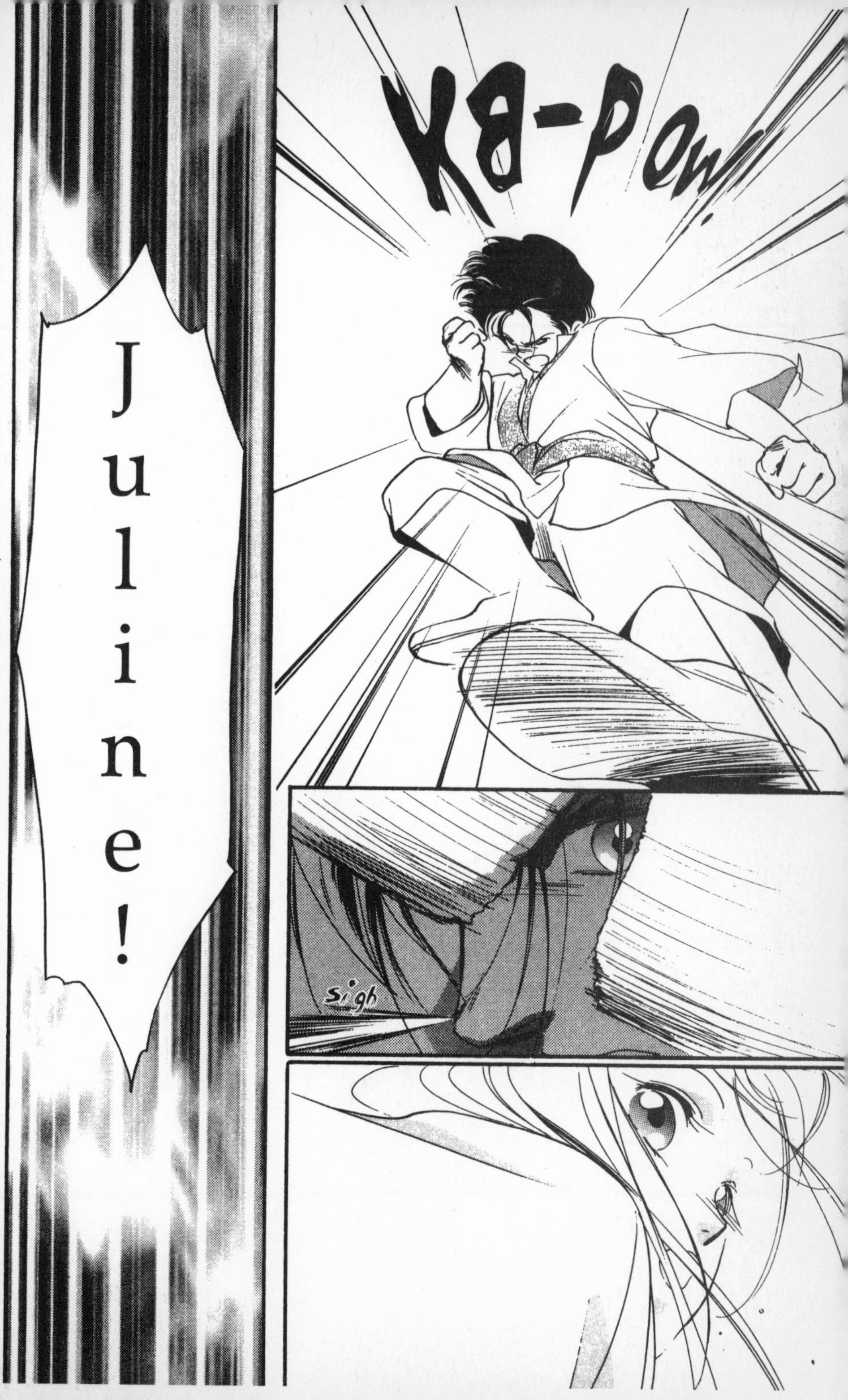
KA-POW!
sigh
Juline!

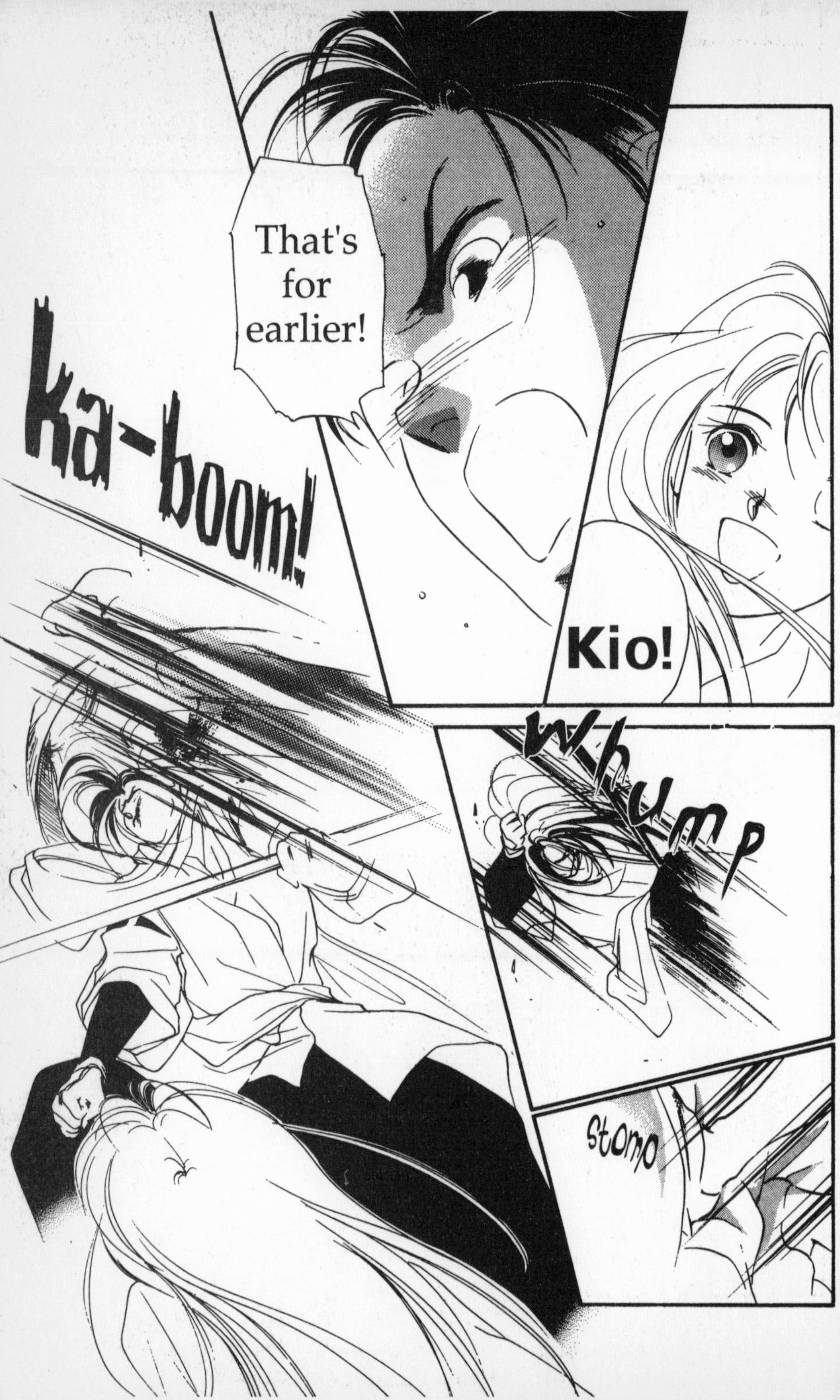
That's for earlier!
Kio!
Ka-boom!
Whump
stomp

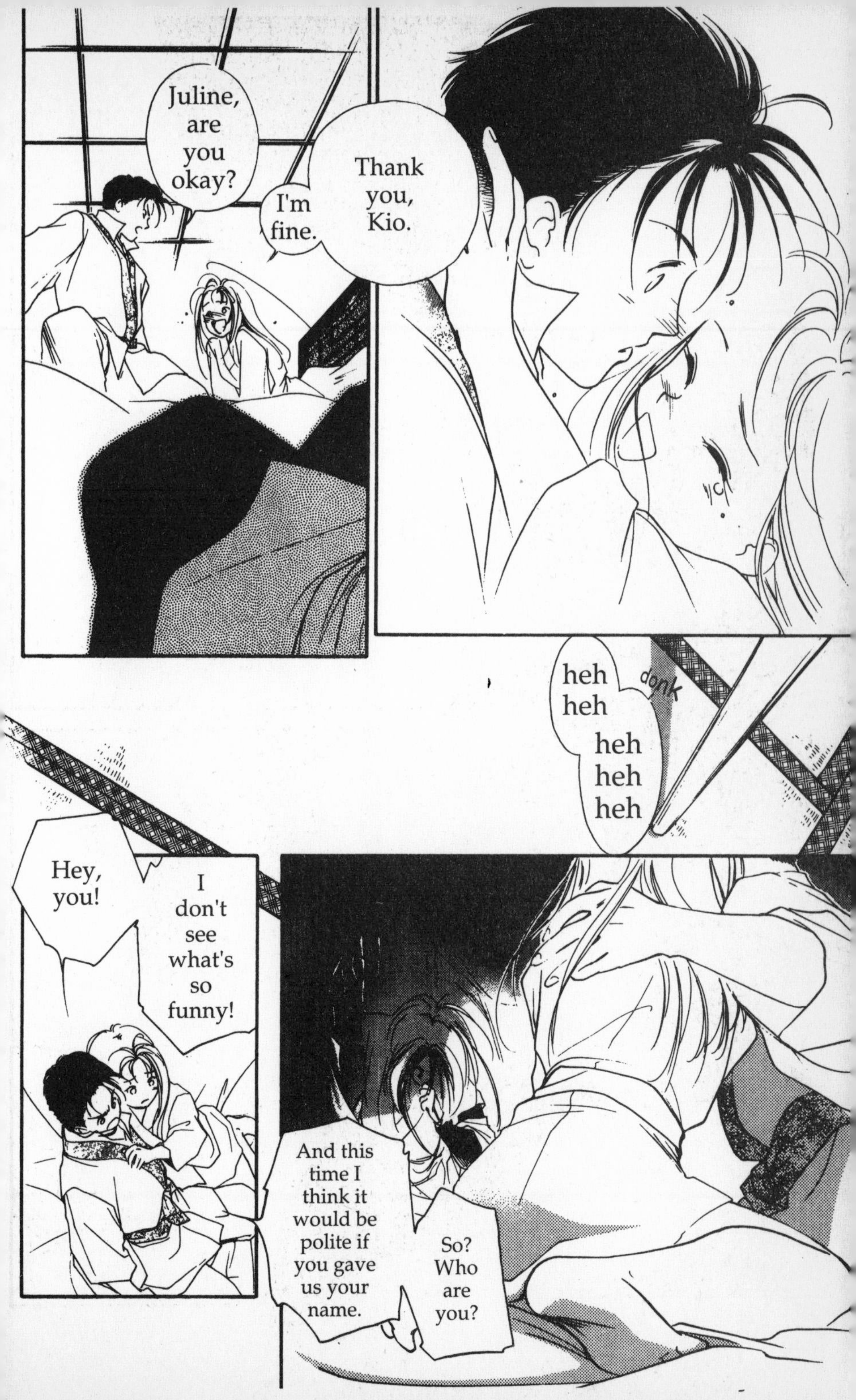
Juline, are you okay?
I'm fine.
Thank you, Kio.
heh heh
donk
heh heh heh
Hey, you!
I don't see what's so funny!
And this time I think it would be polite if you gave us your name.
So? Who are you?

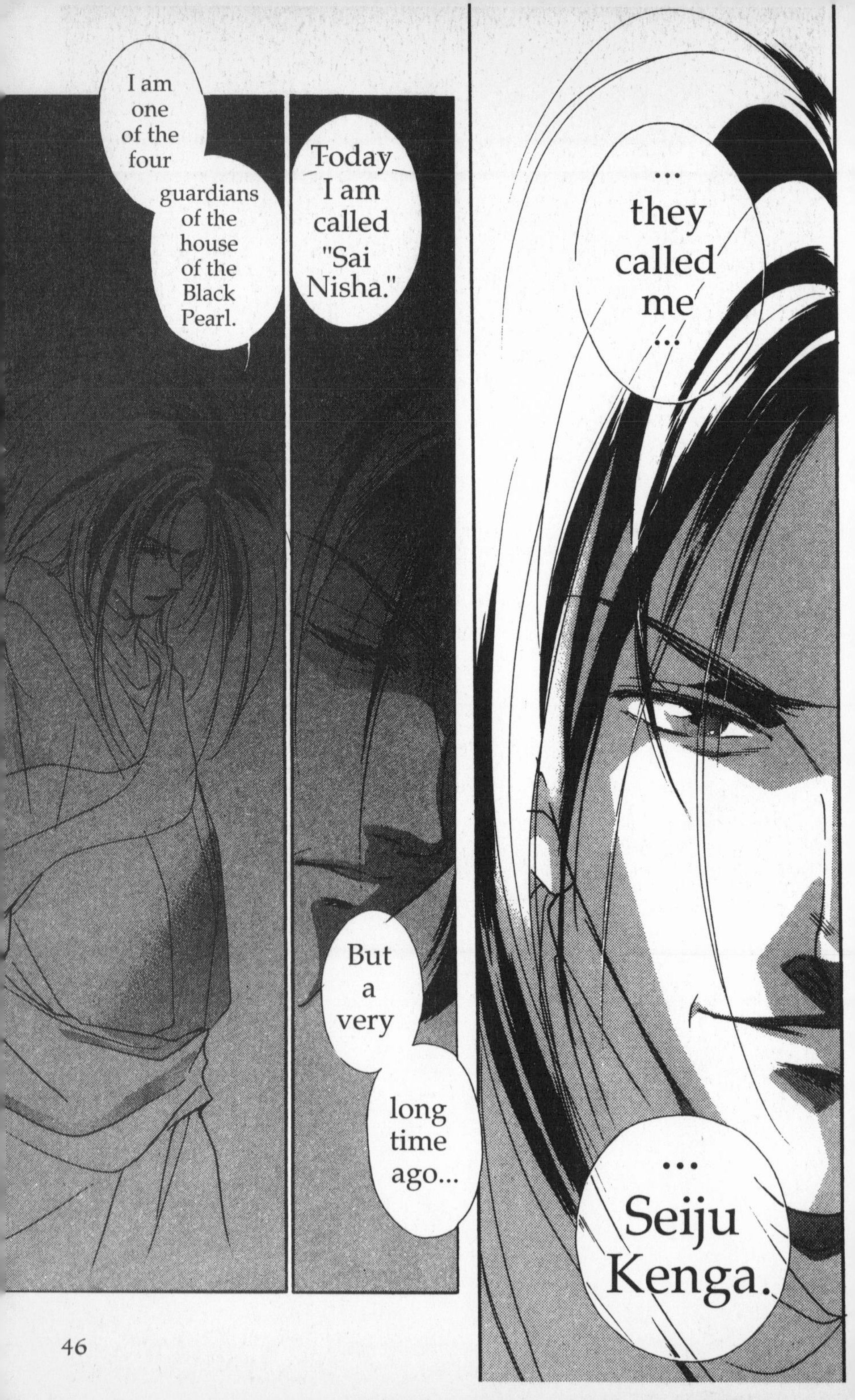
I am one of the four guardians of the house of the Black Pearl.
Today I am called "Sai Nisha."
But a very long time ago...
... they called me ...
... Seiju Kenga.

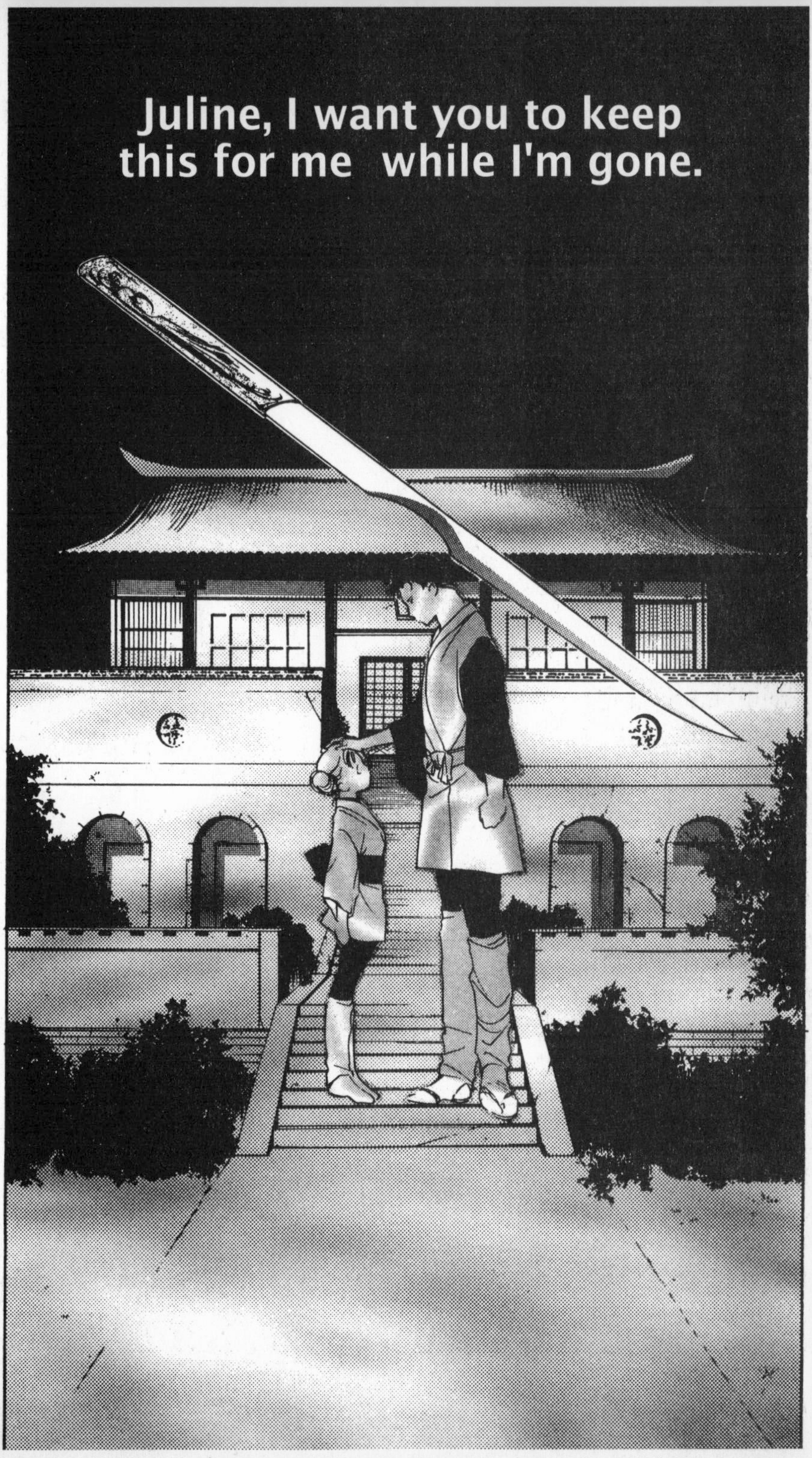
Juline, I want you to keep this for me while I'm gone.

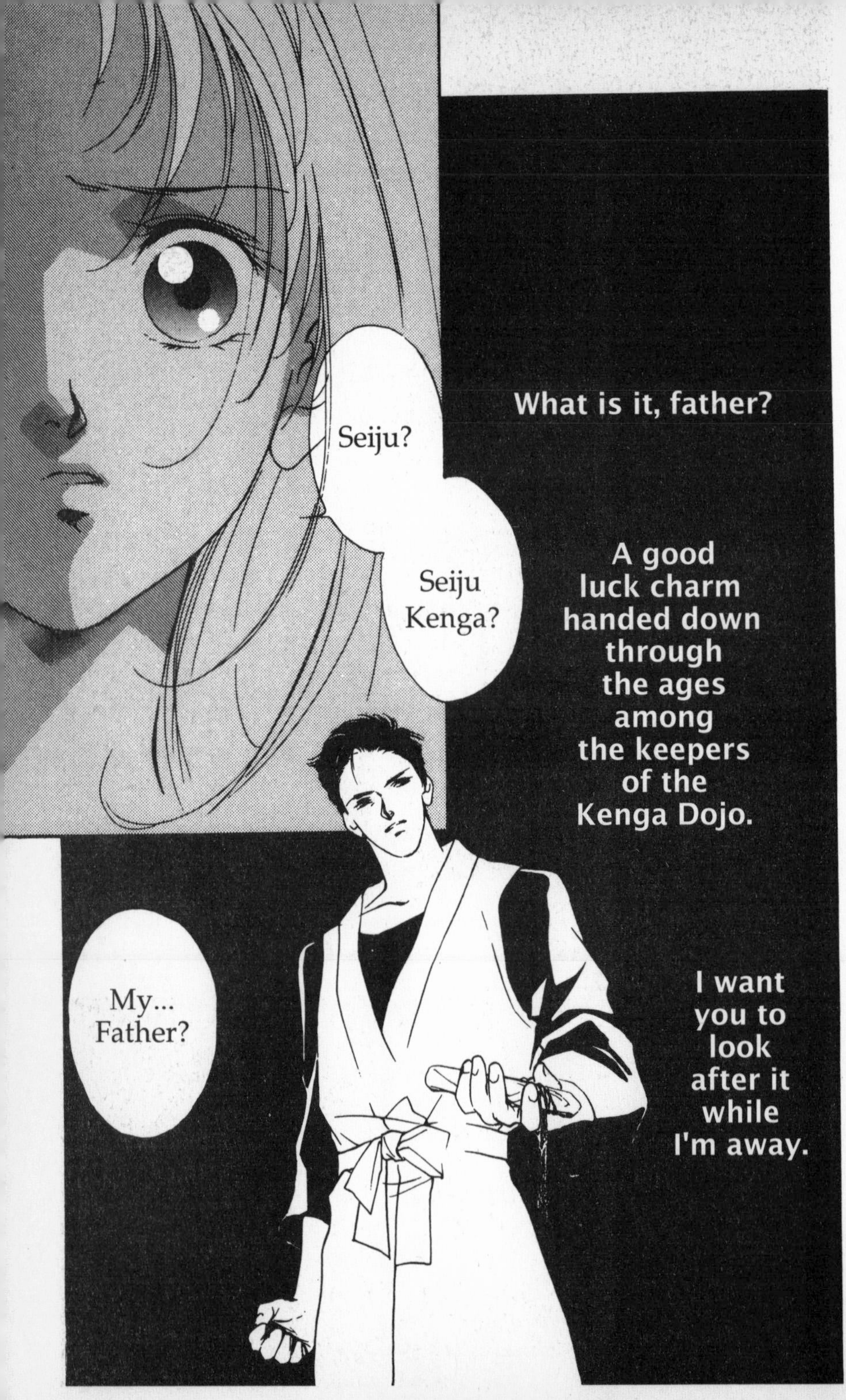
Seiju?
Seiju Kenga?
What is it, father?
A good luck charm handed down through the ages among the keepers of the Kenga Dojo.
My... Father?
I want you to look after it while I'm away.

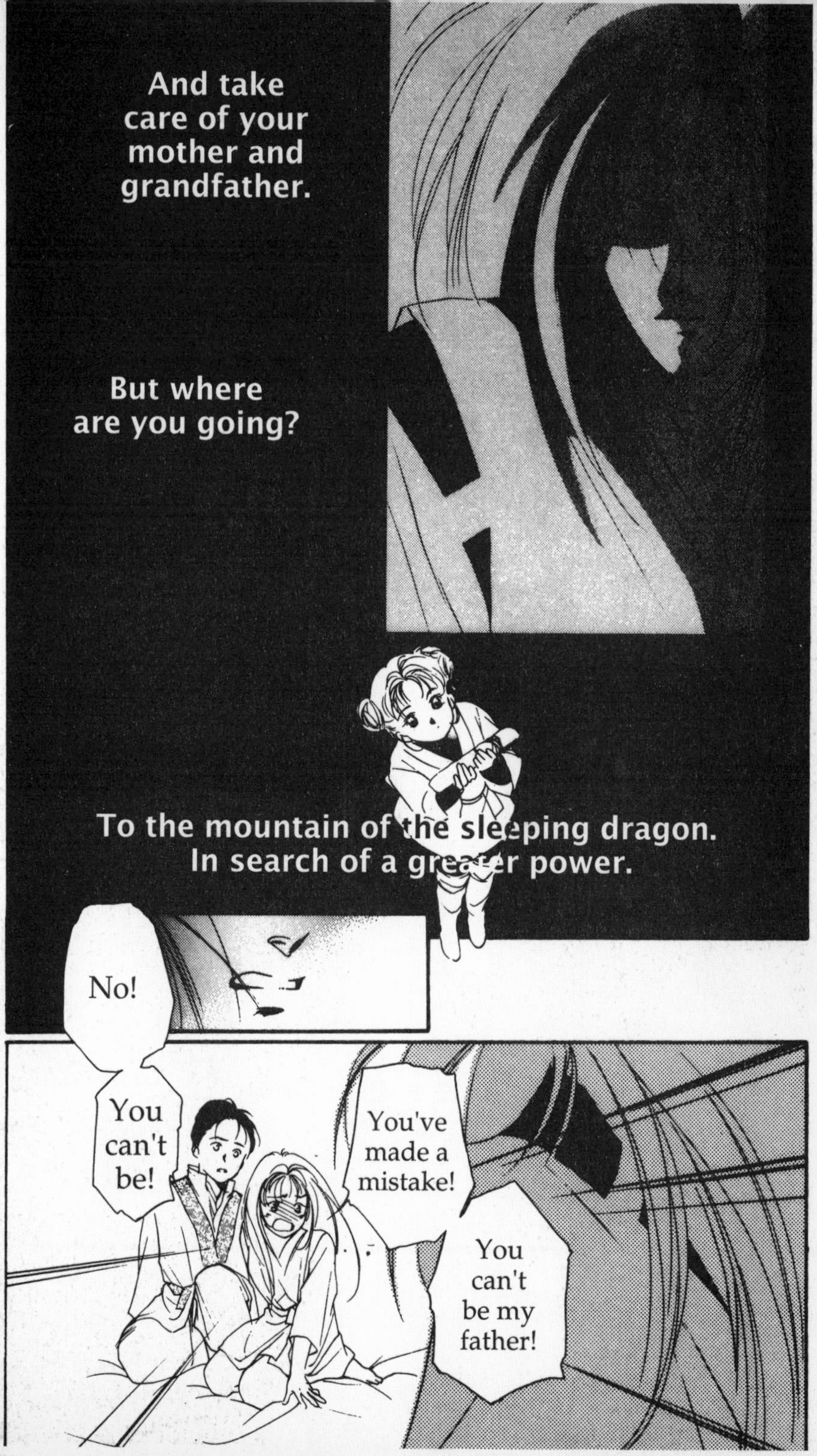

And take care of your mother and grandfather.
But where are you going?
To the mountain of the sleeping dragon. In search of a greater power.
No!
You can't be!
You've made a mistake!
You can't be my father!

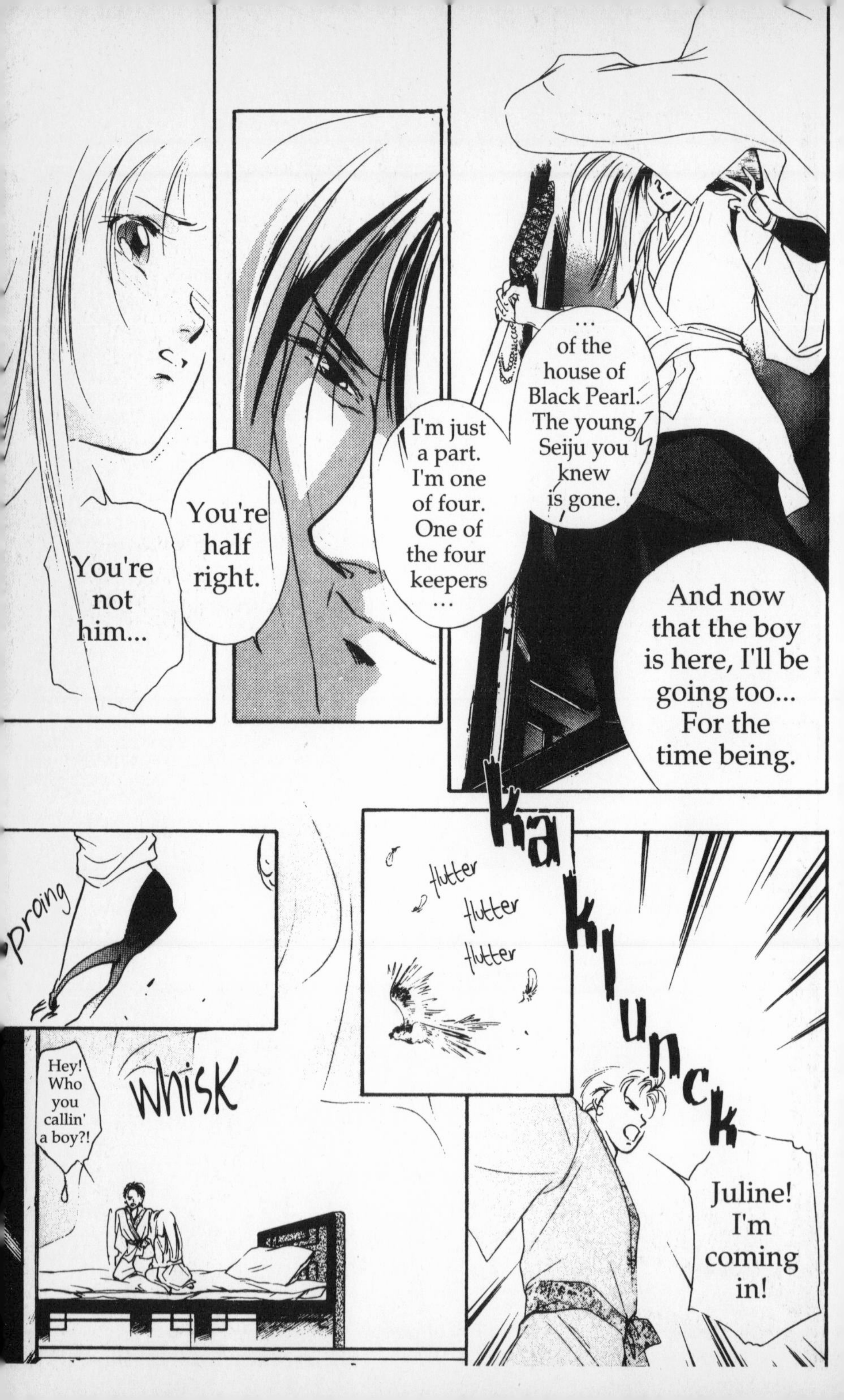

You're not him...
You're half right.
I'm just a part. I'm one of four. One of the four keepers ...
... of the house of Black Pearl. The young Seiju you knew is gone.
And now that the boy is here, I'll be going too... For the time being.
proing
whisk
Hey! Who you callin' a boy?!
flutter
flutter
flutter
Kaklunck
Juline! I'm coming in!

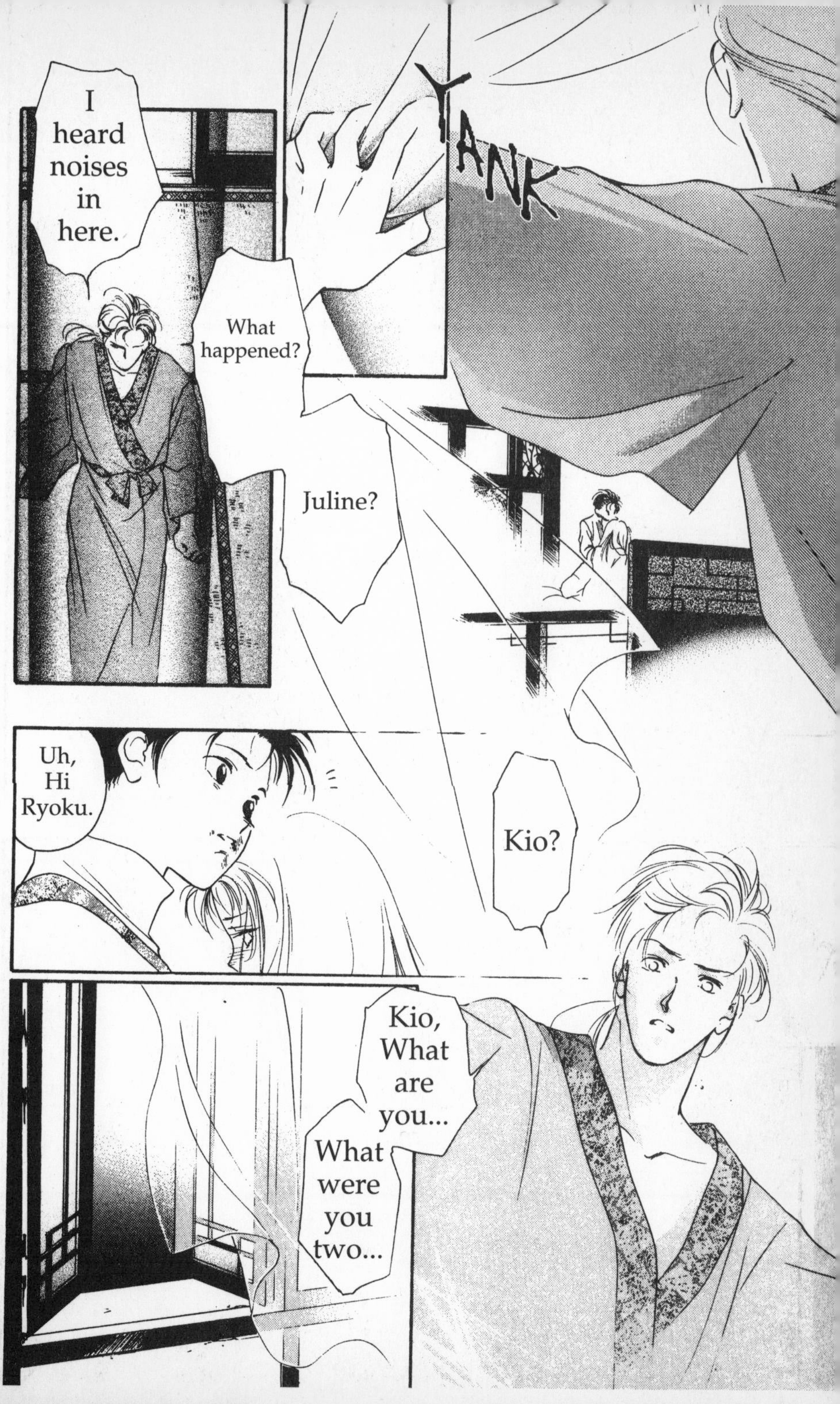

I heard noises in here.
What happened?
YANK
Juline?
Uh, Hi Ryoku.
Kio?
Kio, What are you...
What were you two...

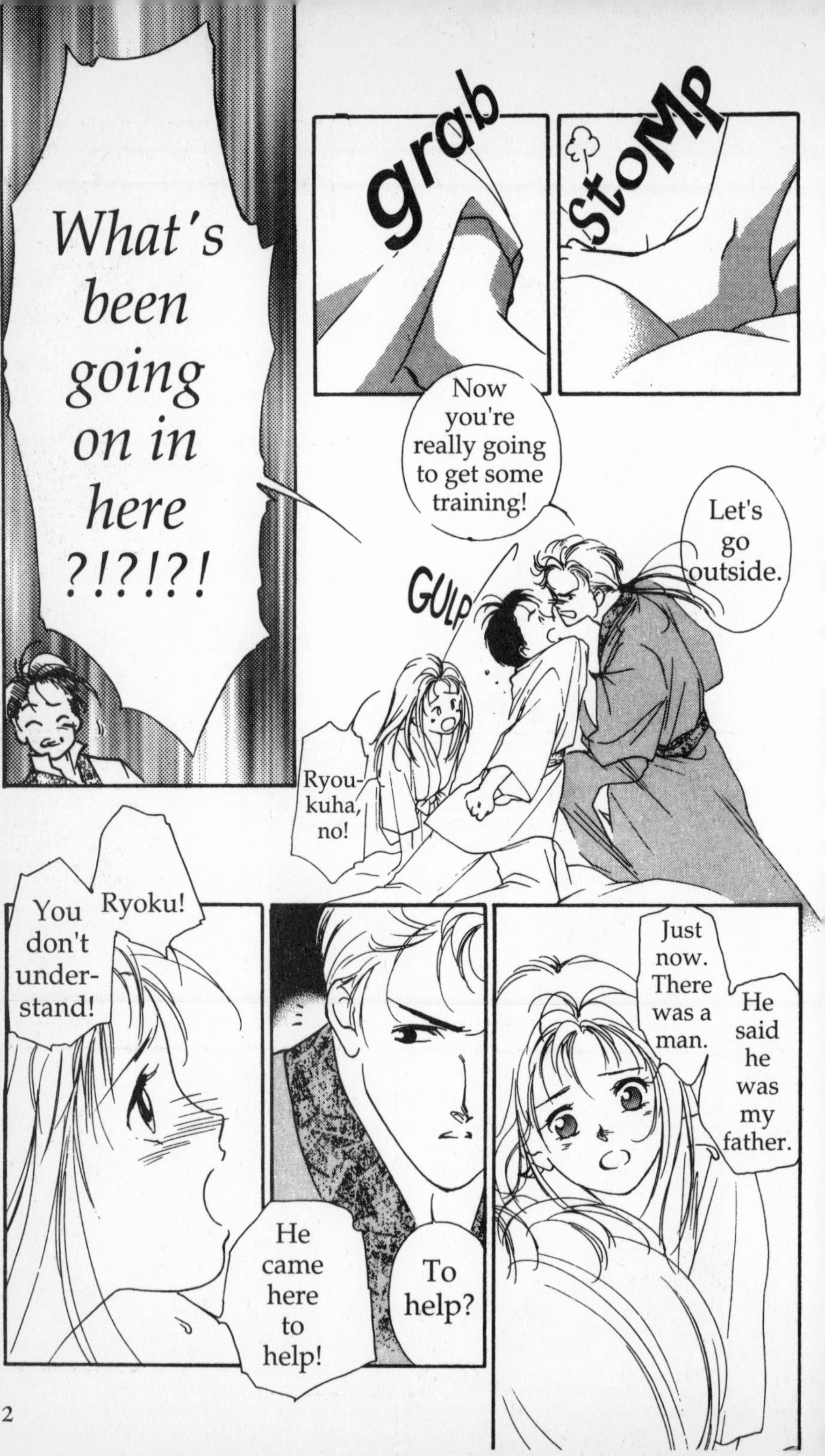

What's been going on in here?!?!?!
grab
stomp
Now you're really going to get some training!
Let's go outside.
GULP
Ryou-kuha, no!
Ryoku!
You don't under-stand!
He came here to help!
To help?
Just now. There was a man.
He said he was my father.

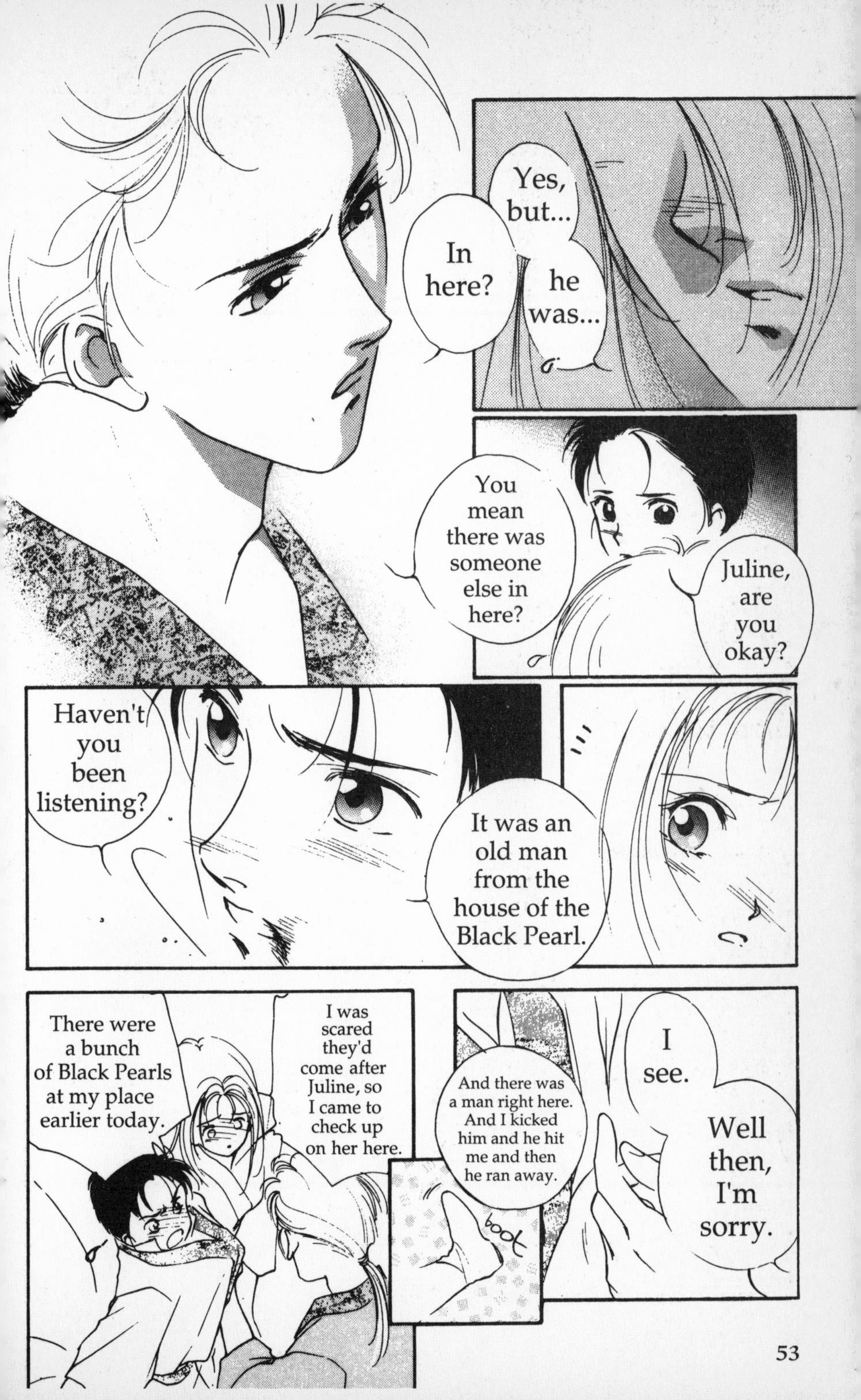

In here?
Yes, but... he was...
You mean there was someone else in here?
Juline, are you okay?
Haven't you been listening?
It was an old man from the house of the Black Pearl.
There were a bunch of Black Pearls at my place earlier today.
I was scared they'd come after Juline, so I came to check up on her here.
And there was a man right here. And I kicked him and he hit me and then he ran away.
boot
I see.
Well then, I'm sorry.

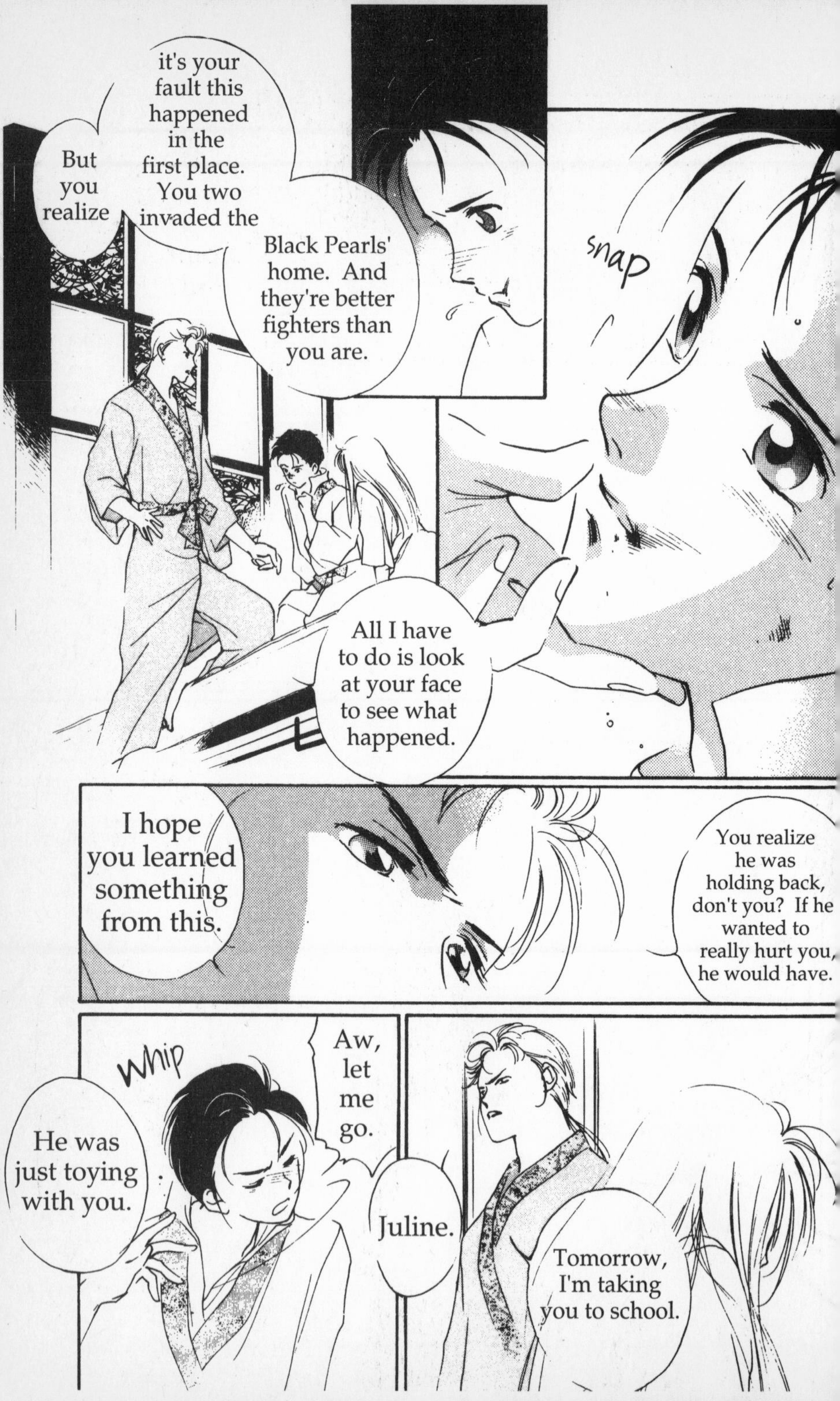
But you realize
it's your fault this happened in the first place. You two invaded the
Black Pearls' home. And they're better fighters than you are.
snap
All I have to do is look at your face to see what happened.
I hope you learned something from this.
You realize he was holding back, don't you? If he wanted to really hurt you, he would have.
Whip
He was just toying with you.
Aw, let me go.
Juline.
Tomorrow, I'm taking you to school.

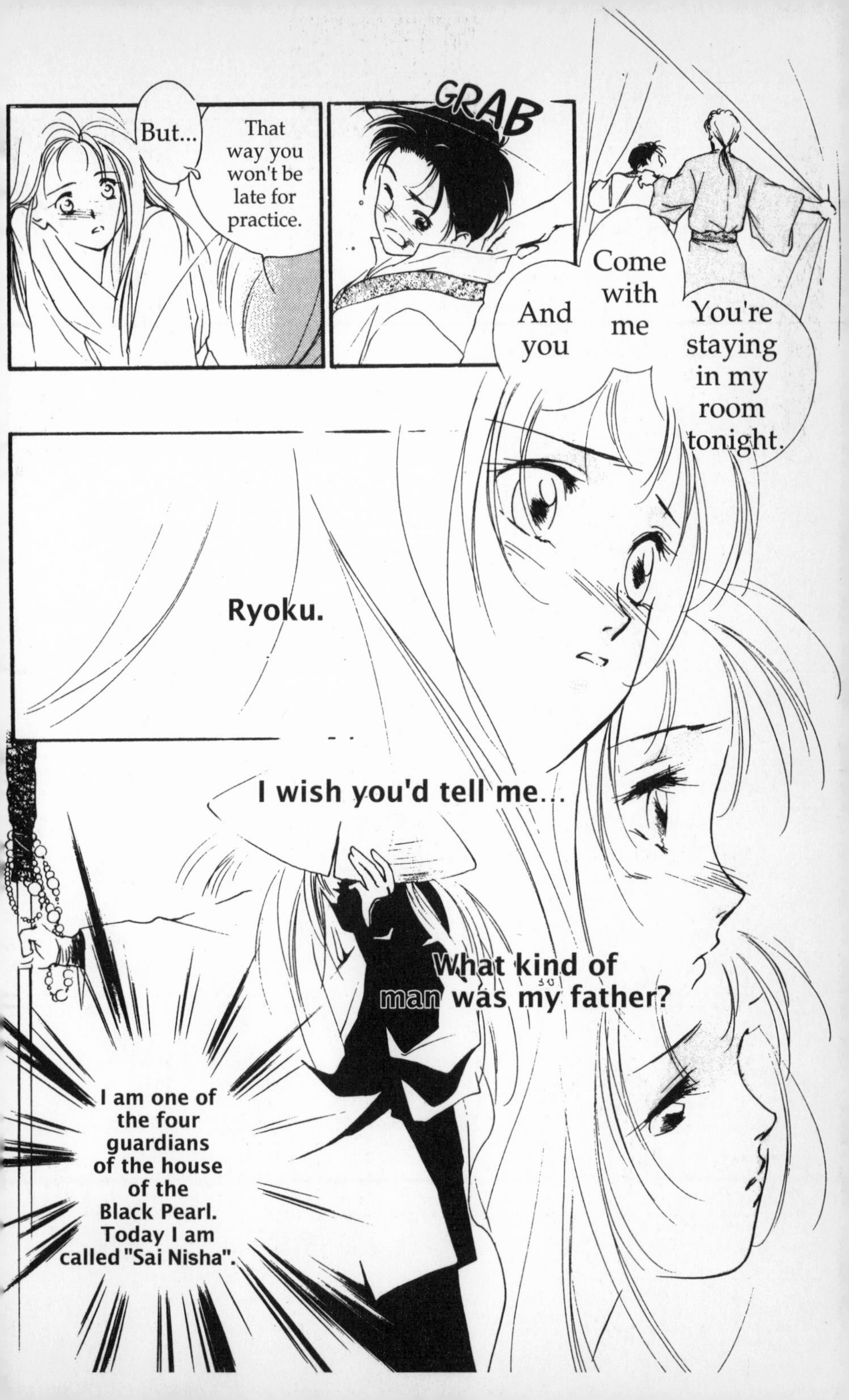

But...
That way you won't be late for practice.
GRAB
And you
Come with me
You're staying in my room tonight.
Ryoku.
I wish you'd tell me...
What kind of man was my father?
I am one of the four guardians of the house of the Black Pearl. Today I am called "Sai Nisha".

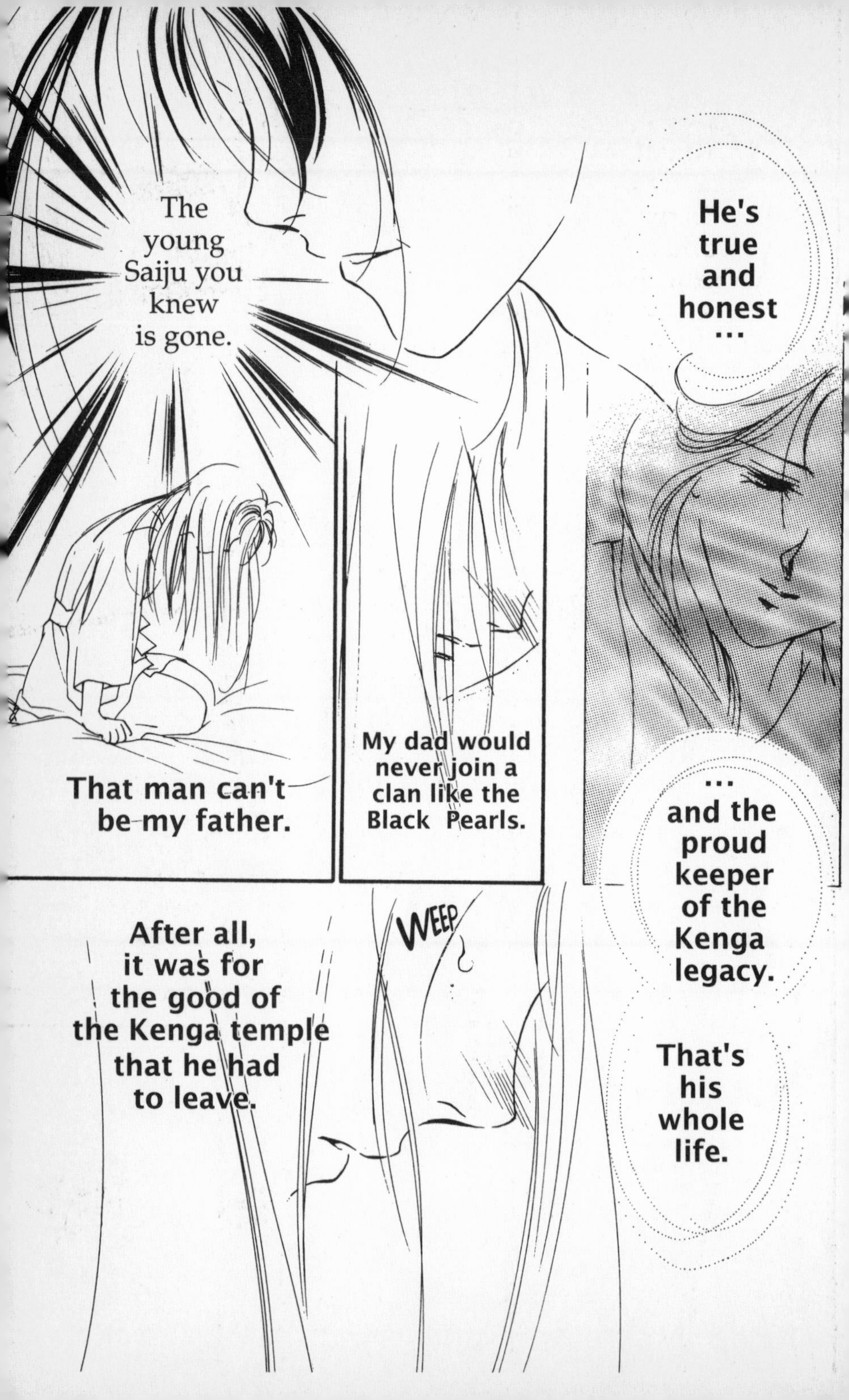
The young Saiju you knew is gone.
He's true and honest ...
That man can't be my father.
My dad would never join a clan like the Black Pearls.
... and the proud keeper of the Kenga legacy.
After all, it was for the good of the Kenga temple that he had to leave.
WEEP
That's his whole life.

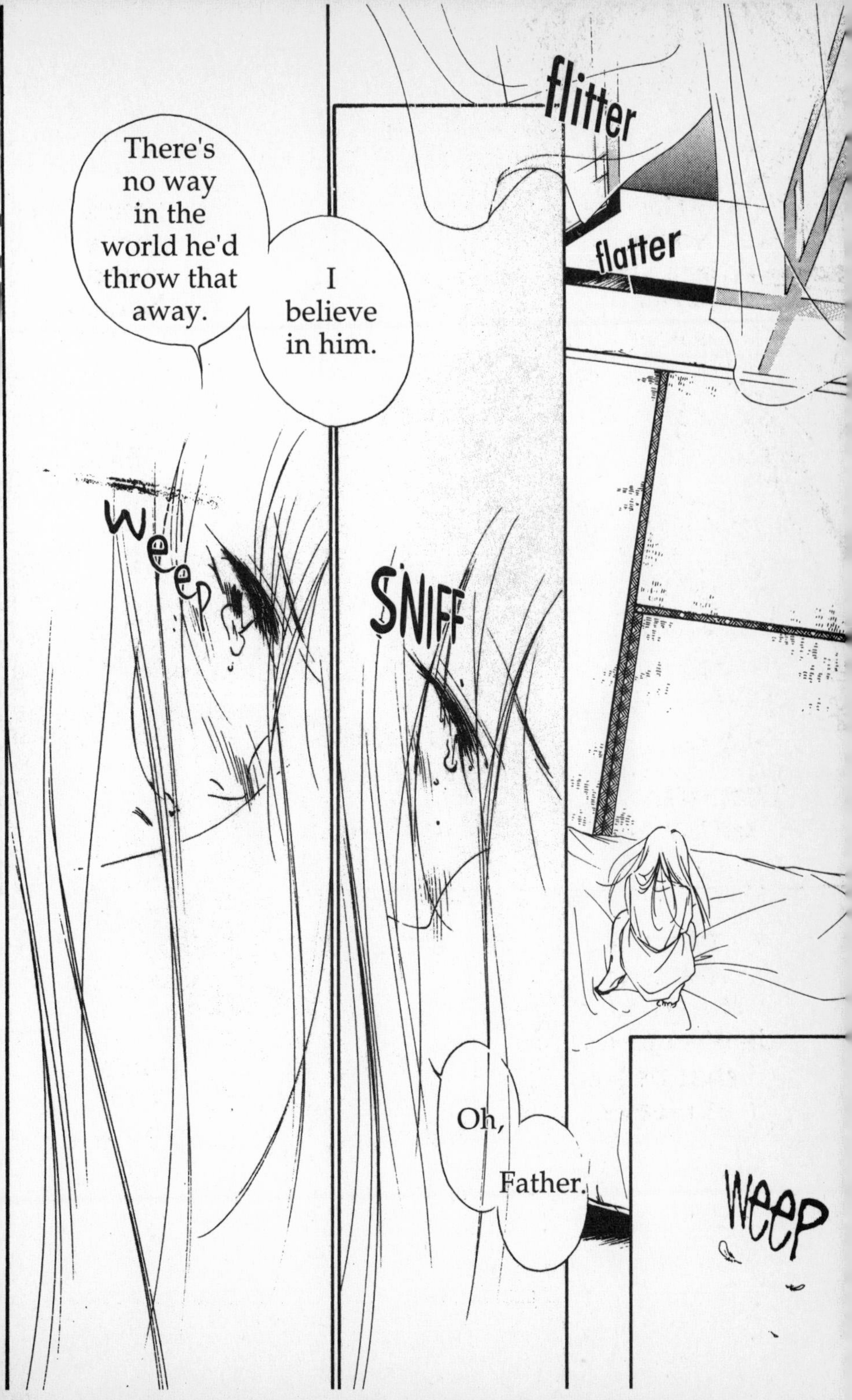
There's no way in the world he'd throw that away.
I believe in him.
weep
SNIFF
flitter
flatter
Oh,
Father.
weep

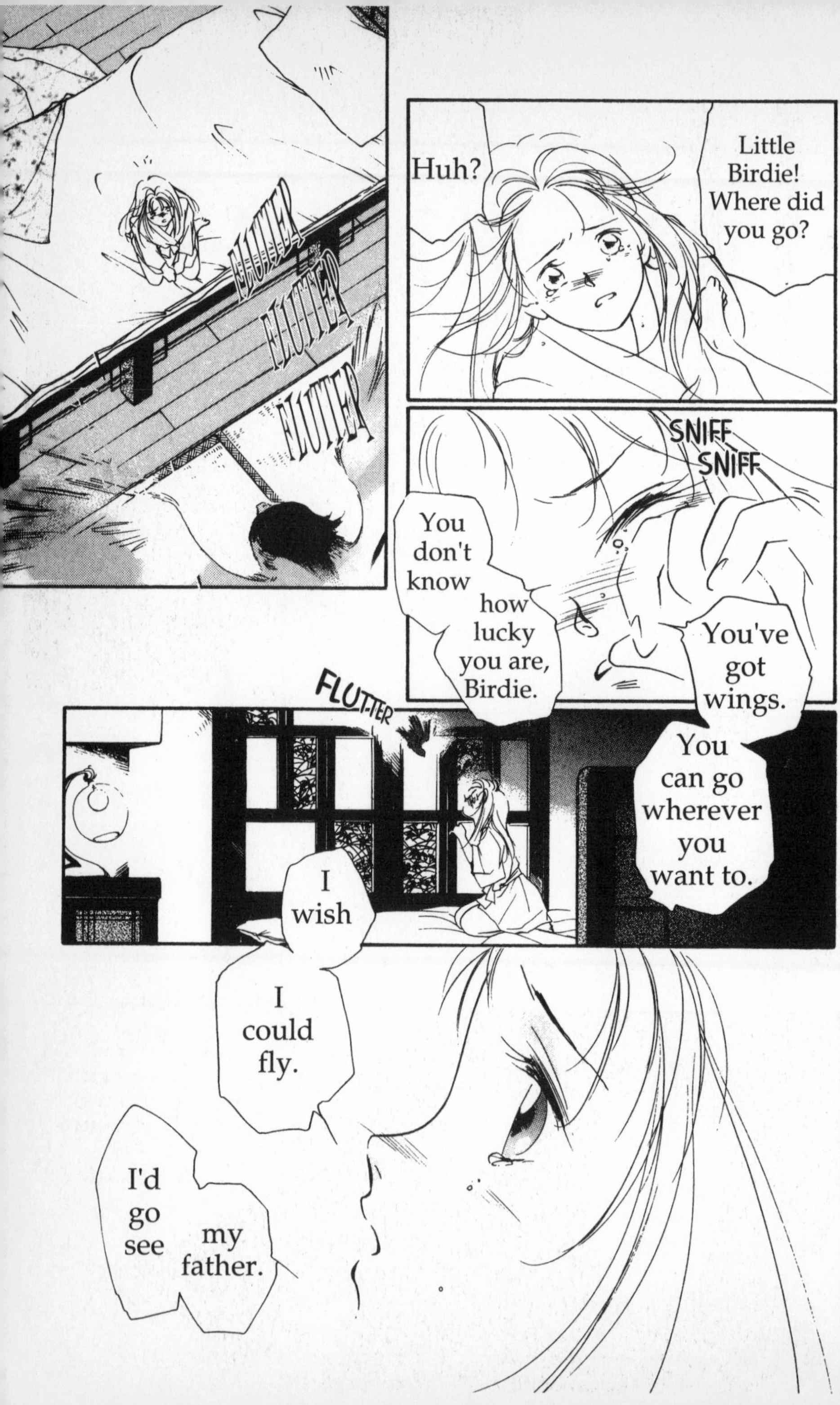
FLUTTER
FLUTTER
FLUTTER
Huh?
Little Birdie! Where did you go?
SNIFF SNIFF
You don't know how lucky you are, Birdie.
You've got wings.
FLUT-TER
You can go wherever you want to.
I wish
I could fly.
I'd go see my father.

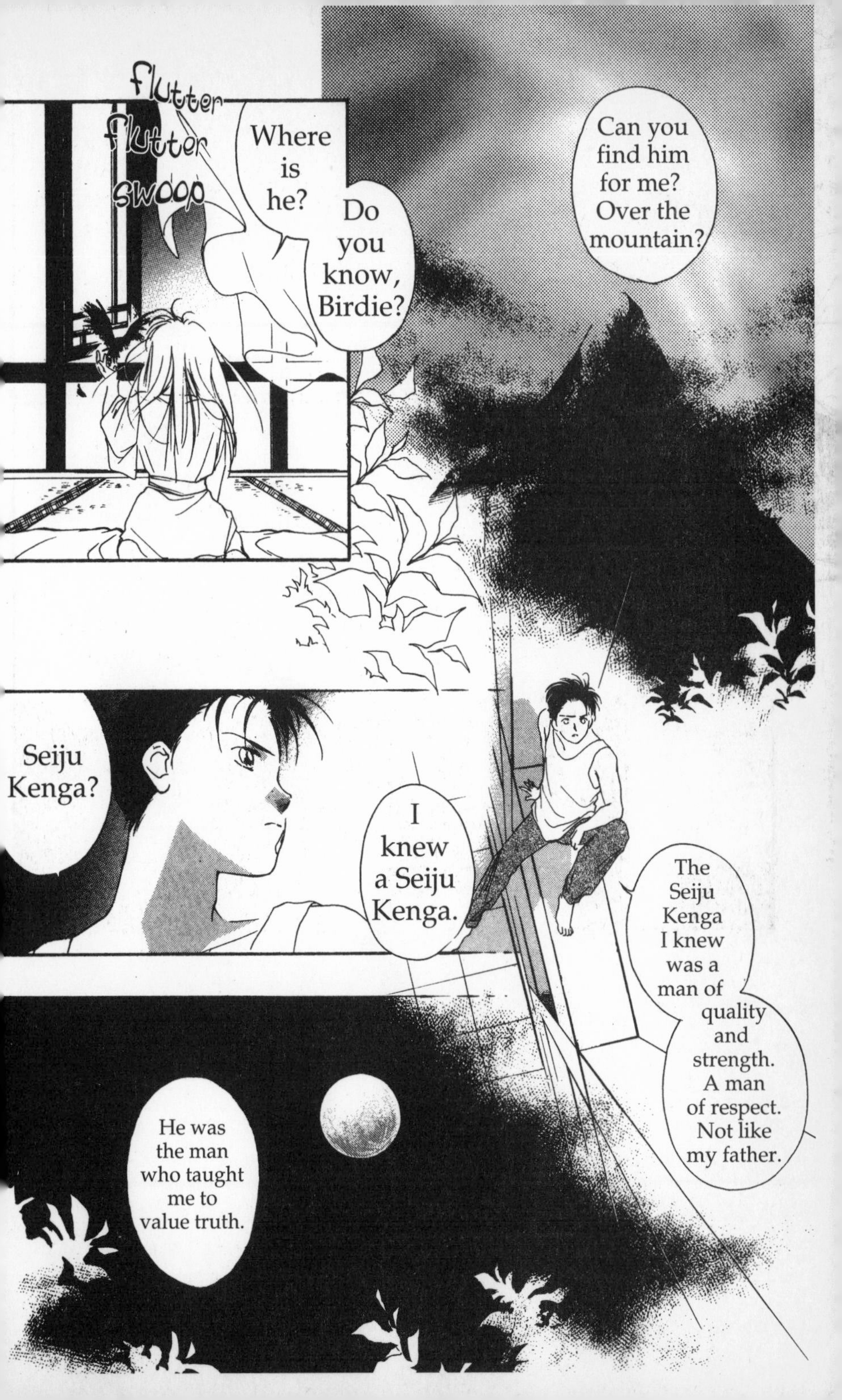
flutter
flutter
swoop
Where is he?
Do you know, Birdie?
Can you find him for me? Over the mountain?
Seiju Kenga?
I knew a Seiju Kenga.
The Seiju Kenga I knew was a man of quality and strength. A man of respect. Not like my father.
He was the man who taught me to value truth.

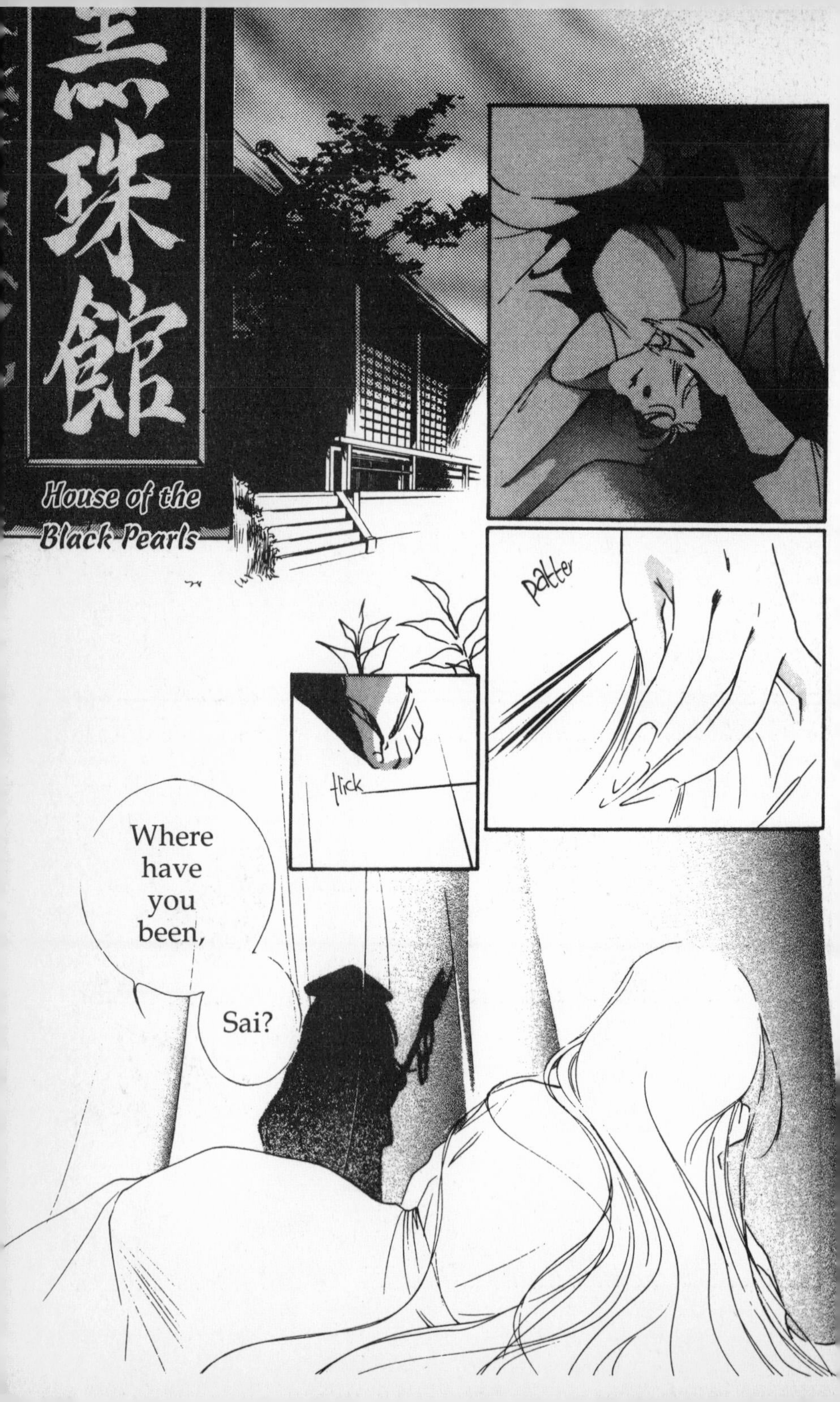

黒珠館
House of the Black Pearls
patter
flick
Where have you been,
Sai?

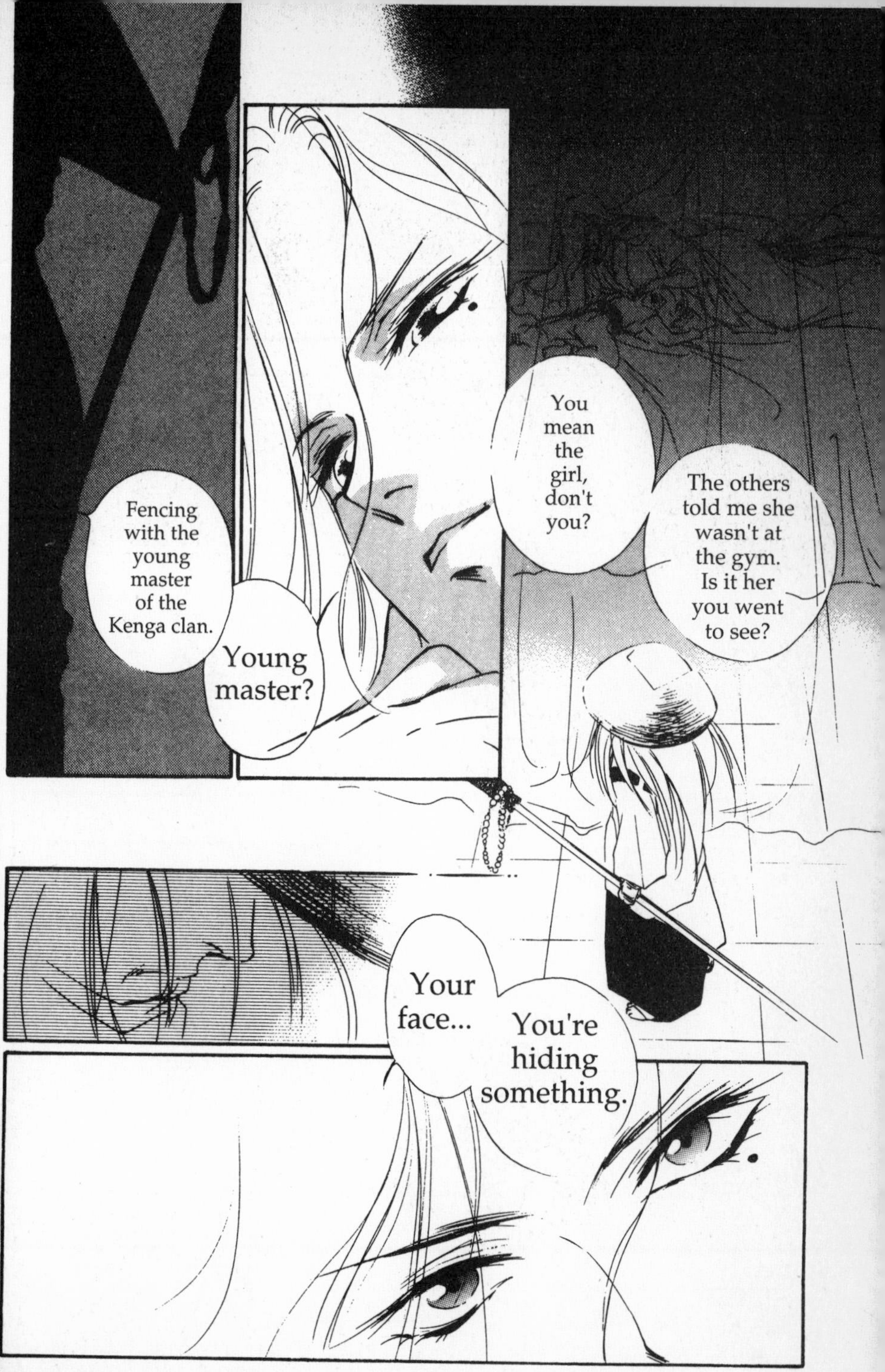
Fencing with the young master of the Kenga clan.
Young master?
You mean the girl, don't you?
The others told me she wasn't at the gym. Is it her you went to see?
Your face...
You're hiding something.

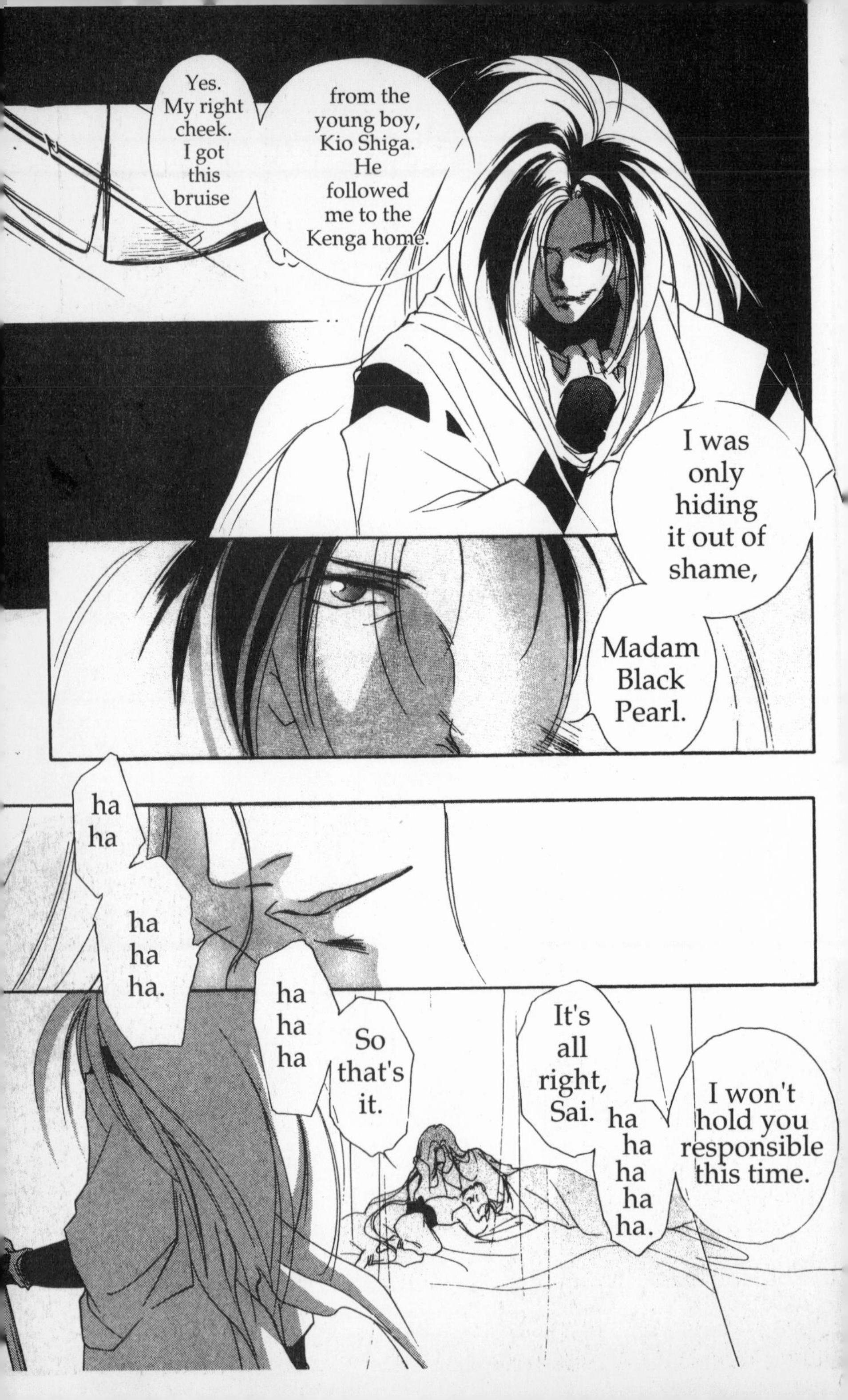

Yes. My right cheek. I got this bruise
from the young boy, Kio Shiga. He followed me to the Kenga home.
I was only hiding it out of shame,
Madam Black Pearl.
ha ha
ha ha ha.
ha ha ha
So that's it.
It's all right, Sai.
ha ha ha ha ha.
I won't hold you responsible this time.

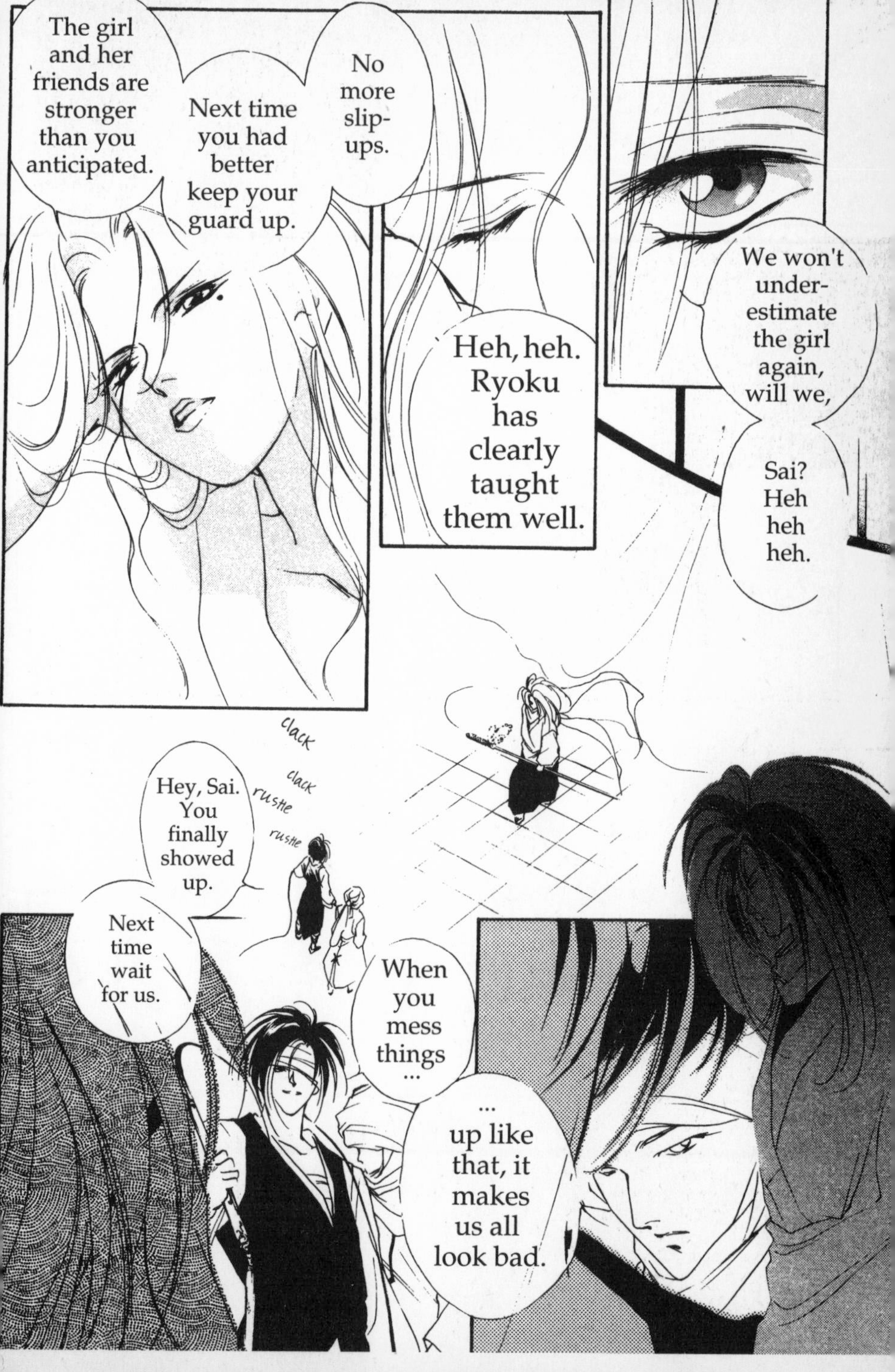
The girl and her friends are stronger than you anticipated.
Next time you had better keep your guard up.
No more slip-ups.
Heh, heh. Ryoku has clearly taught them well.
We won't under-estimate the girl again, will we,
Sai? Heh heh heh.
clack
clack
rustle
rustle
Hey, Sai. You finally showed up.
Next time wait for us.
When you mess things ...
... up like that, it makes us all look bad.

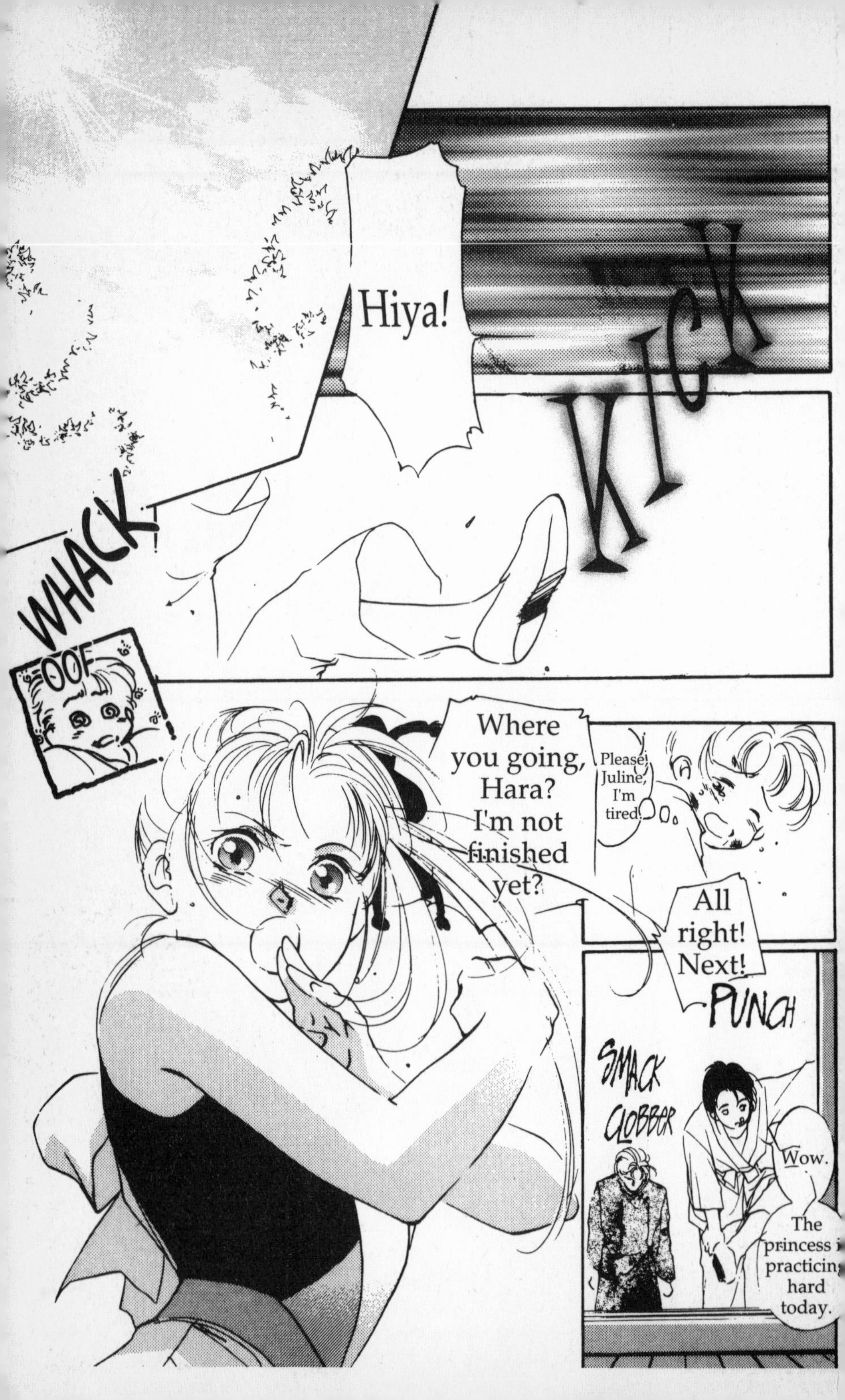

Hiya!
KICK
WHACK
OOF
Where you going, Hara? I'm not finished yet?
Please! Juline, I'm tired.
All right! Next!
PUNCH
SMACK
CLOBBER
Wow.
The princess i practicin hard today.

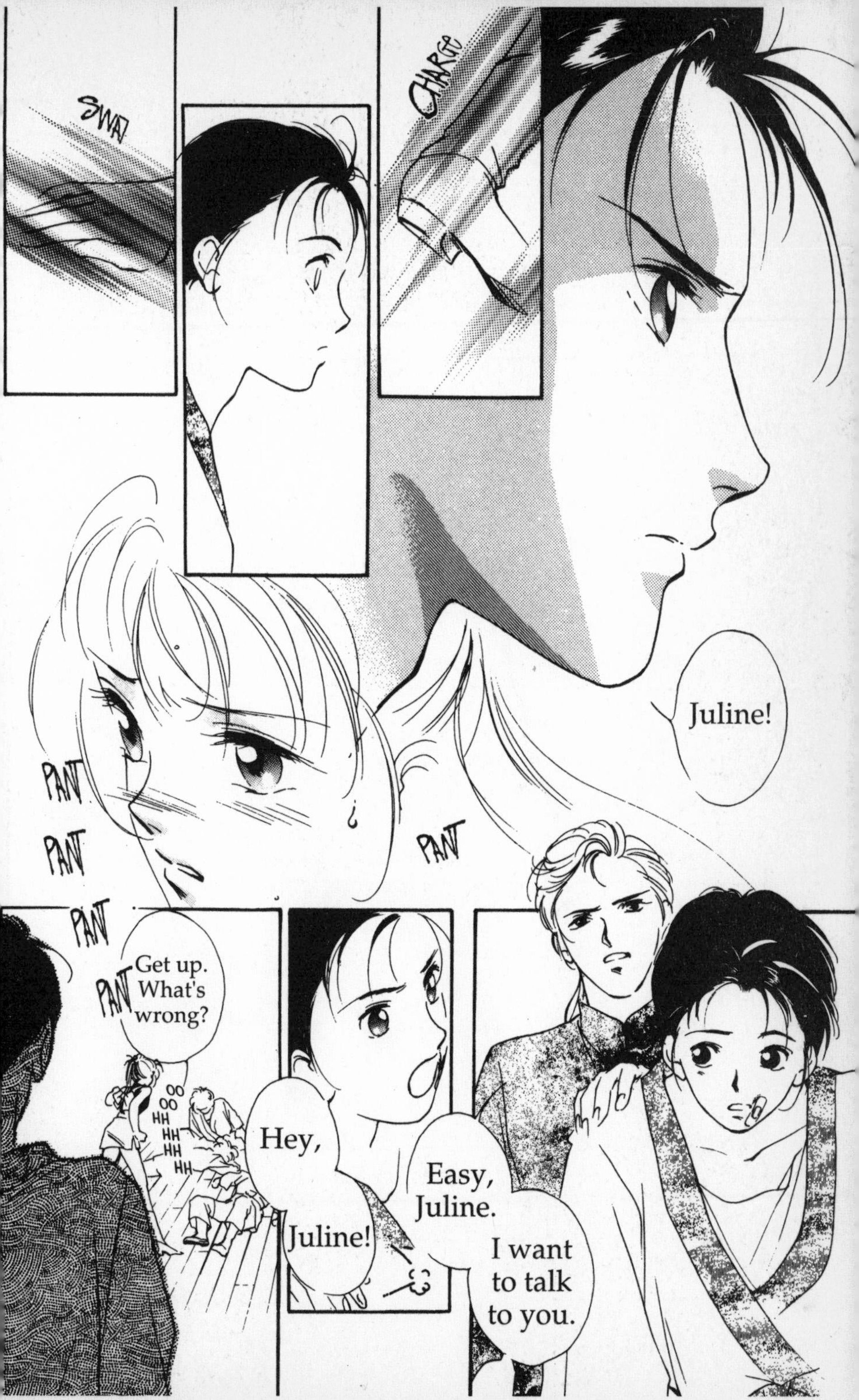

CHARGE
Juline!
PANT
PANT
PANT
PANT
PANT
Get up. What's wrong?
Hey,
Juline!
Easy, Juline.
I want to talk to you.

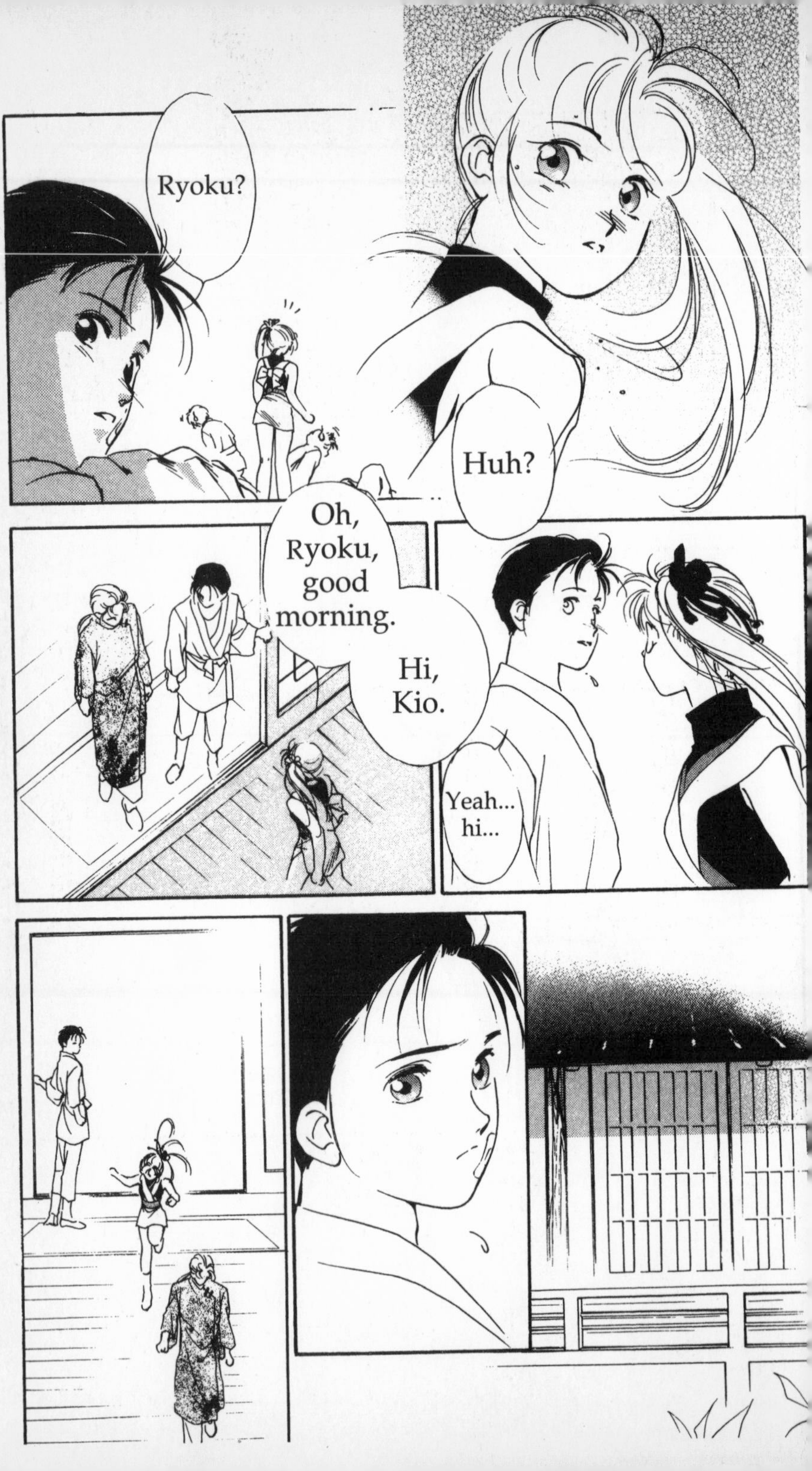
Ryoku?
Huh?
Oh, Ryoku, good morning.
Hi, Kio.
Yeah... hi...

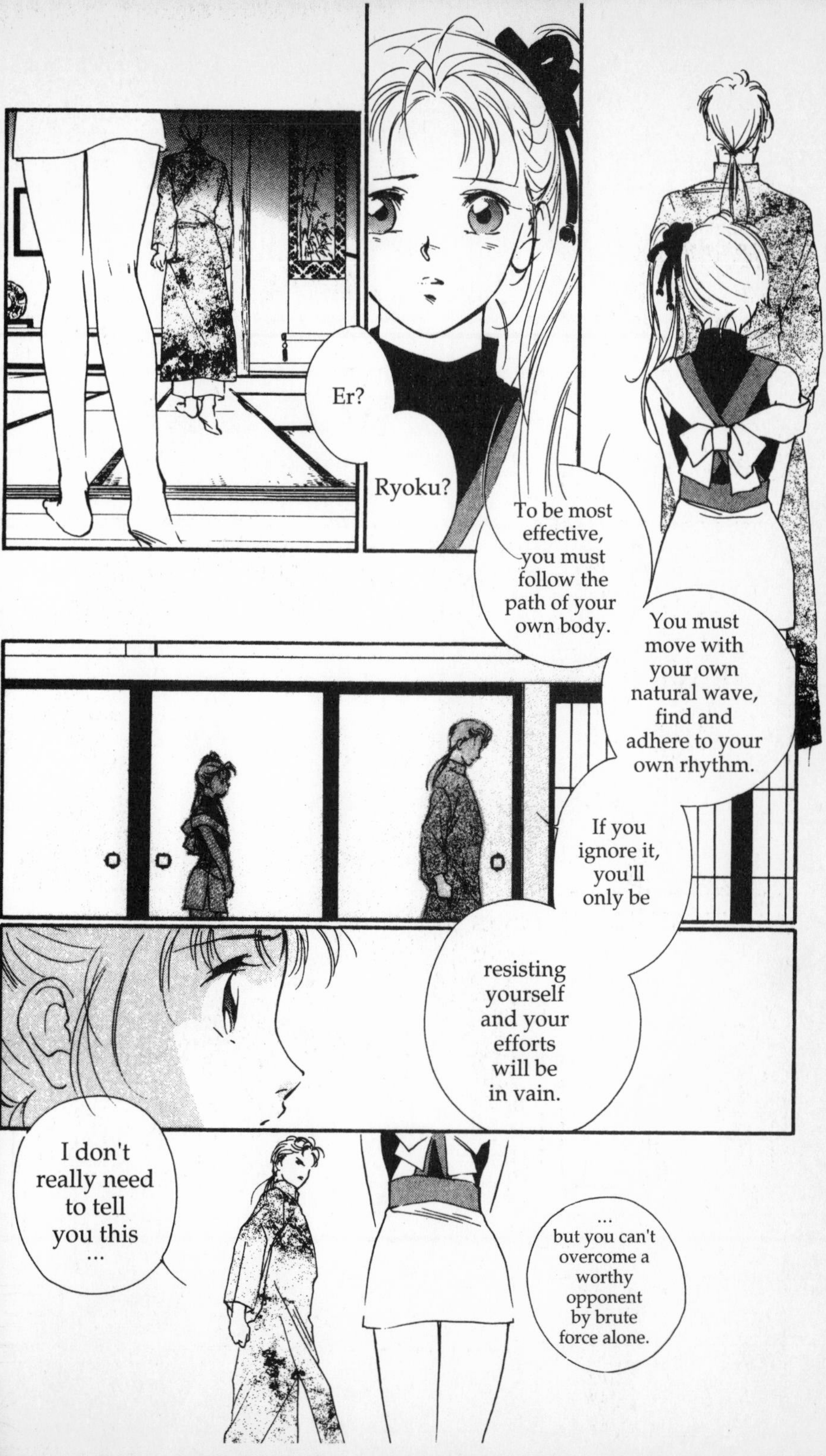
Er?
Ryoku?
To be most effective, you must follow the path of your own body.
You must move with your own natural wave, find and adhere to your own rhythm.
If you ignore it, you'll only be
resisting yourself and your efforts will be in vain.
I don't really need to tell you this ...
... but you can't overcome a worthy opponent by brute force alone.

Yes, I know, Ryoku.

Juline, tonight your sensei will return to the dojo.

Grandpa?

That's right. I guess the tournament's over by now, isn't it?

Juline, listen.

If something is troubling you, something you feel you can't talk to your mother about, you can always talk to your grandfather.

Huh?

I can tell from your eyes you haven't been sleeping well.

And I'm supposed to be taking care of you in your father's absence.

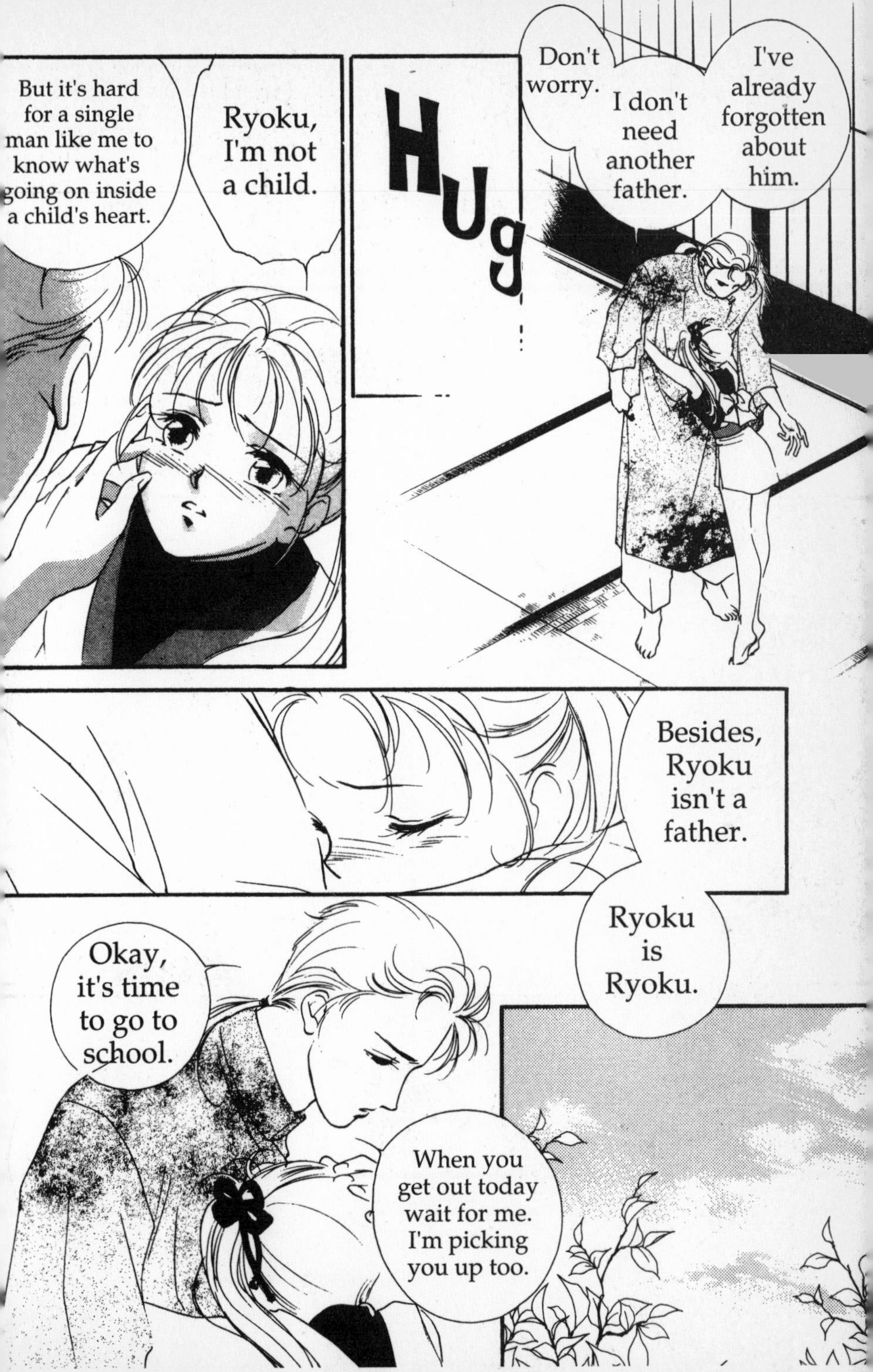
But it's hard for a single man like me to know what's going on inside a child's heart.
Ryoku, I'm not a child.
HUG
Don't worry.
I don't need another father.
I've already forgotten about him.
Besides, Ryoku isn't a father.
Ryoku is Ryoku.
Okay, it's time to go to school.
When you get out today wait for me. I'm picking you up too.

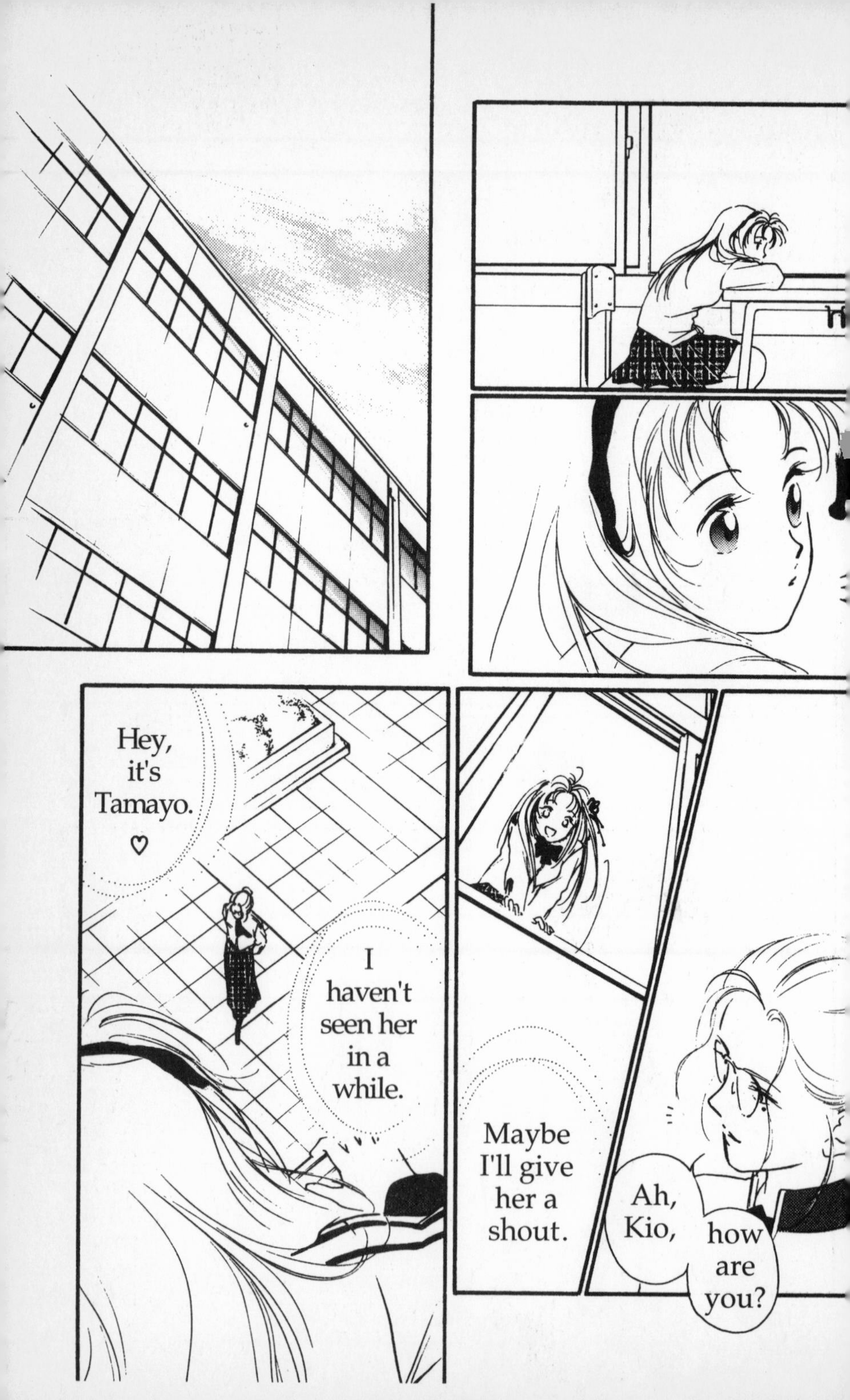
Hey, it's Tamayo. ♡
I haven't seen her in a while.
Maybe I'll give her a shout.
Ah, Kio,
how are you?

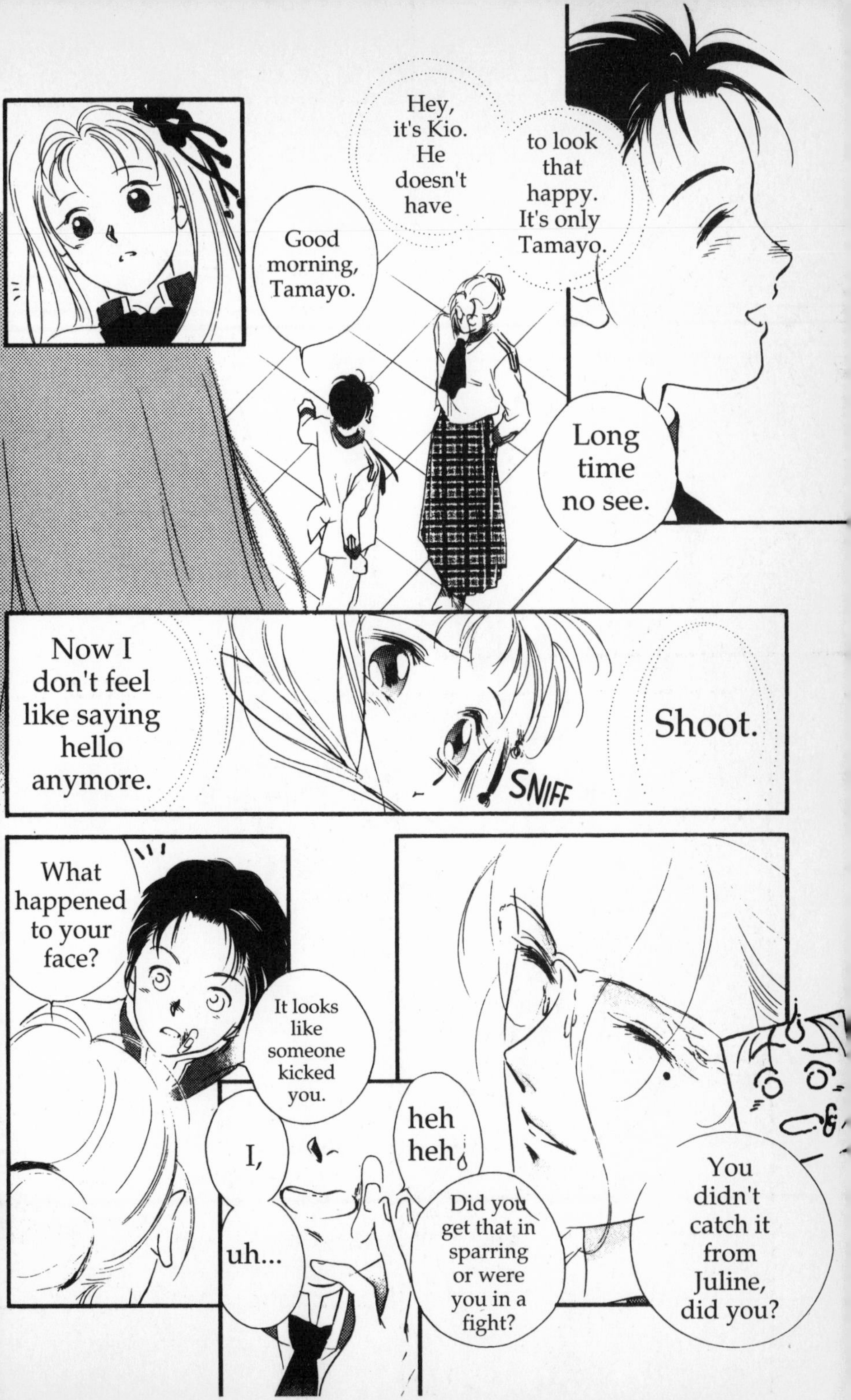

Good morning, Tamayo.
Hey, it's Kio. He doesn't have
to look that happy. It's only Tamayo.
Long time no see.
Now I don't feel like saying hello anymore.
SNIFF
Shoot.
What happened to your face?
It looks like someone kicked you.
I,
uh...
heh heh
Did you get that in sparring or were you in a fight?
You didn't catch it from Juline, did you?

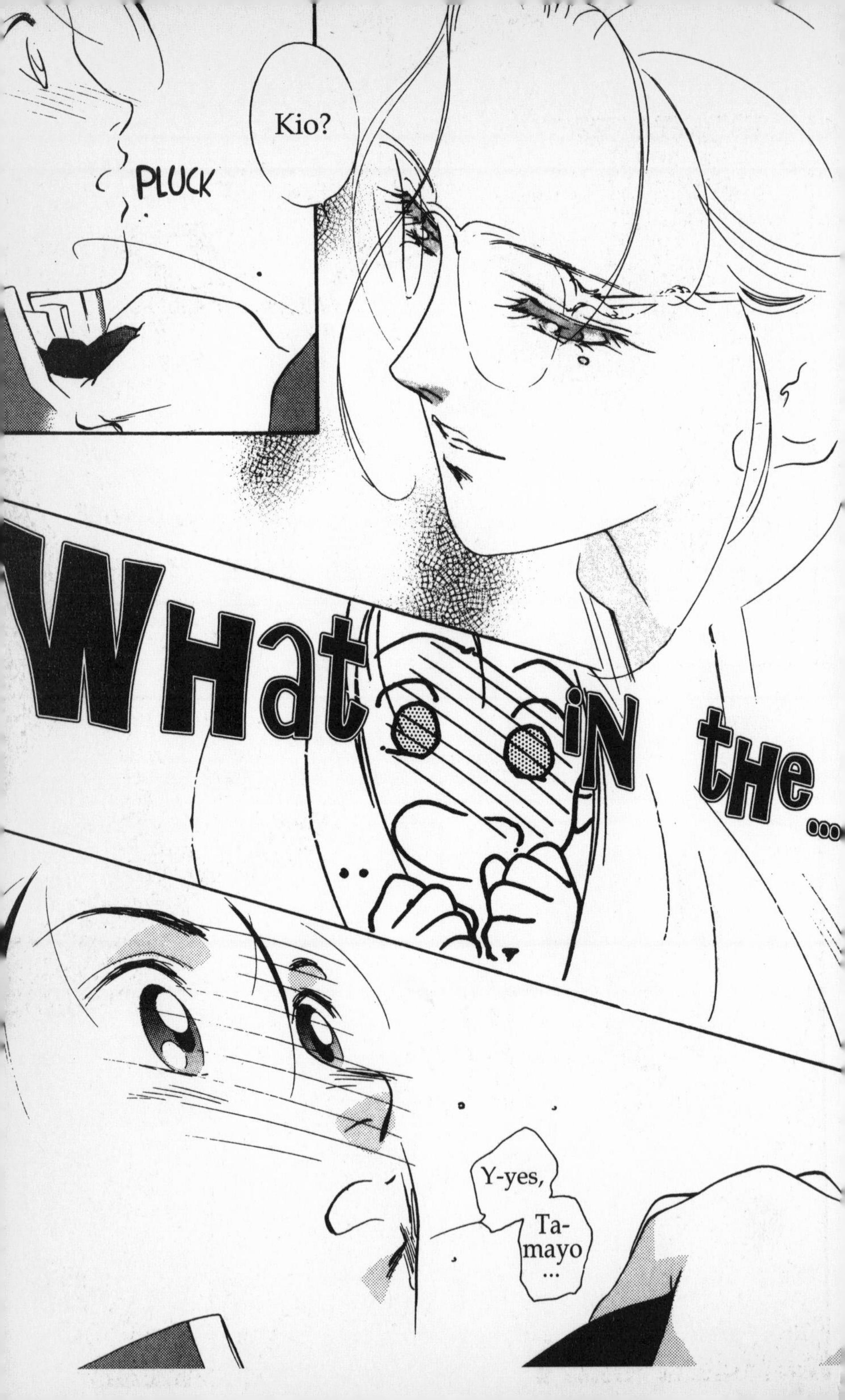
Kio?
PLUCK
What in the...
Y-yes, Tamayo...

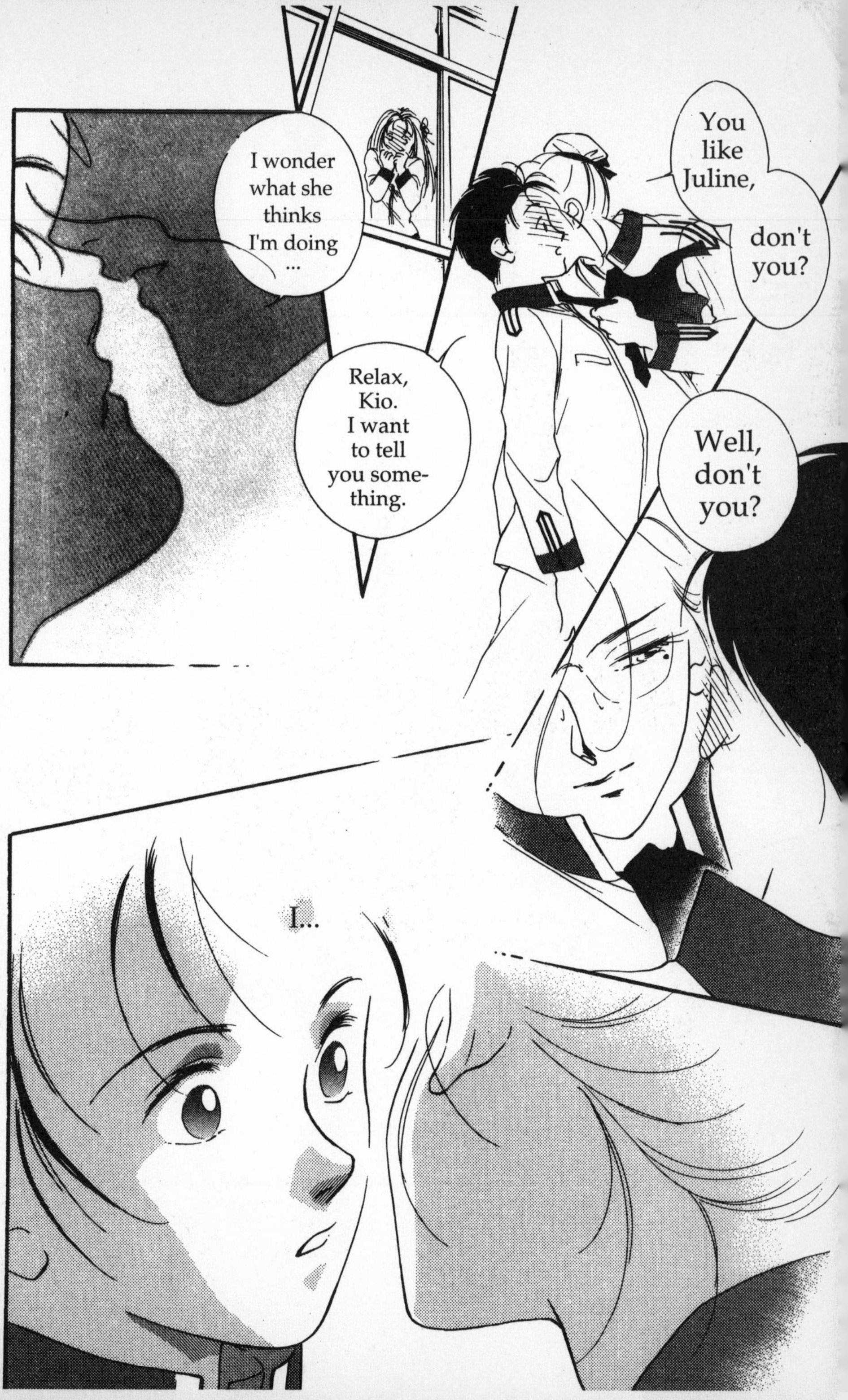
I wonder what she thinks I'm doing ...
Relax, Kio. I want to tell you some-thing.
You like Juline,
don't you?
Well, don't you?
I...

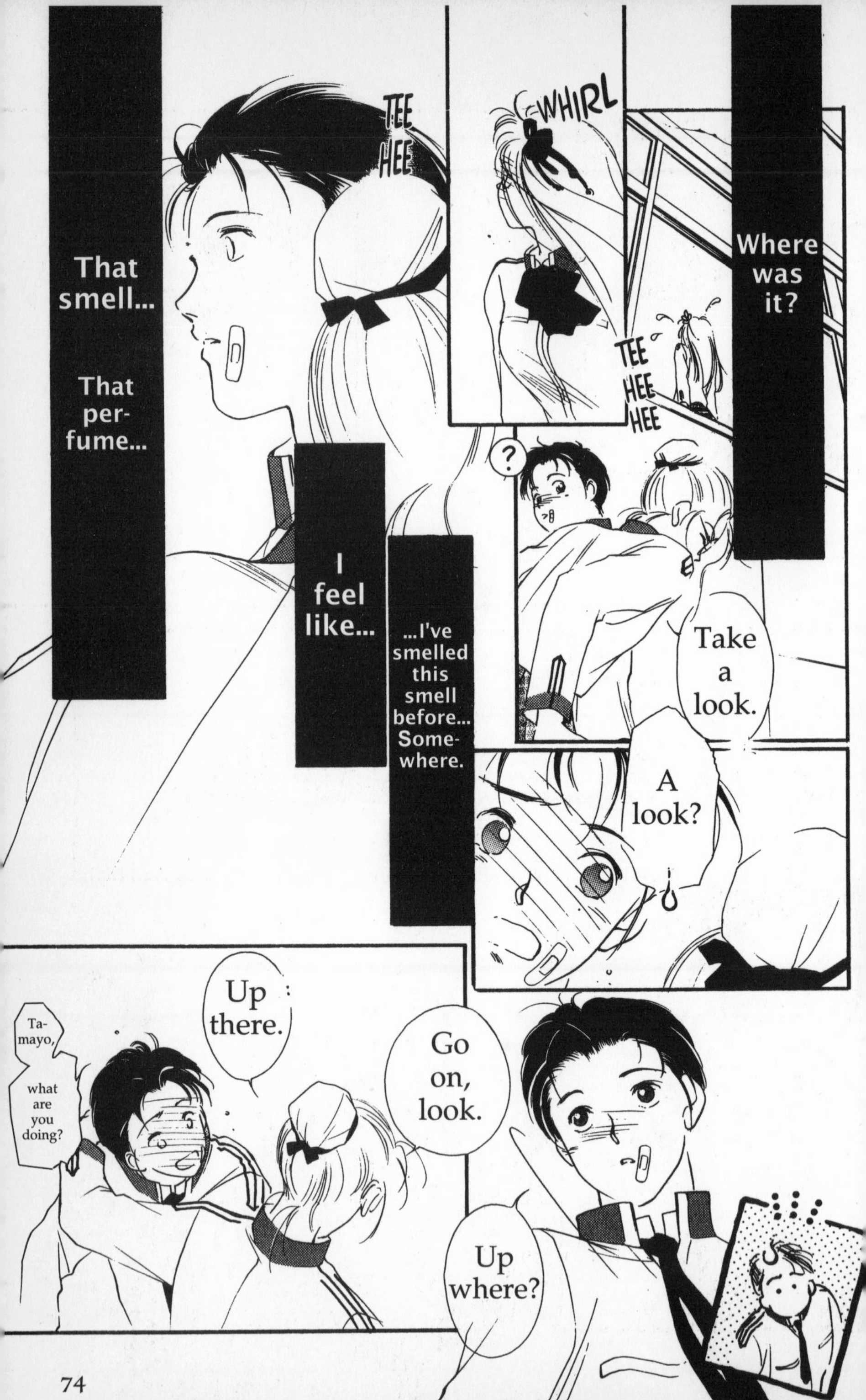
That smell...
That perfume...
TEE HEE
I feel like...
...I've smelled this smell before... Somewhere.
WHIRL
Where was it?
TEE HEE HEE
?
Take a look.
A look?
Tamayo, what are you doing?
Up there.
Go on, look.
Up where?

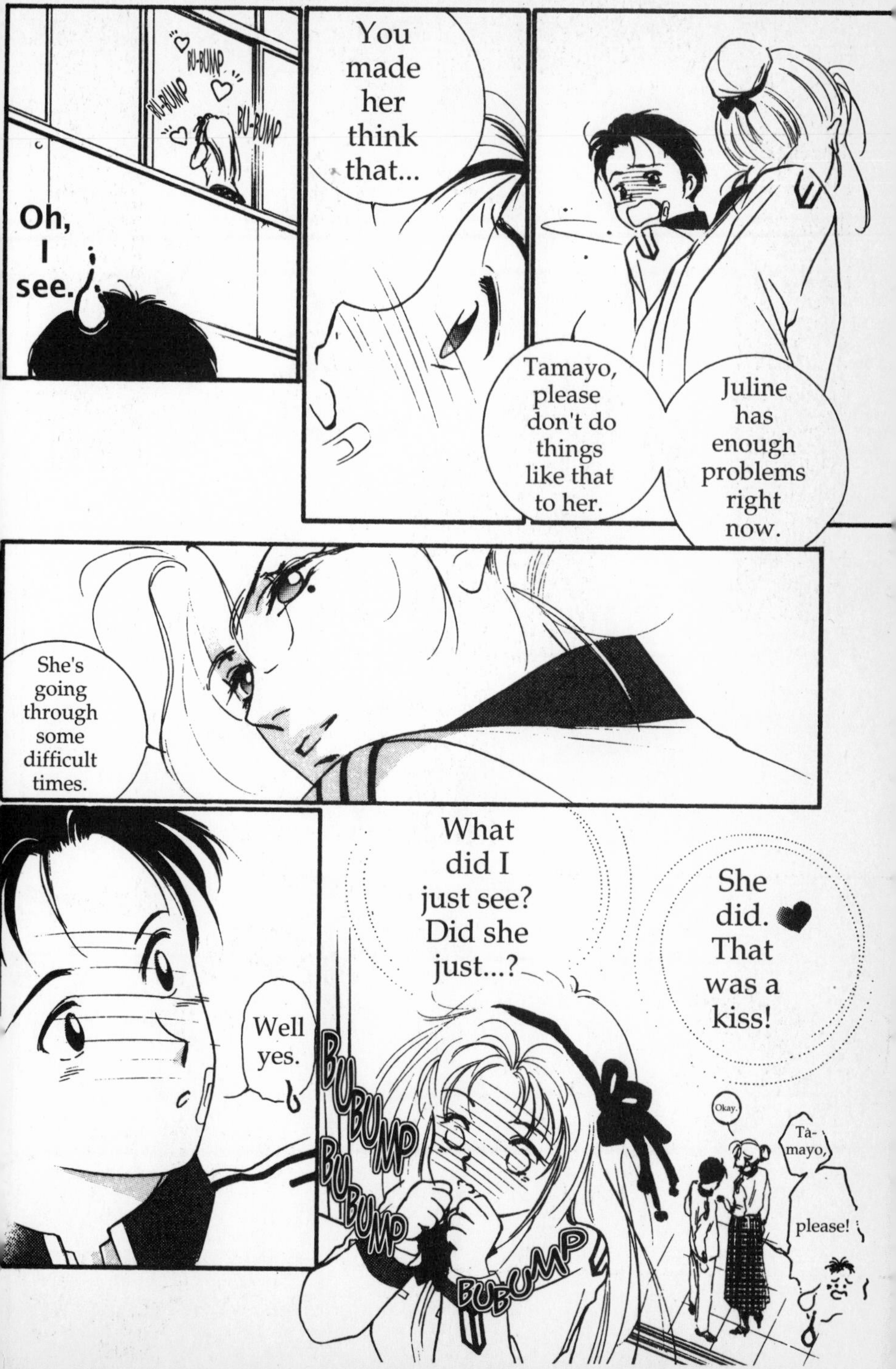
BU-BUMP
BU-BUMP
BU-BUMP
Oh, I see.
You made her think that...
Tamayo, please don't do things like that to her.
Juline has enough problems right now.
She's going through some difficult times.
Well yes.
What did I just see? Did she just...?
She did. That was a kiss!
BUBUMP BUBUMP BUBUMP
Okay.
Tamayo, please!

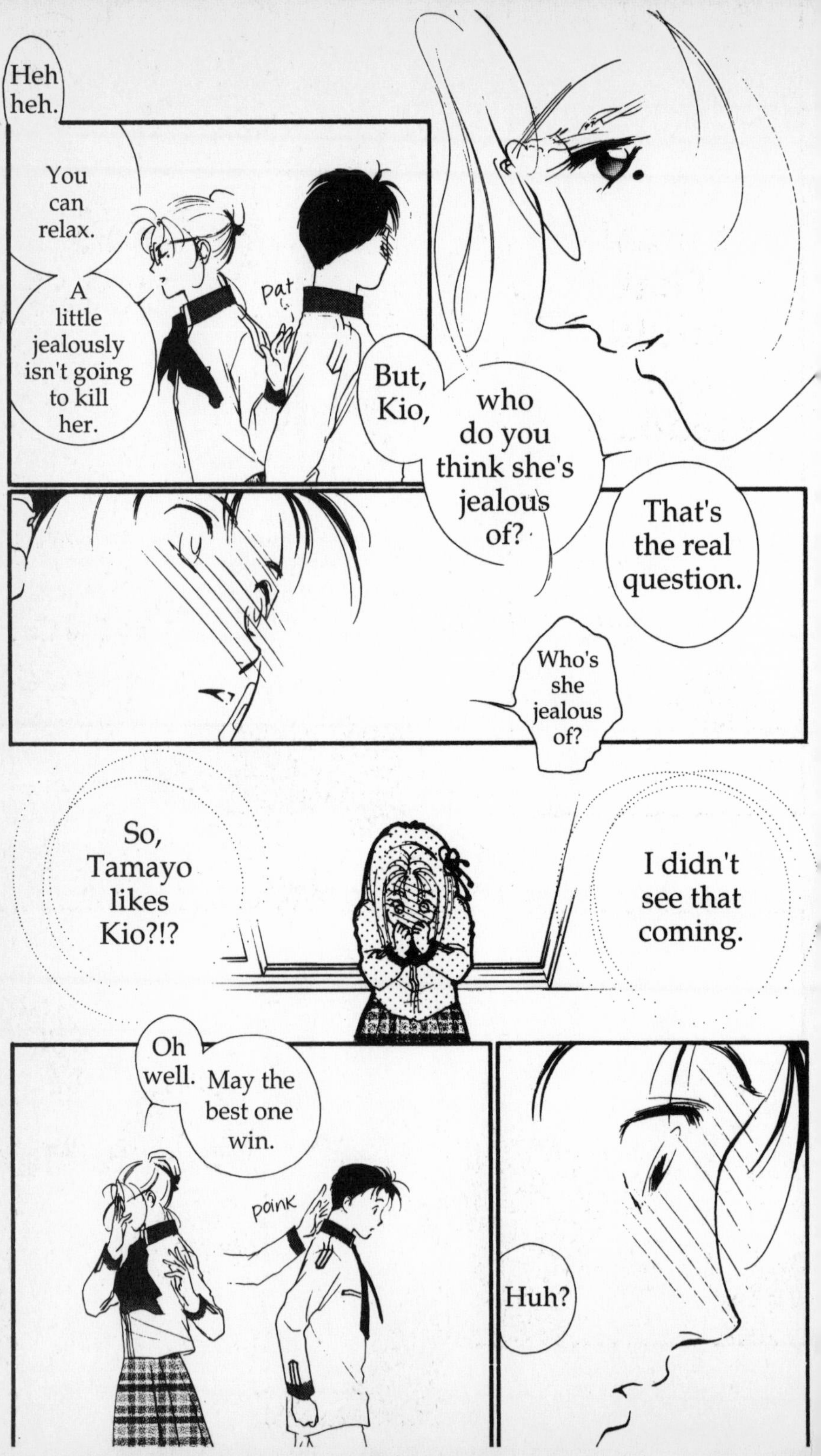
Heh heh.
You can relax.
A little jealously isn't going to kill her.
pat
But, Kio,
who do you think she's jealous of?
That's the real question.
Who's she jealous of?
So, Tamayo likes Kio?!?
I didn't see that coming.
Oh well.
May the best one win.
poink
Huh?

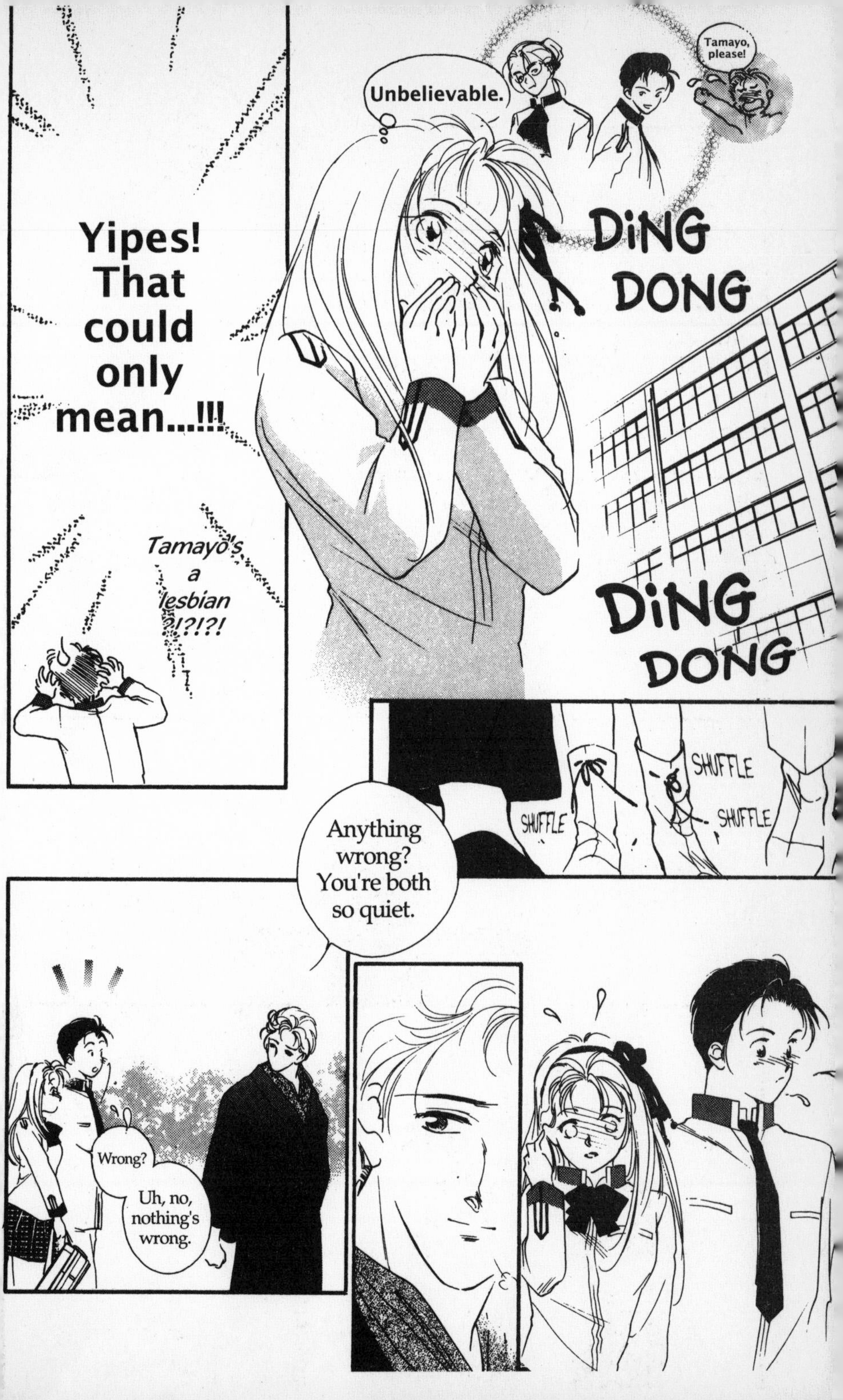
Yipes! That could only mean...!!!
Tamayo's a lesbian ?!?!?!
Unbelievable.
Tamayo, please!
DiNG DONG
DiNG DONG
SHUFFLE
SHUFFLE
SHUFFLE
Anything wrong? You're both so quiet.
Wrong?
Uh, no, nothing's wrong.

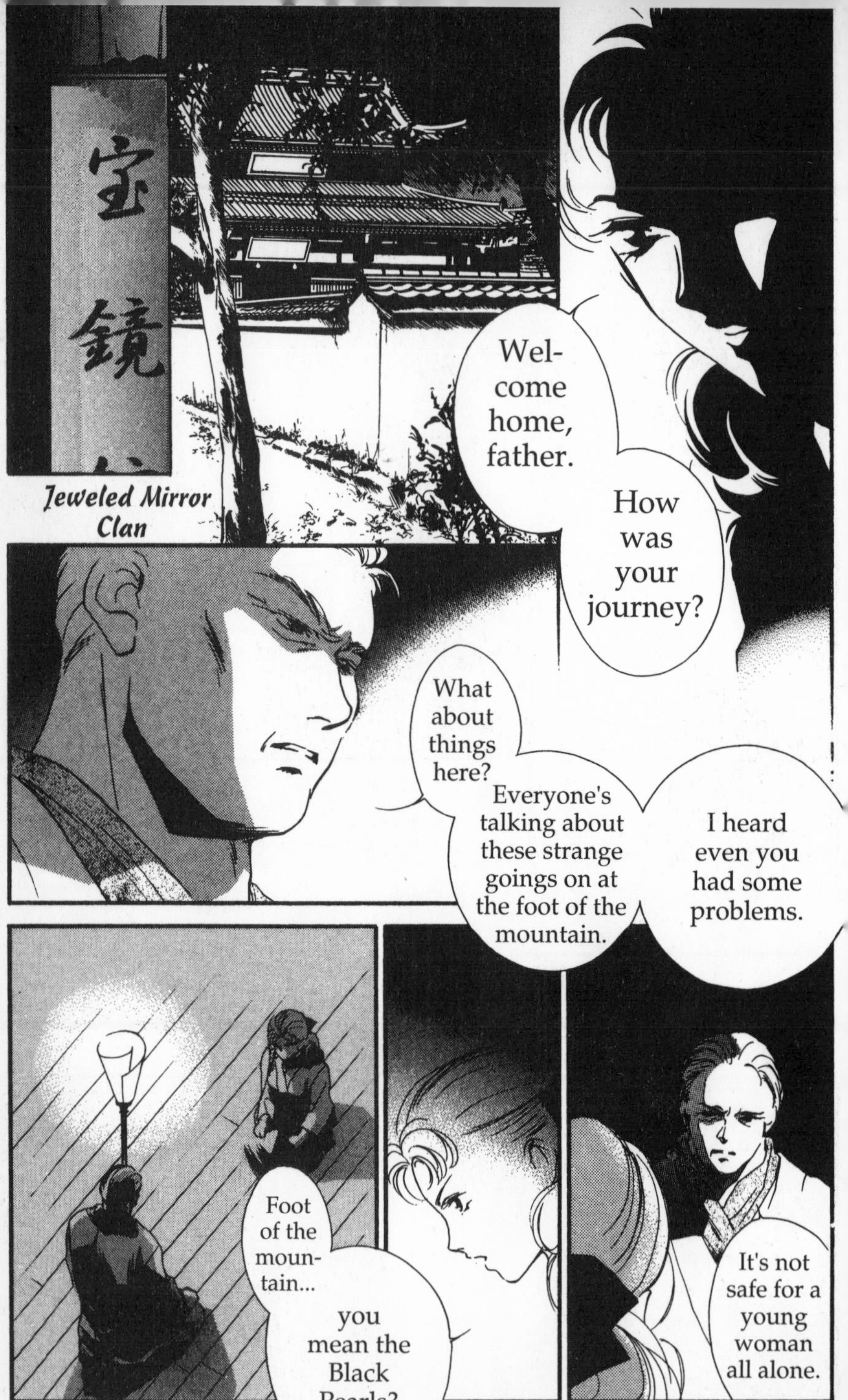
宝鏡
Jeweled Mirror Clan
Wel-come home, father.
How was your journey?
What about things here?
Everyone's talking about these strange goings on at the foot of the mountain.
I heard even you had some problems.
Foot of the moun-tain...
you mean the Black Pearls?
It's not safe for a young woman all alone.

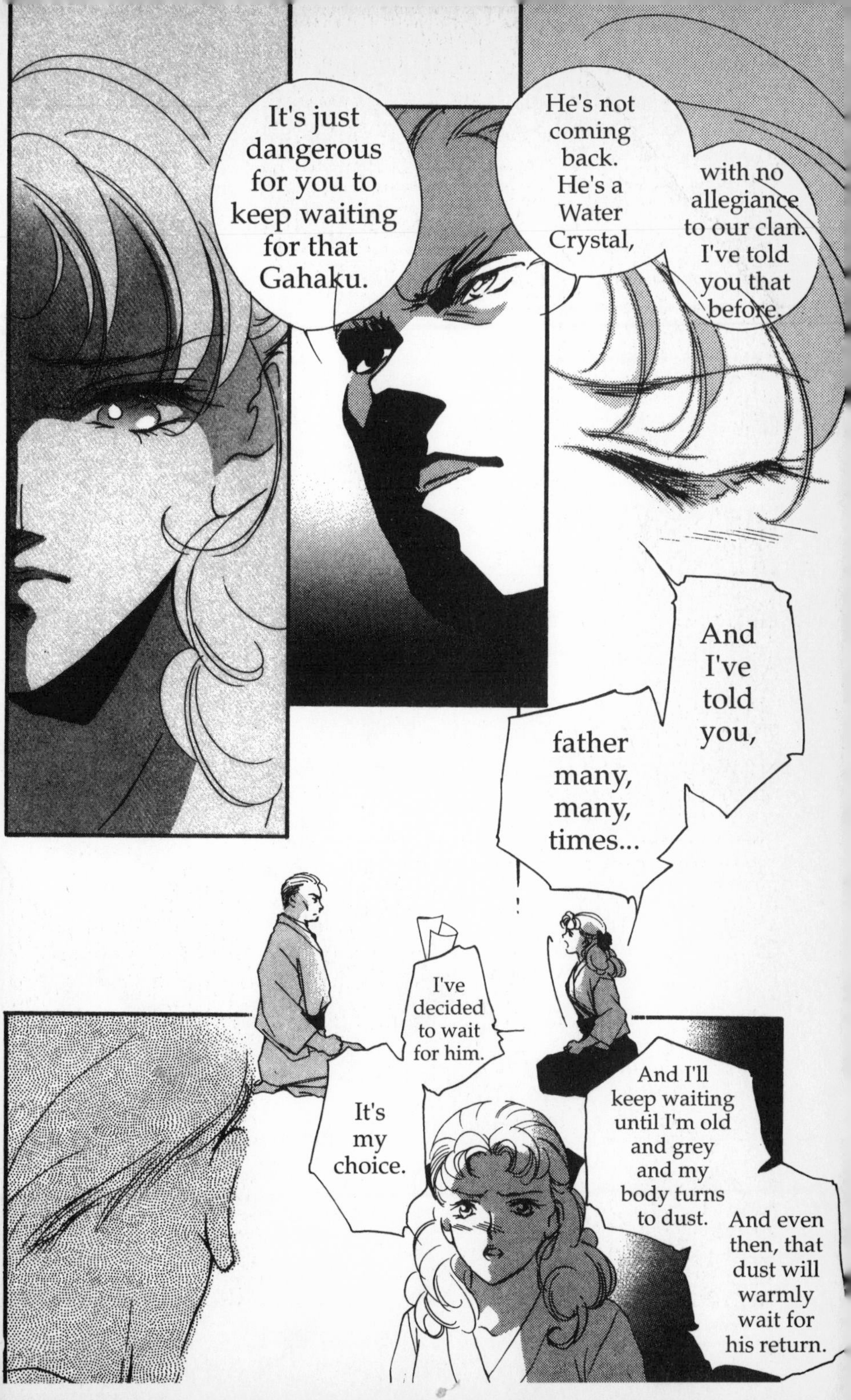
It's just dangerous for you to keep waiting for that Gahaku.
He's not coming back. He's a Water Crystal,
with no allegiance to our clan. I've told you that before.
And I've told you,
father many, many, times...
I've decided to wait for him.
It's my choice.
And I'll keep waiting until I'm old and grey and my body turns to dust.
And even then, that dust will warmly wait for his return.

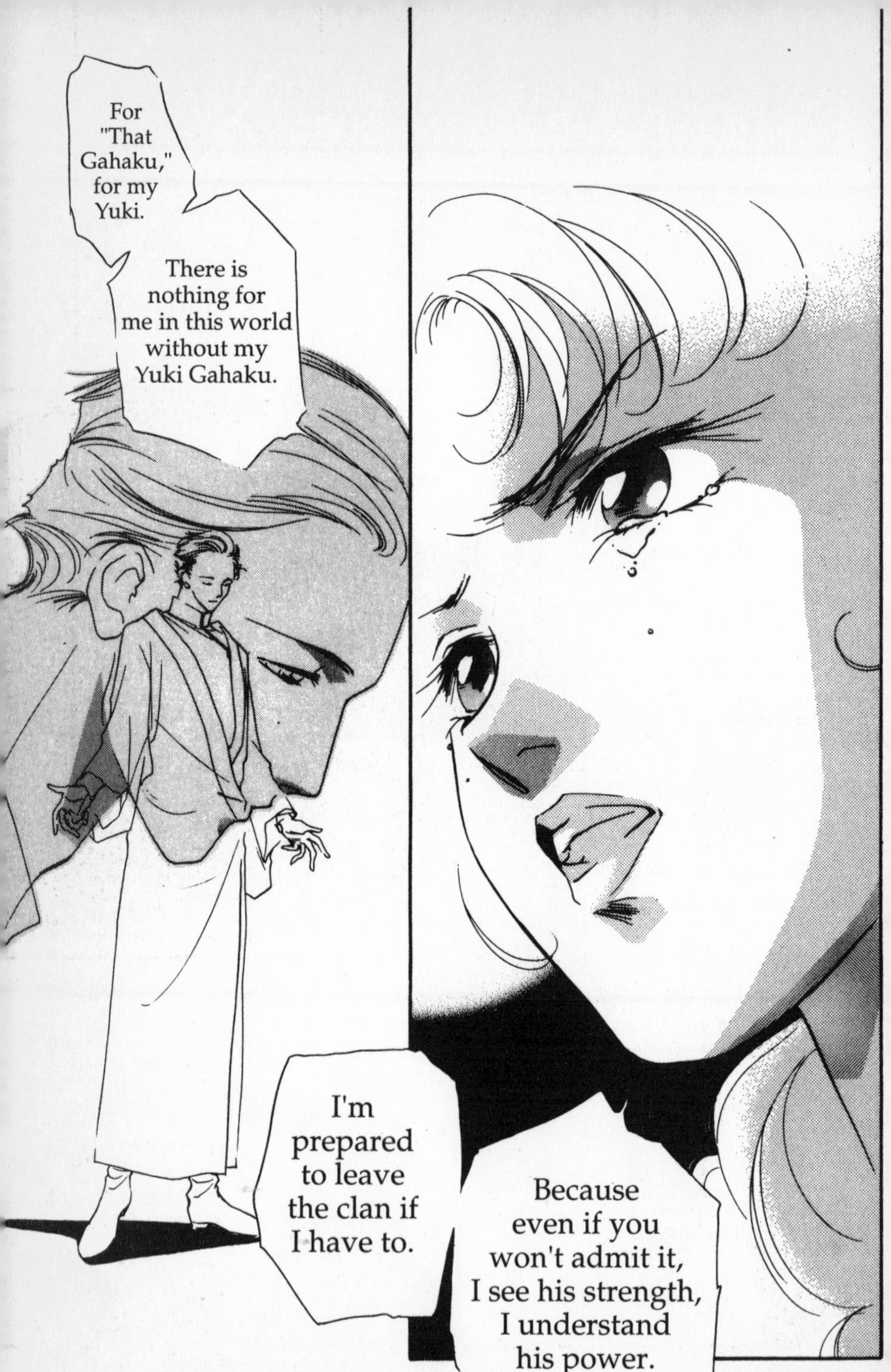

For "That Gahaku," for my Yuki.
There is nothing for me in this world without my Yuki Gahaku.
I'm prepared to leave the clan if I have to.
Because even if you won't admit it, I see his strength, I understand his power.

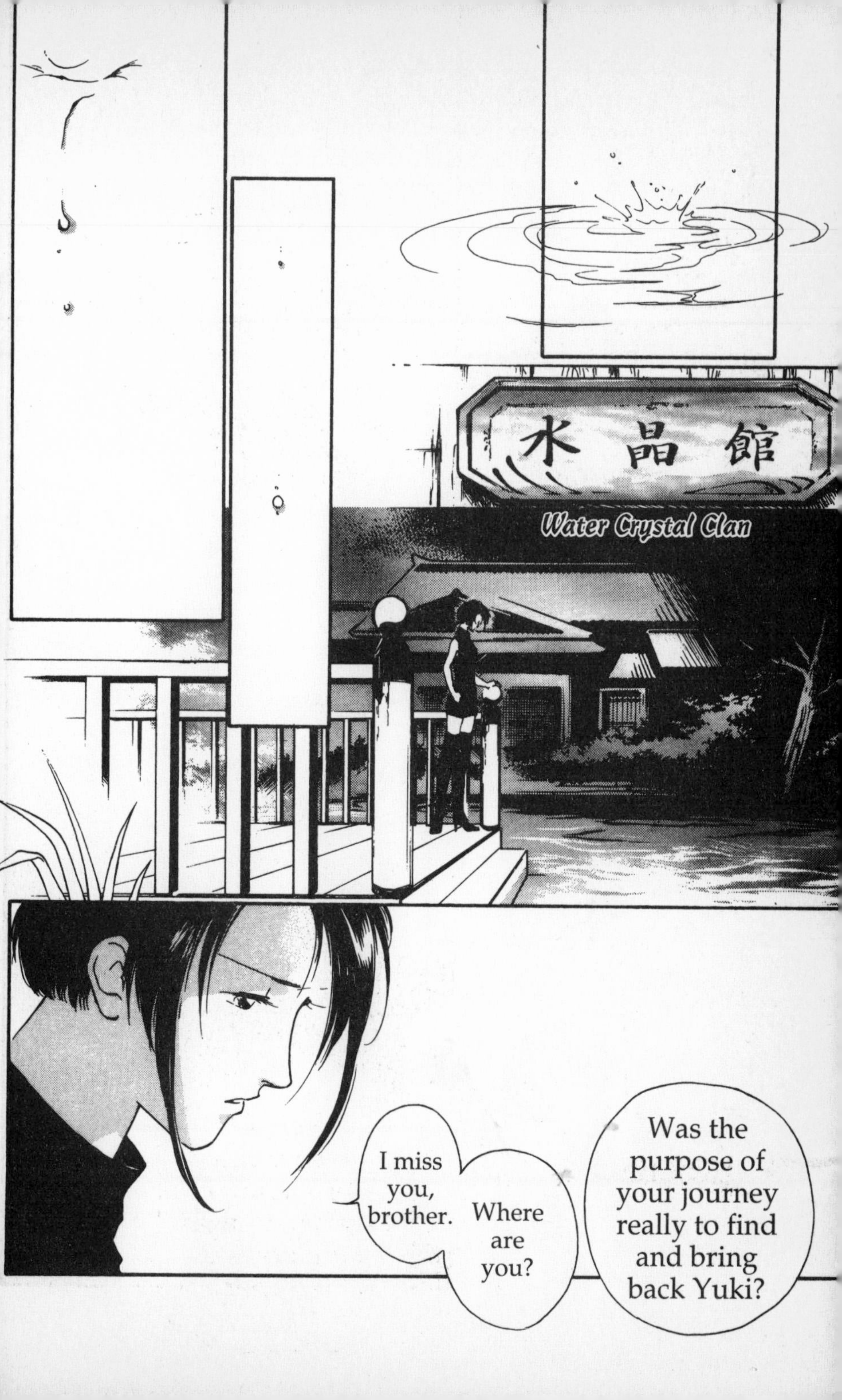
水晶館
Water Crystal Clan
I miss you, brother.
Where are you?
Was the purpose of your journey really to find and bring back Yuki?

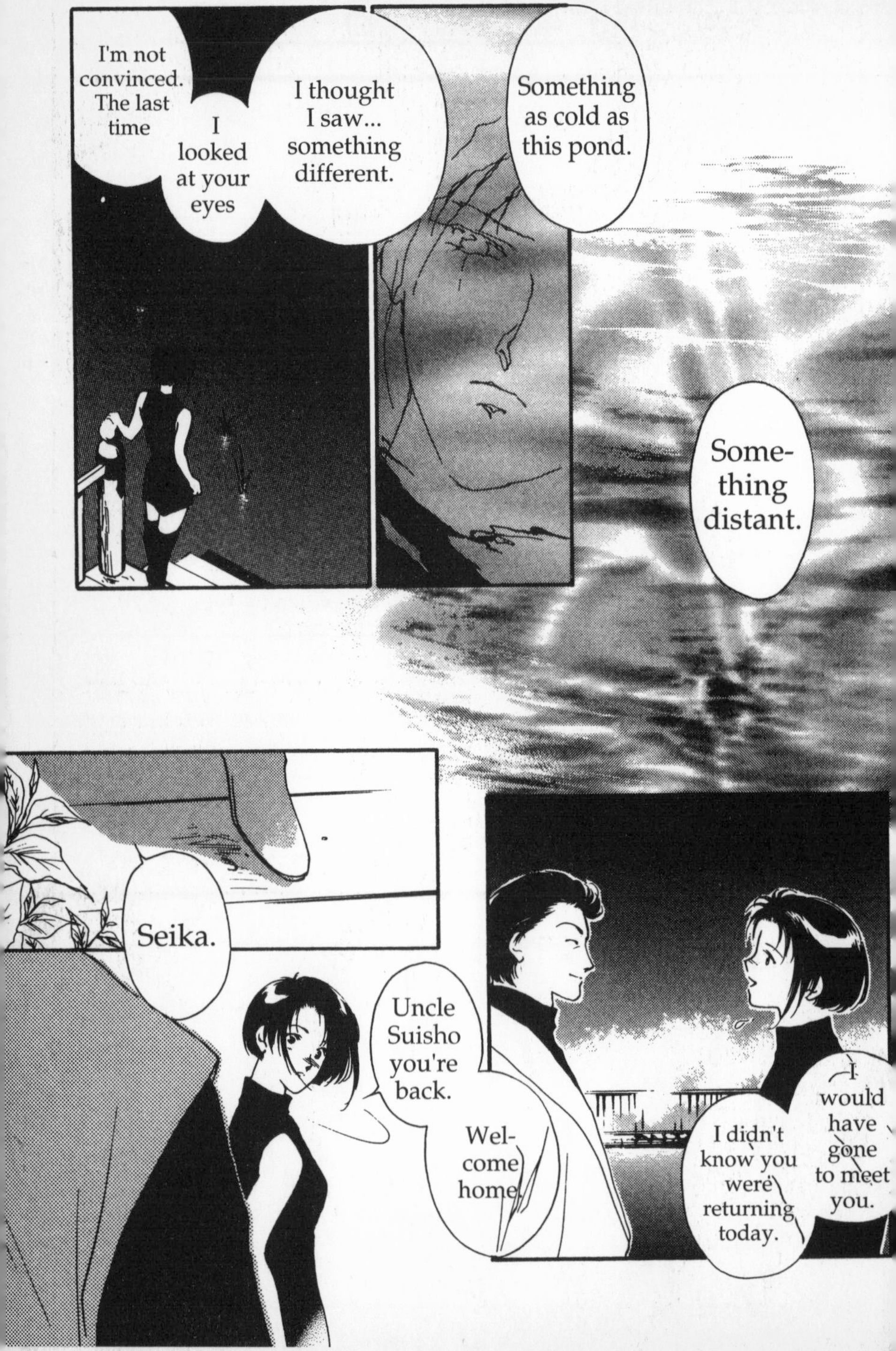
I'm not convinced. The last time
I looked at your eyes
I thought I saw... something different.
Something as cold as this pond.
Some-thing distant.
Seika.
Uncle Suisho you're back.
Wel-come home
I didn't know you were returning today.
I would have gone to meet you.

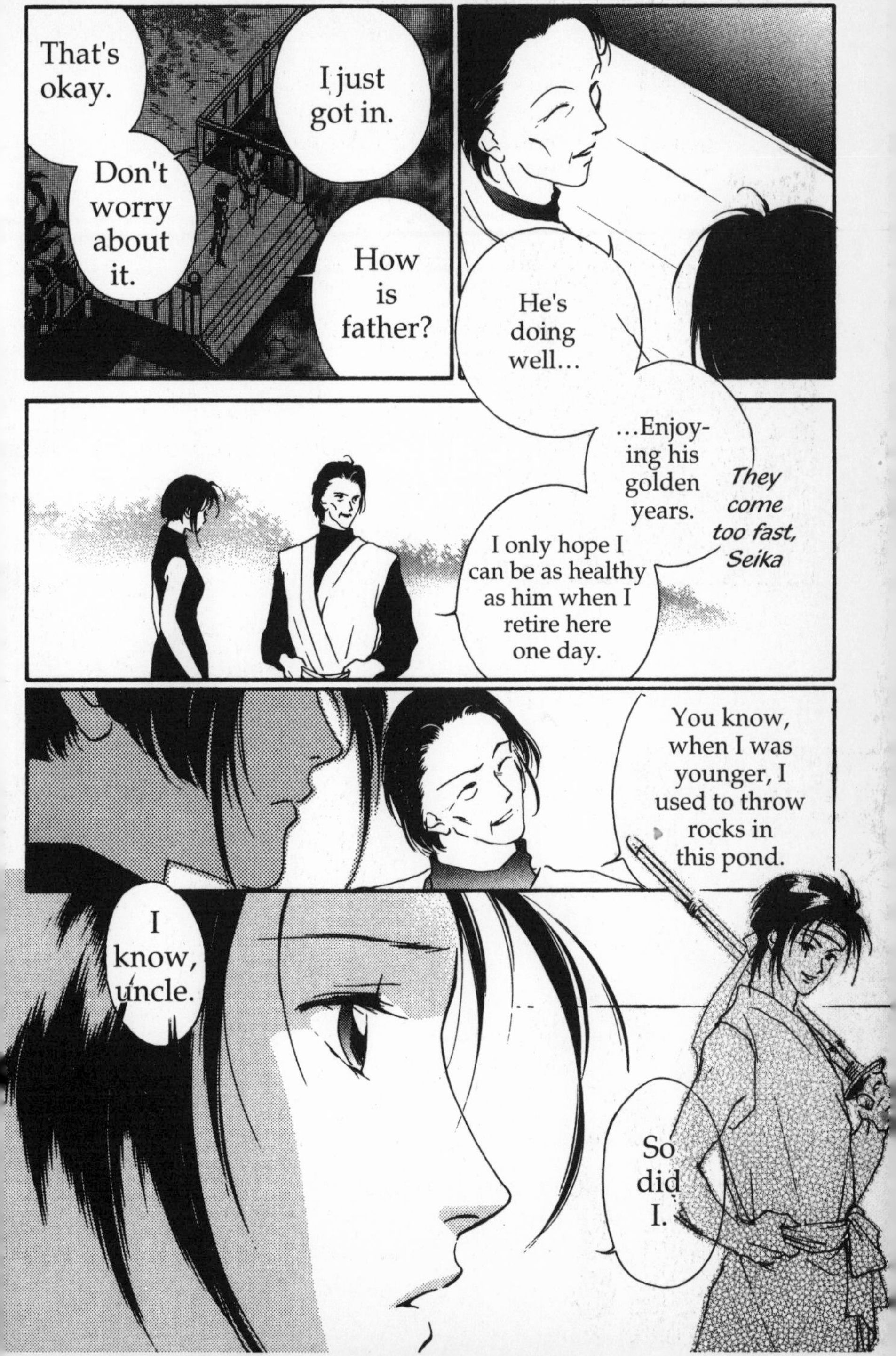
That's okay.
I just got in.
Don't worry about it.
How is father?
He's doing well...
...Enjoying his golden years.
They come too fast, Seika
I only hope I can be as healthy as him when I retire here one day.
You know, when I was younger, I used to throw rocks in this pond.
I know, uncle.
So did I.

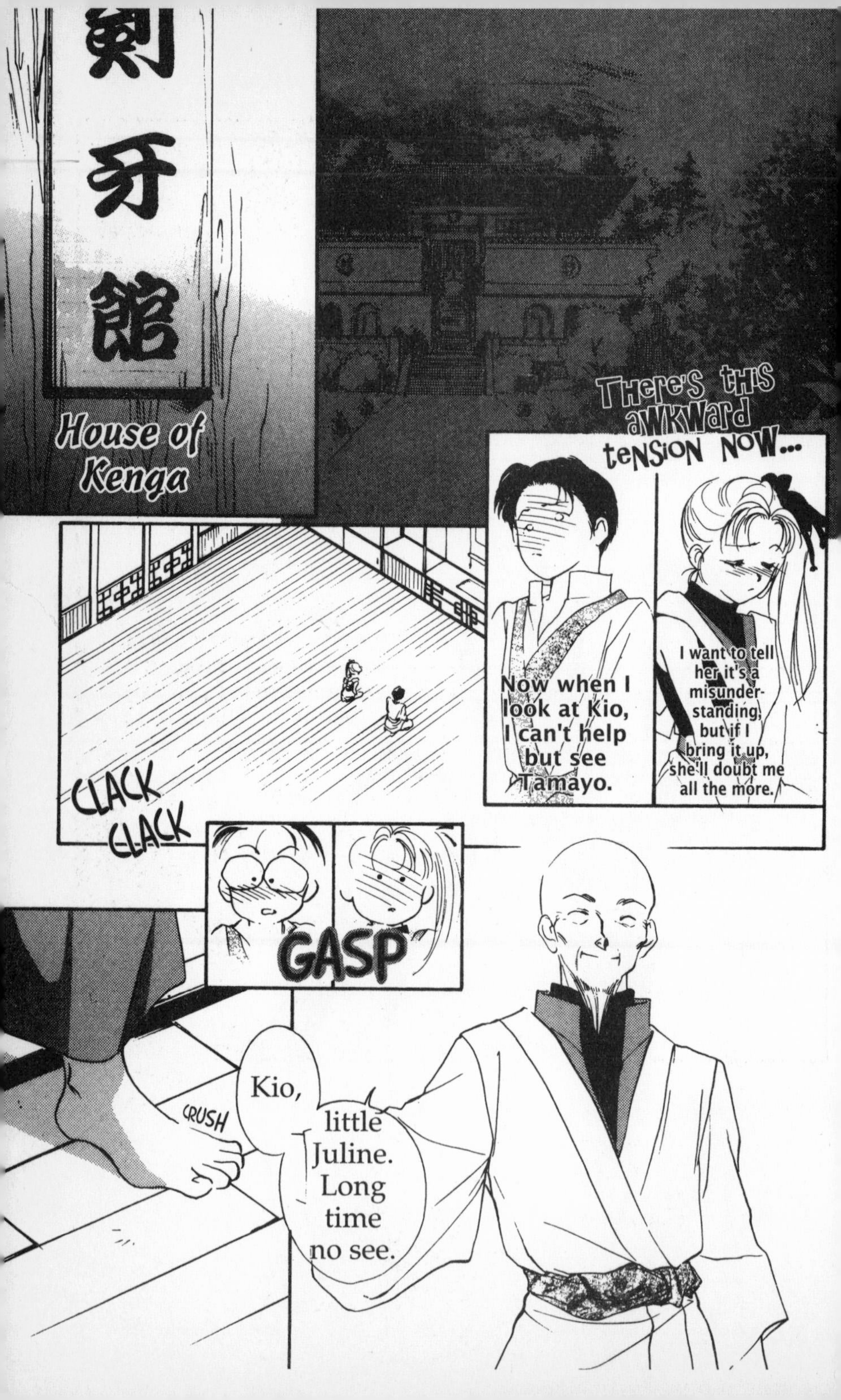
剣
牙
館
House of Kenga
There's this awkward tension now...
CLACK CLACK
Now when I look at Kio, I can't help but see Tamayo.
I want to tell her it's a misunder-standing, but if I bring it up, she'll doubt me all the more.
GASP
CRUSH
Kio,
little Juline. Long time no see.

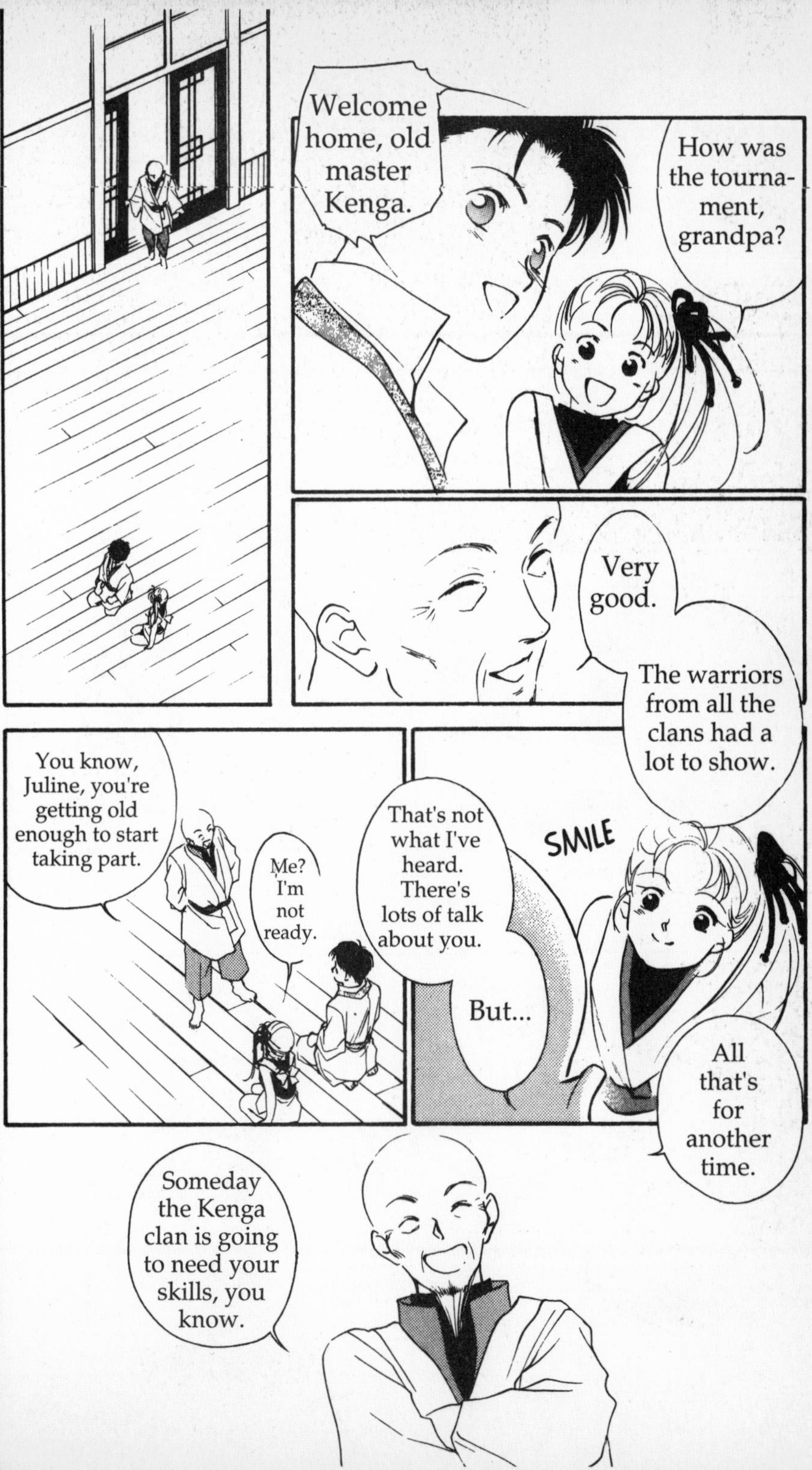
Welcome home, old master Kenga.
How was the tourna-ment, grandpa?
Very good.
The warriors from all the clans had a lot to show.
You know, Juline, you're getting old enough to start taking part.
Me? I'm not ready.
That's not what I've heard. There's lots of talk about you.
But...
SMILE
All that's for another time.
Someday the Kenga clan is going to need your skills, you know.

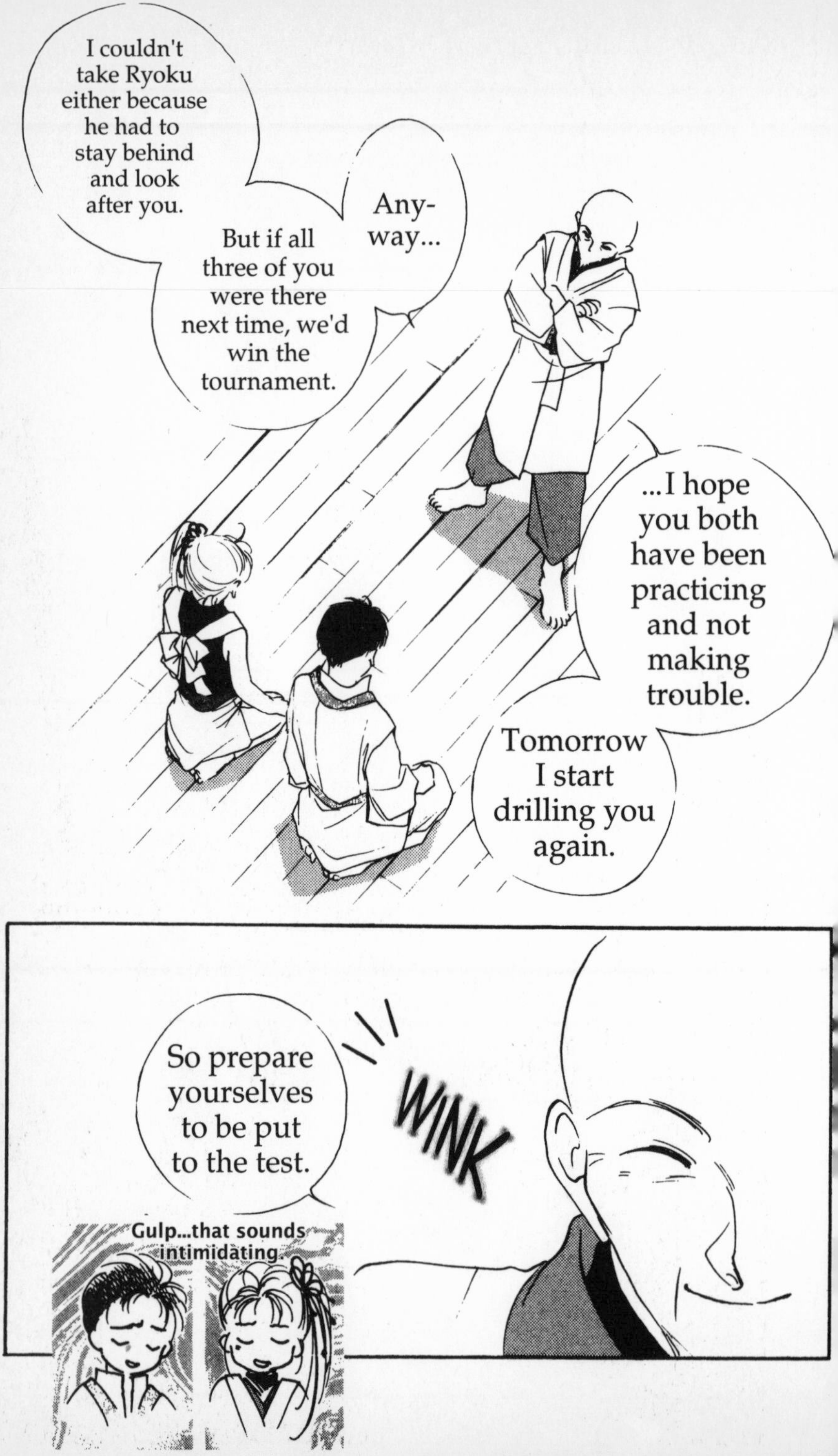
I couldn't take Ryoku either because he had to stay behind and look after you.
But if all three of you were there next time, we'd win the tournament.
Any-way...
...I hope you both have been practicing and not making trouble.
Tomorrow I start drilling you again.
So prepare yourselves to be put to the test.
WINK
Gulp...that sounds intimidating.

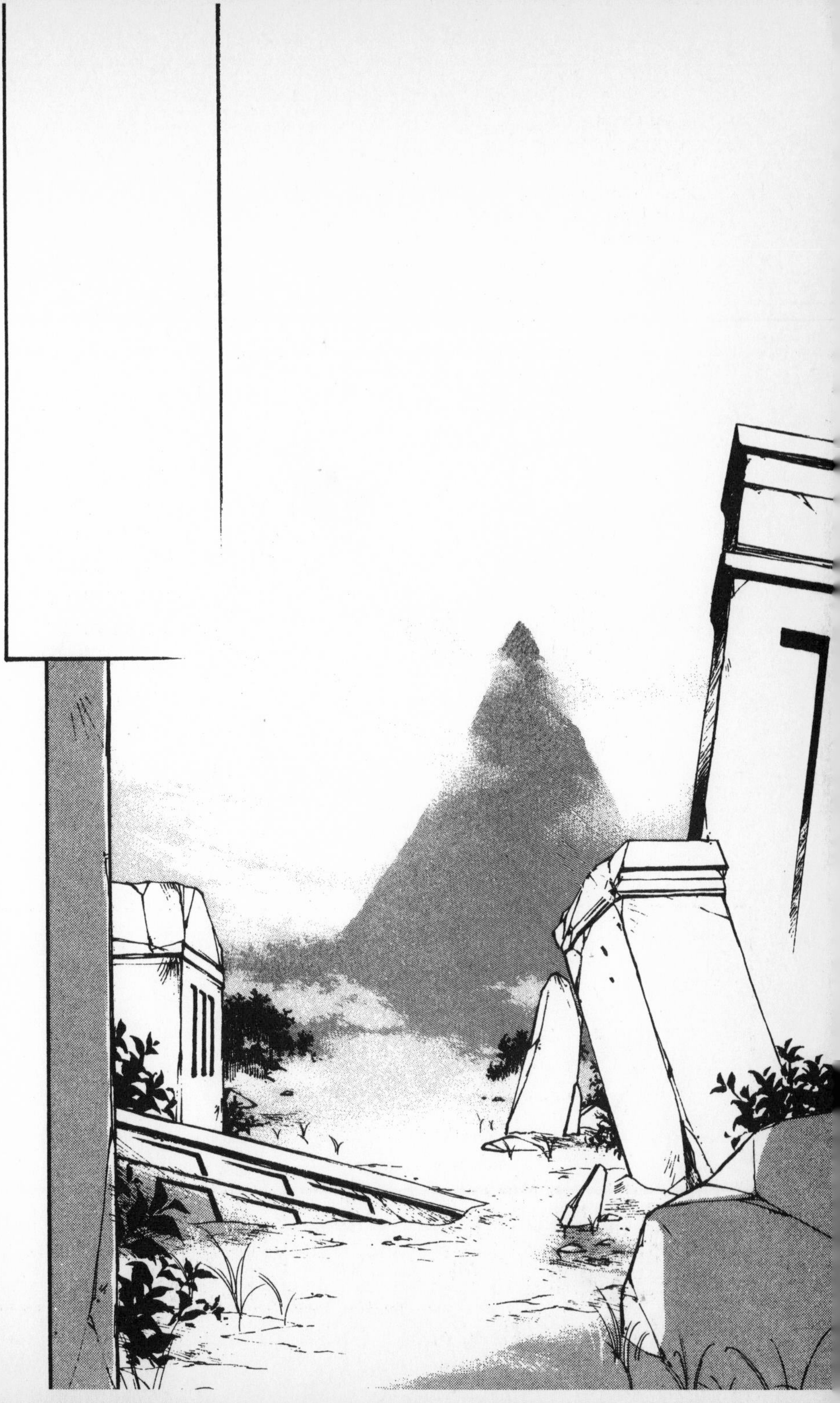

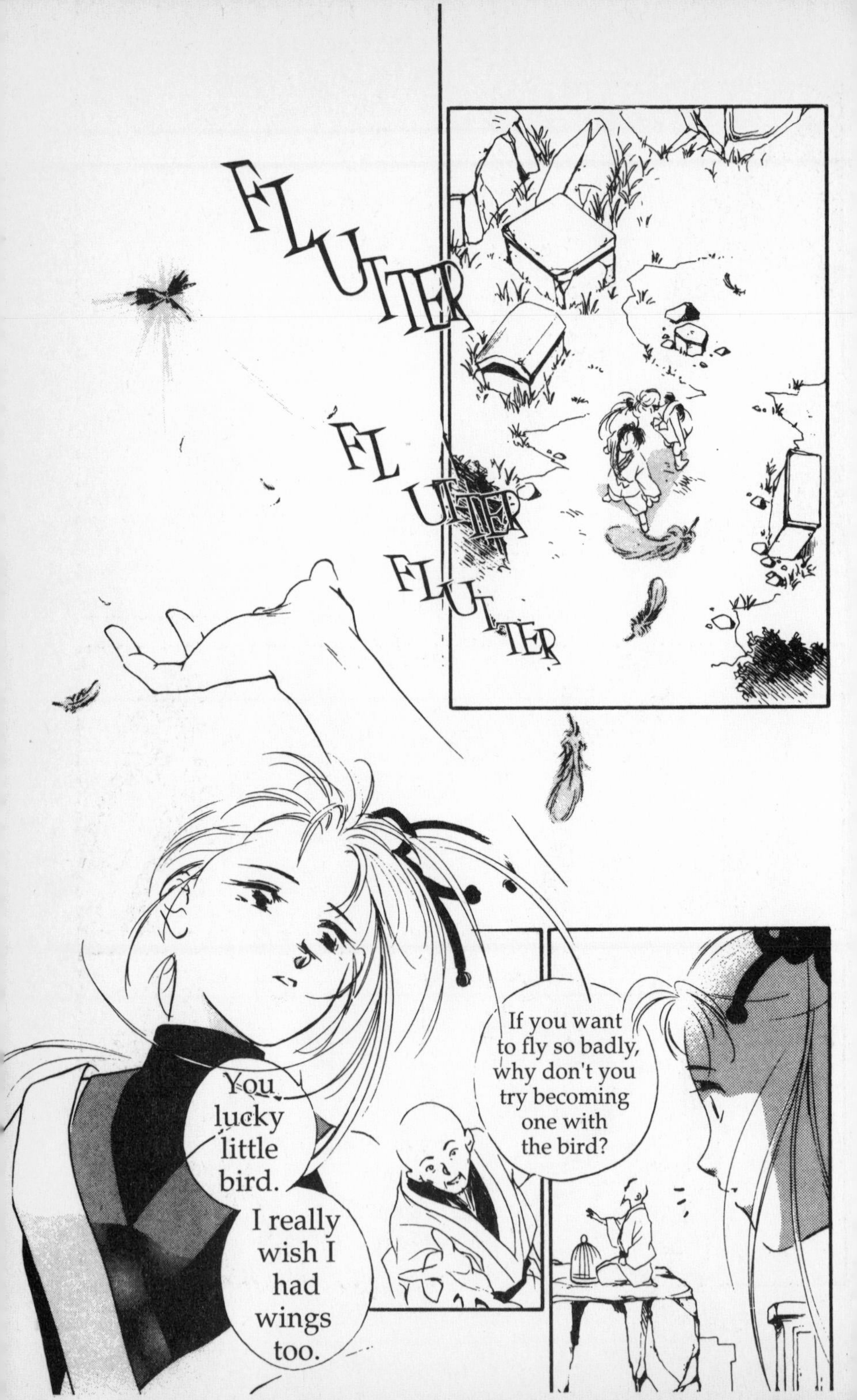
FLUTTER
FLUTTER
FLUTTER
You lucky little bird.
I really wish I had wings too.
If you want to fly so badly, why don't you try becoming one with the bird?

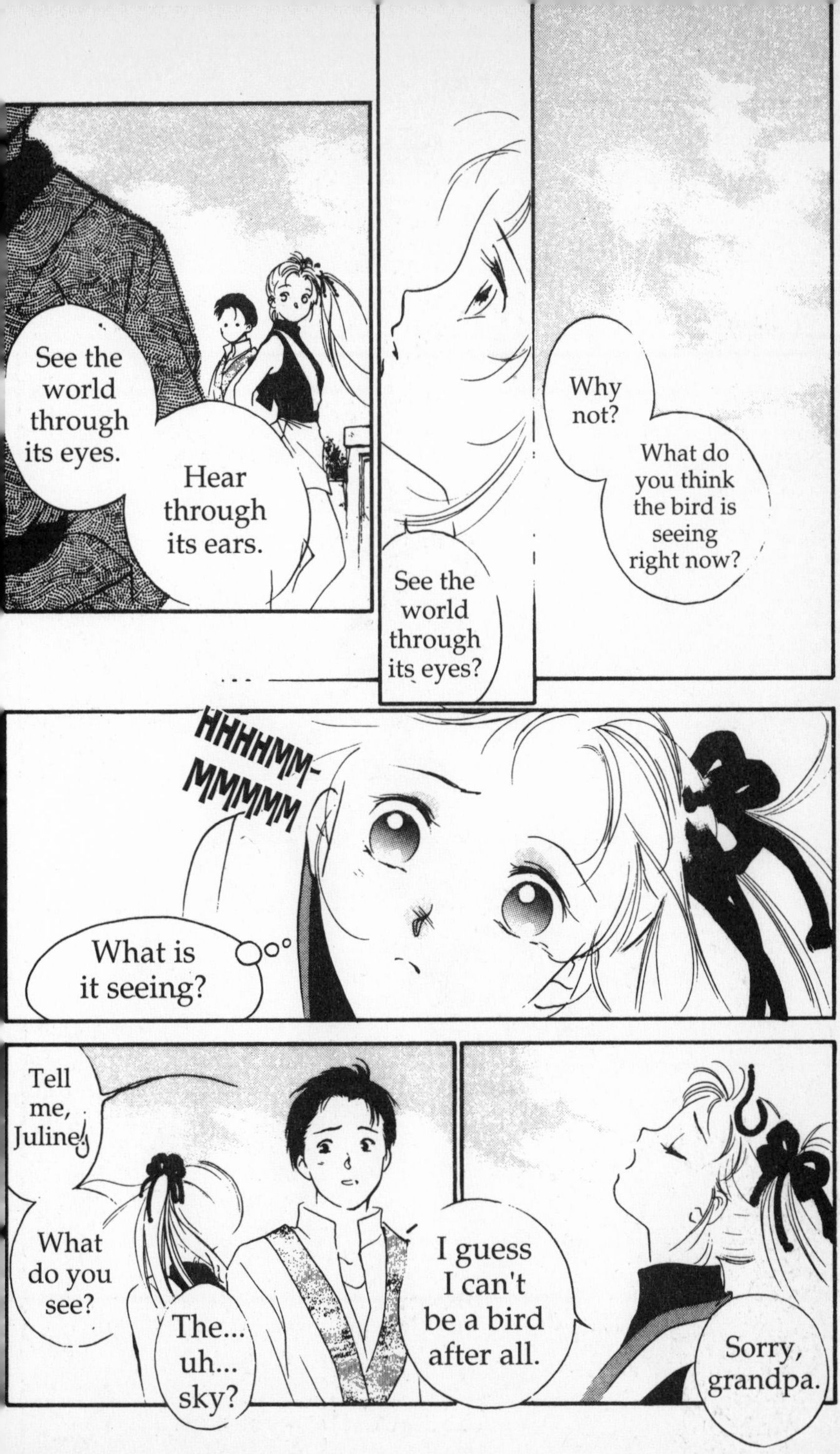
See the world through its eyes.
Hear through its ears.
See the world through its eyes?
Why not?
What do you think the bird is seeing right now?
HHHHMM-MMMMM
What is it seeing?
Tell me, Juline.
What do you see?
The... uh... sky?
I guess I can't be a bird after all.
Sorry, grandpa.

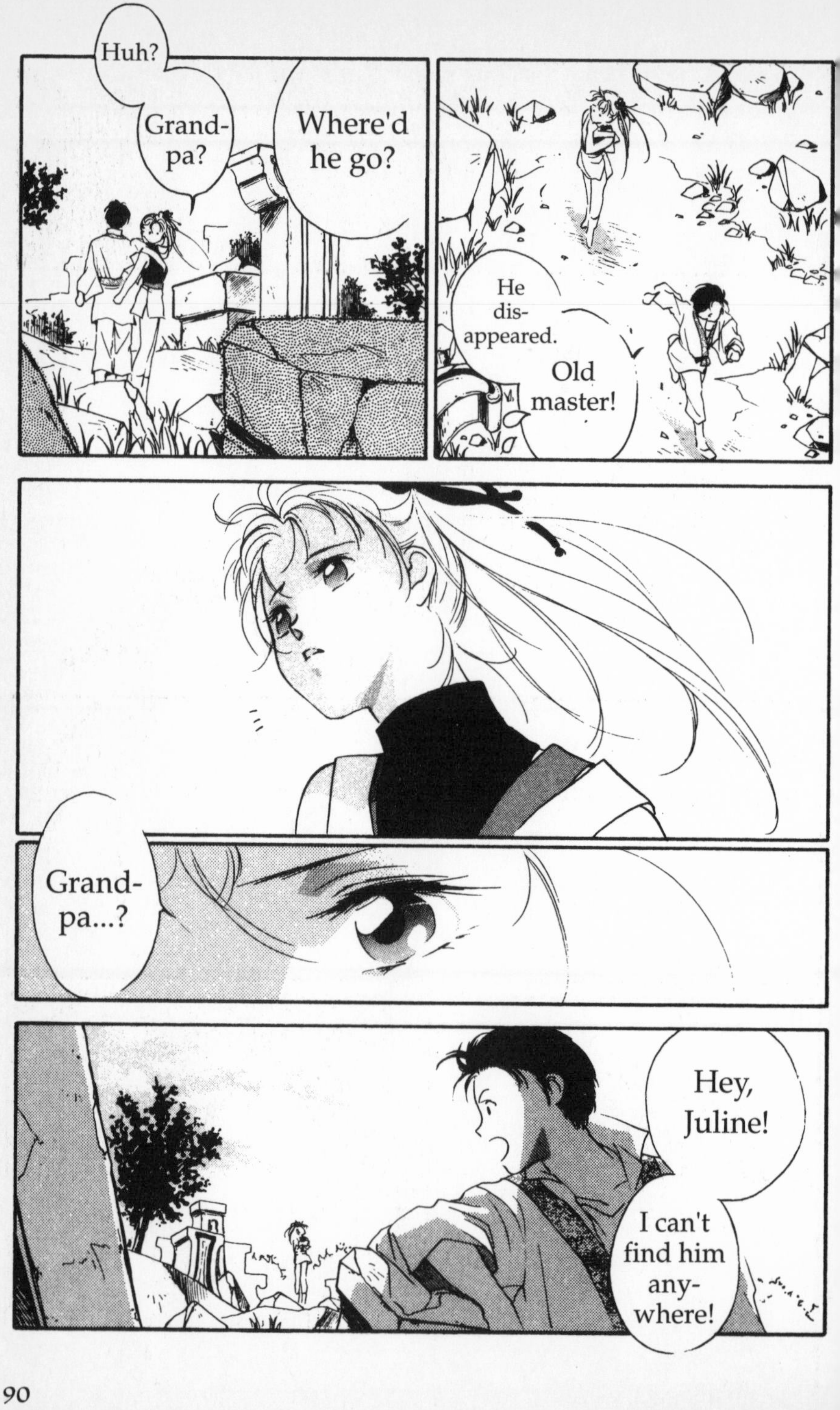
Huh?
Grand-pa?
Where'd he go?
He dis-appeared.
Old master!
Grand-pa...?
Hey, Juline!
I can't find him any-where!

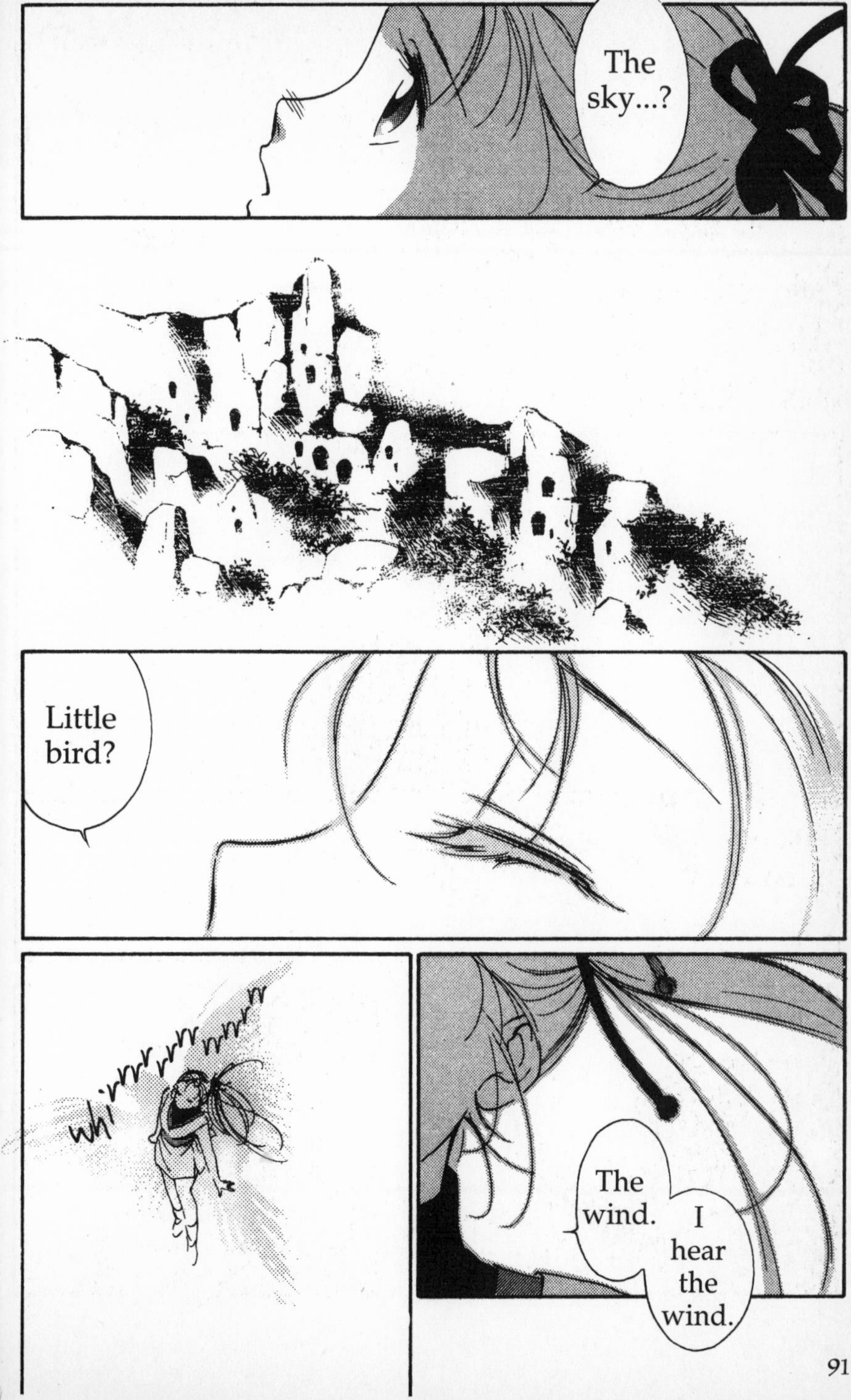
The sky...?
Little bird?
whirrrrrrrrrrrr
The wind.
I hear the wind.

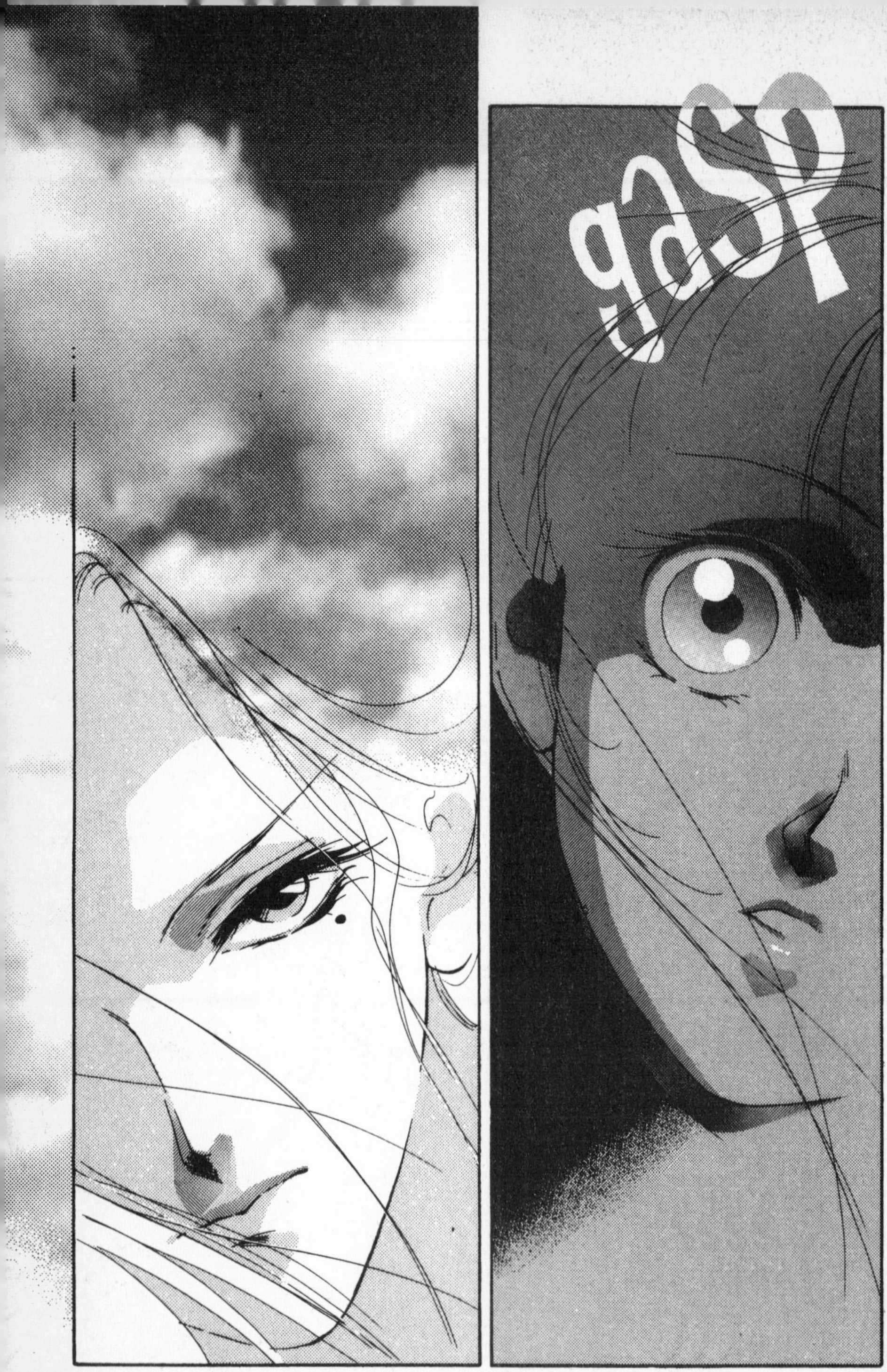
gasp

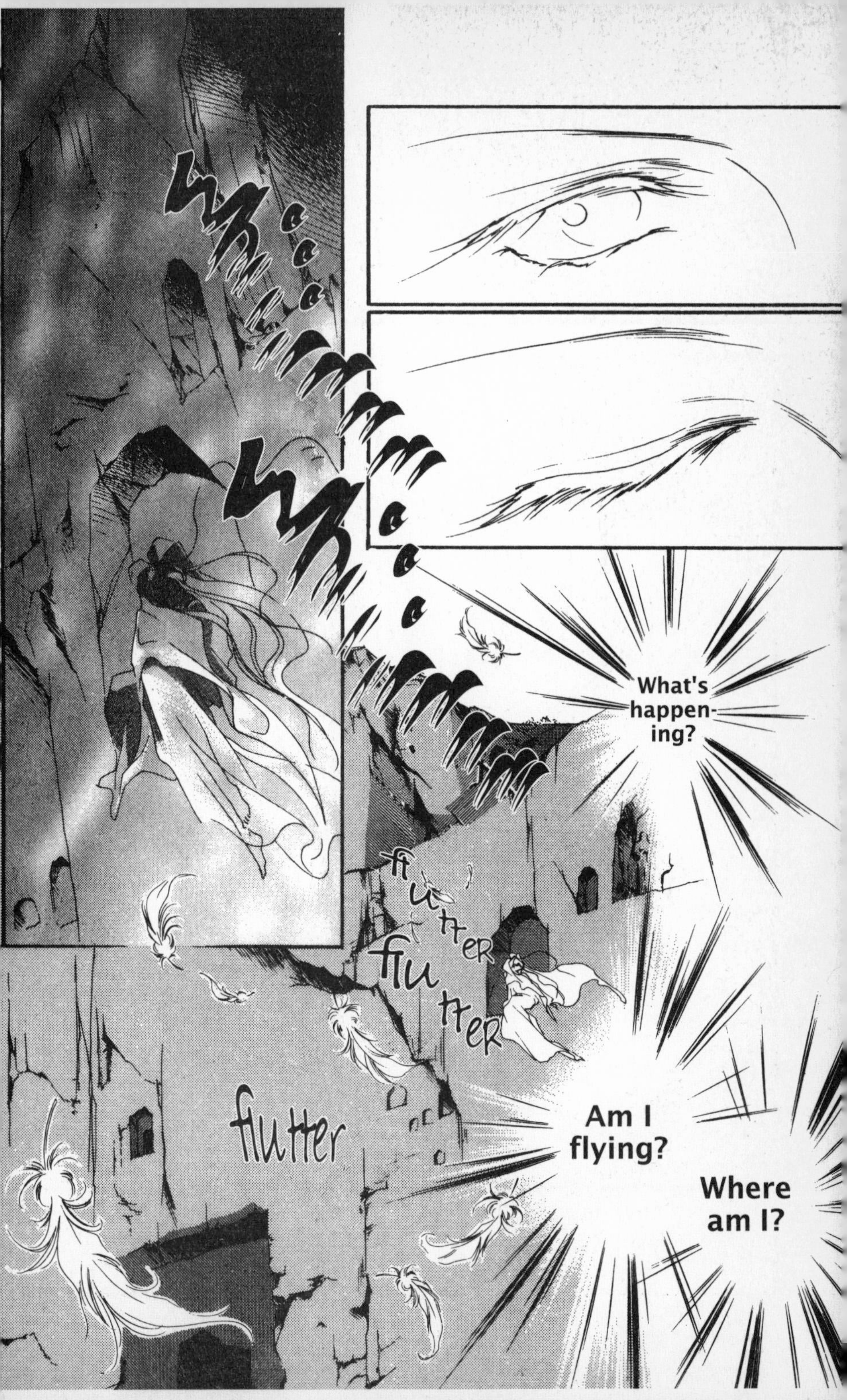
Whoooooshhhh
Whoooooshhhh
What's happen-ing?
flutter
flutter
flutter
Am I flying?
Where am I?

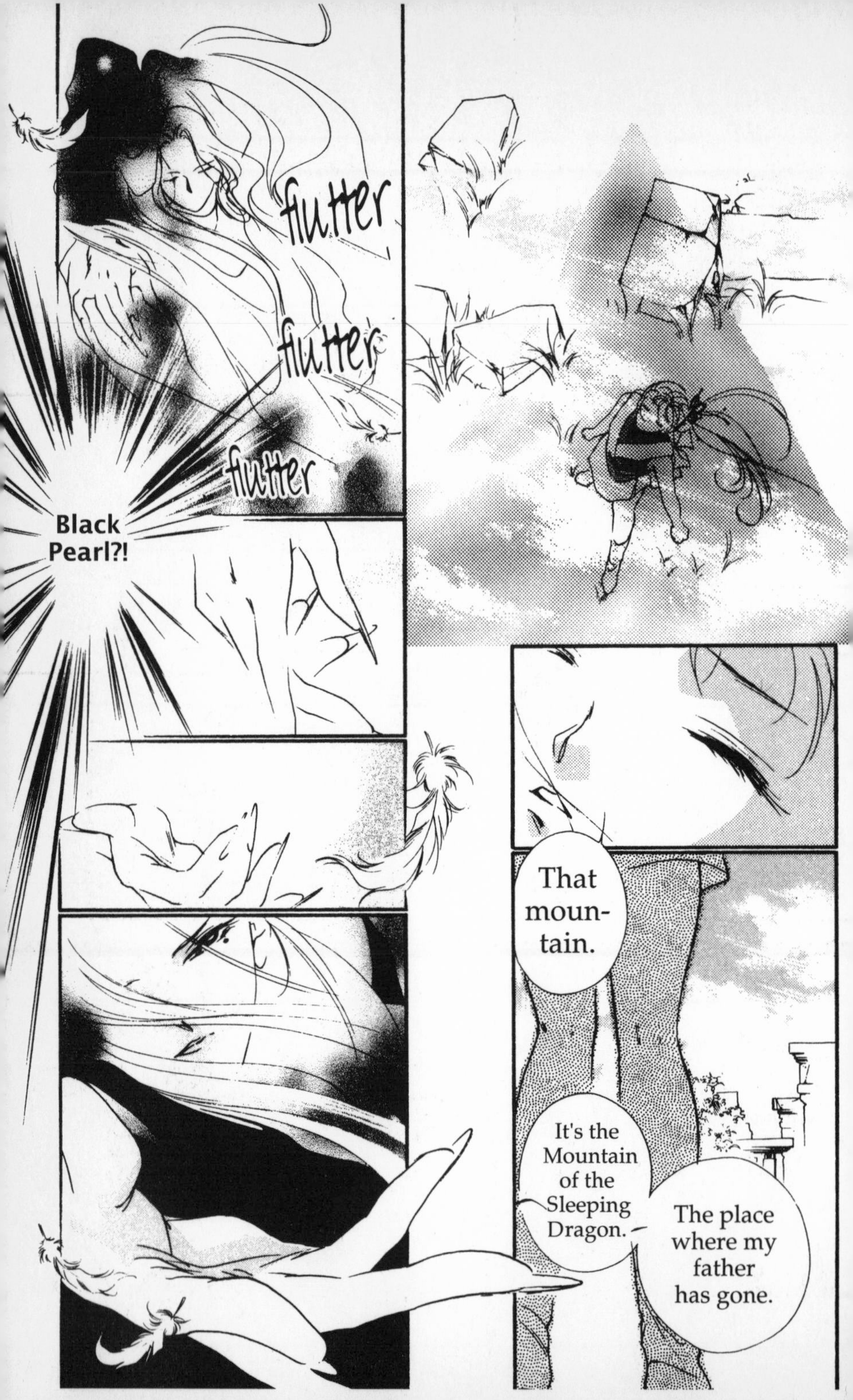

flutter
flutter
flutter
Black Pearl?!
That moun-tain.
It's the Mountain of the Sleeping Dragon.
The place where my father has gone.

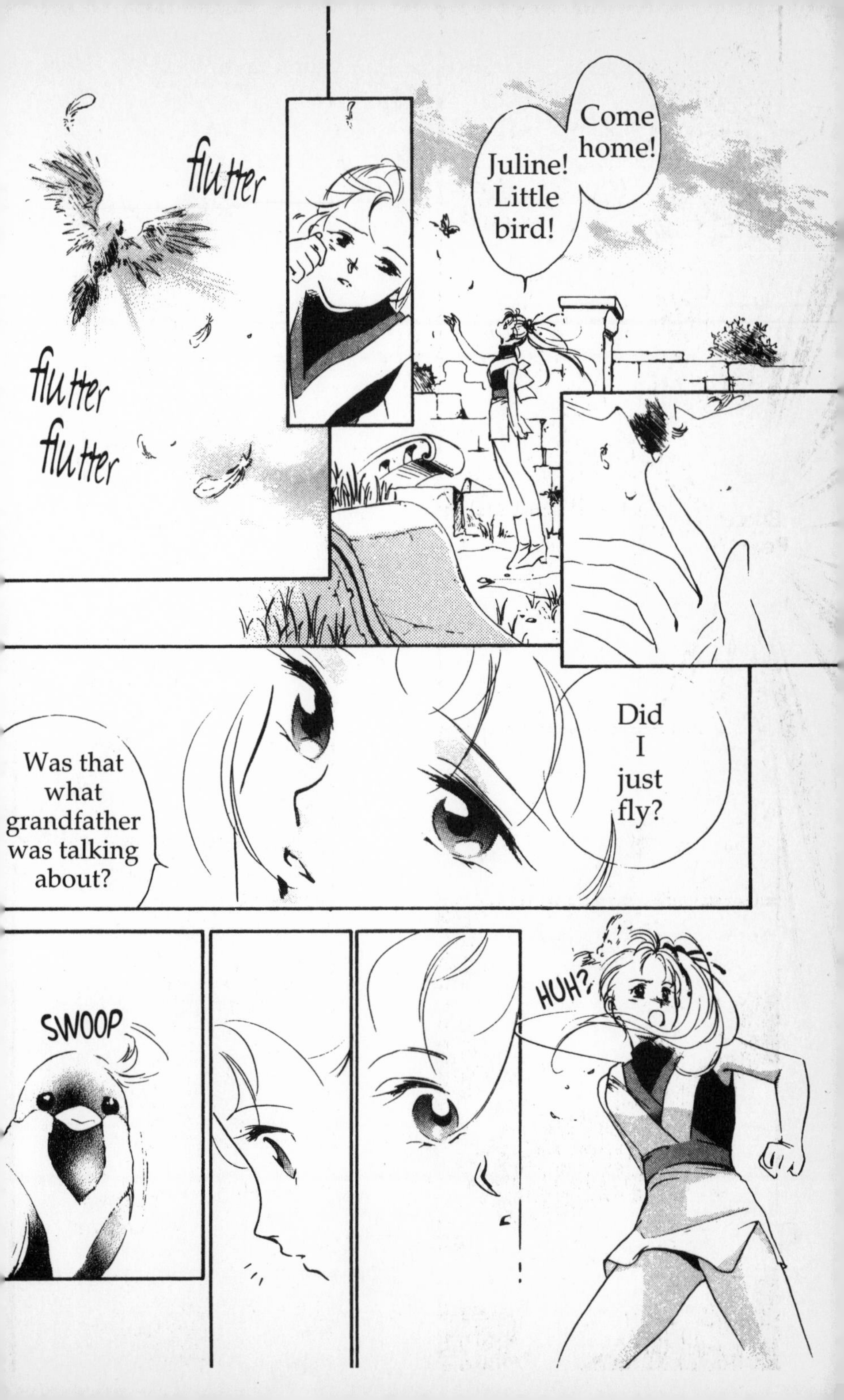
flutter
flutter flutter
Juline! Little bird!
Come home!
Was that what grandfather was talking about?
Did I just fly?
SWOOP
HUH?

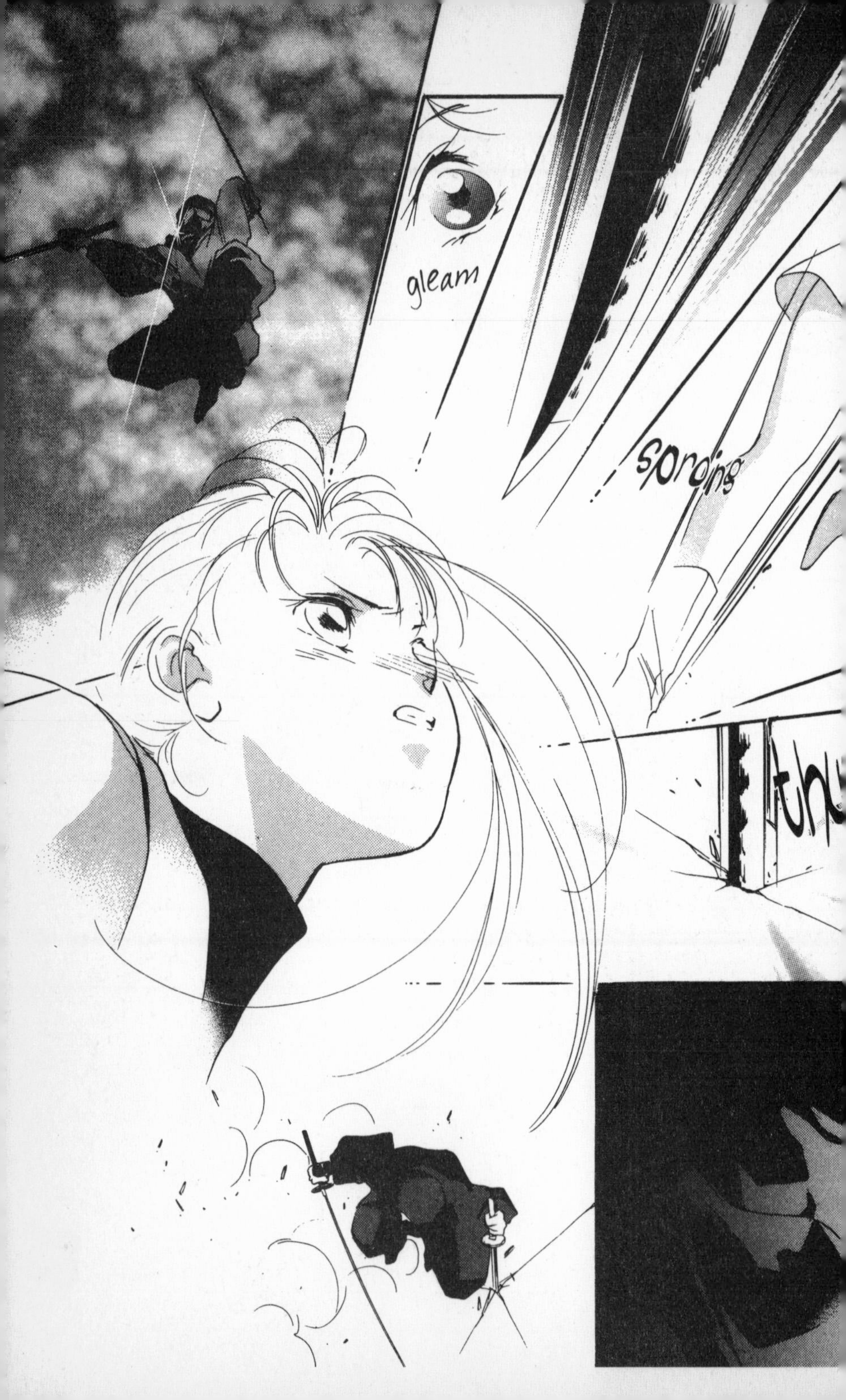
gleam
sproing
thu

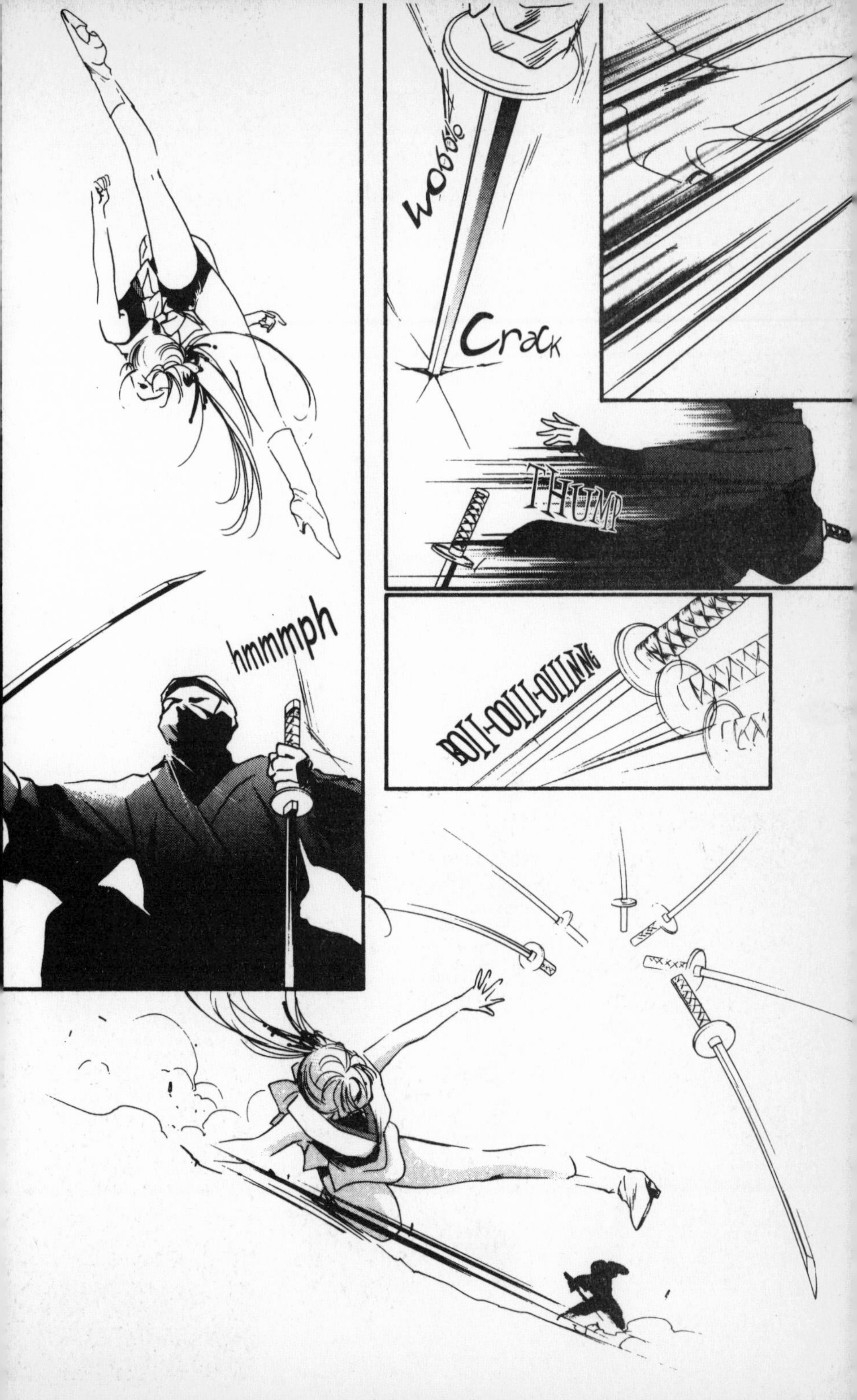
wooooo
Crack
THUMP
BOII-OOIII-OIIINNG
hmmmph

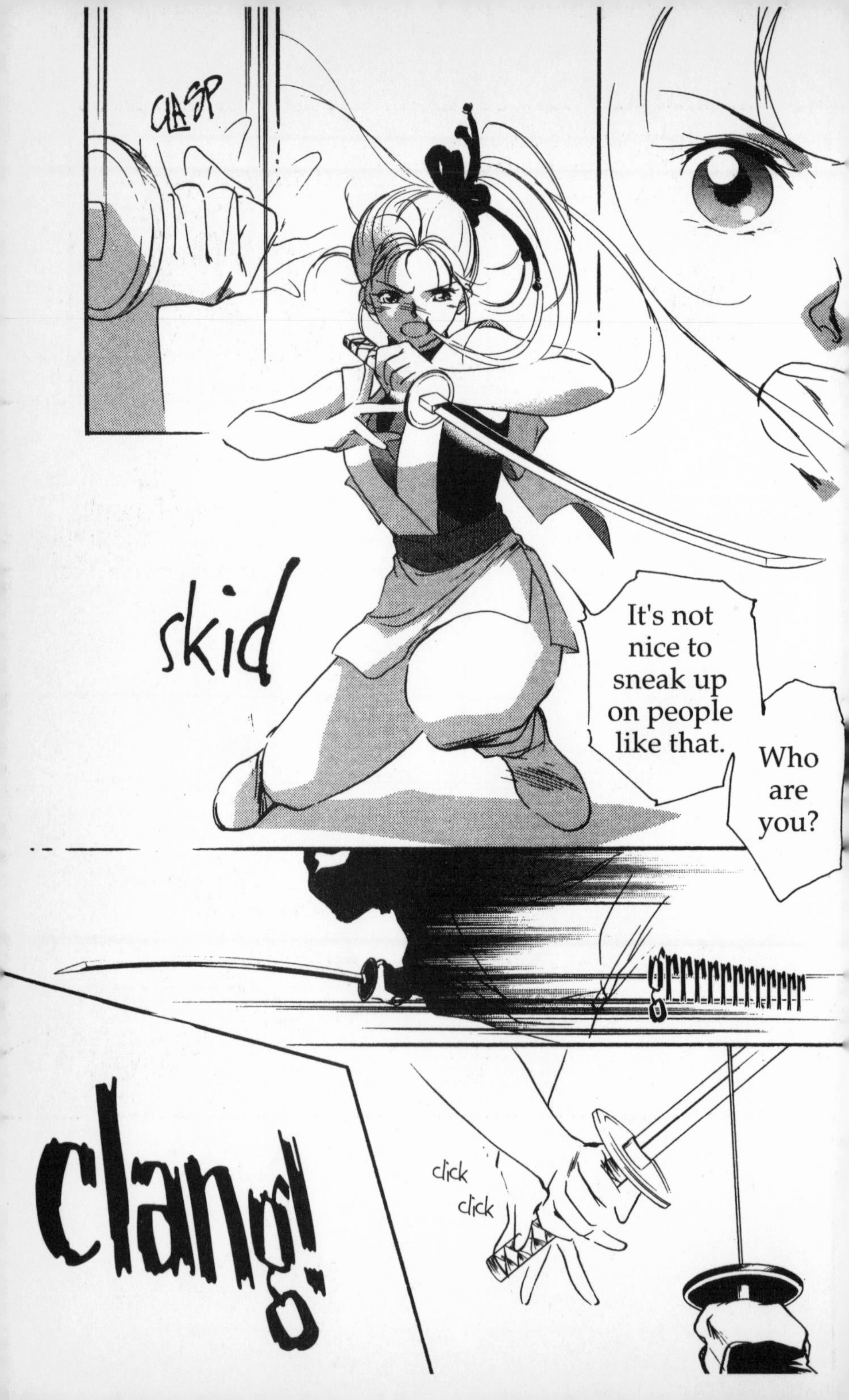
CLASP
skid
It's not nice to sneak up on people like that.
Who are you?
grrrrrrrrrrrr
clang!
click
click

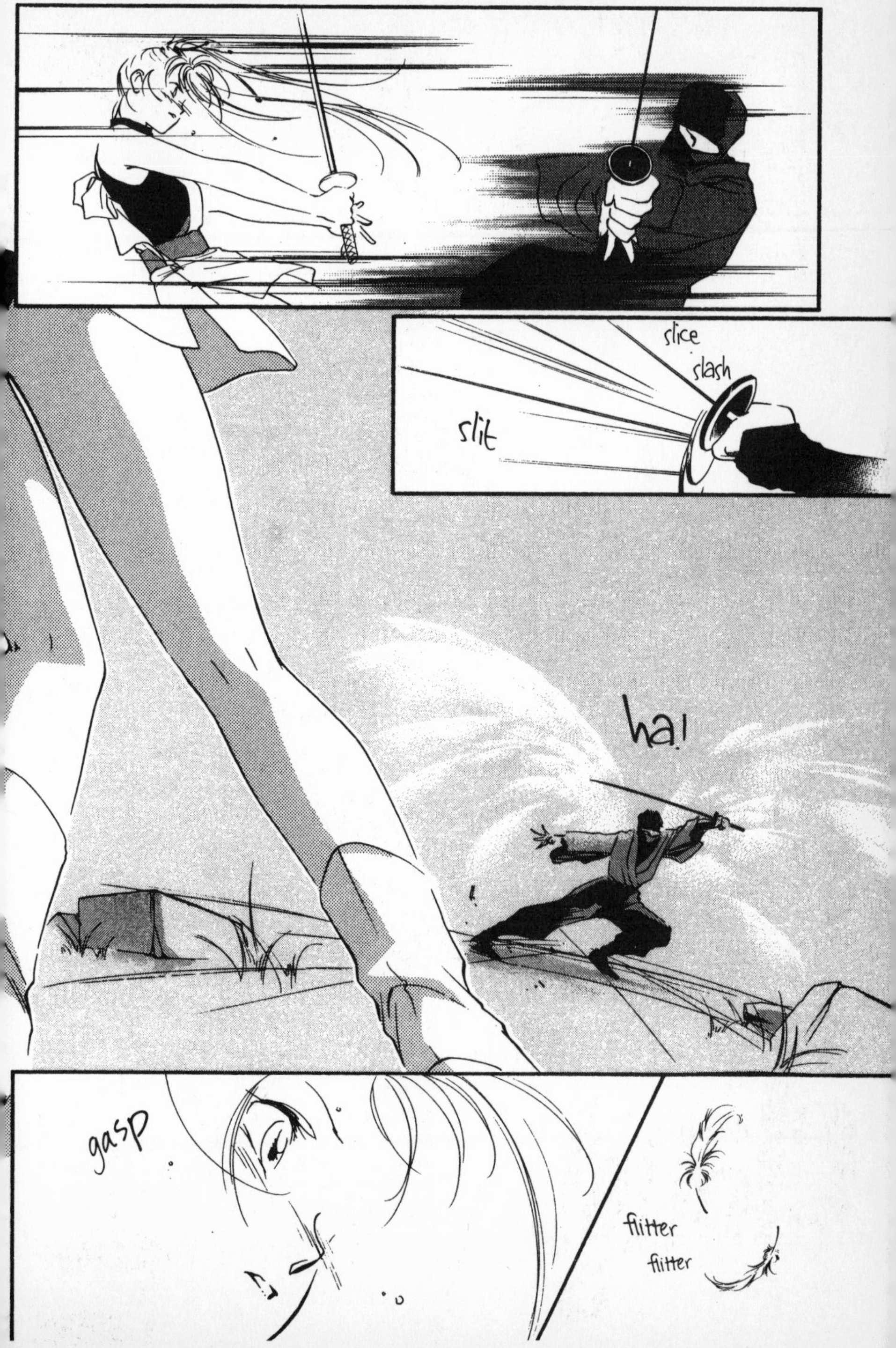
slice
slash
slit
ha!
gasp
flitter
flitter

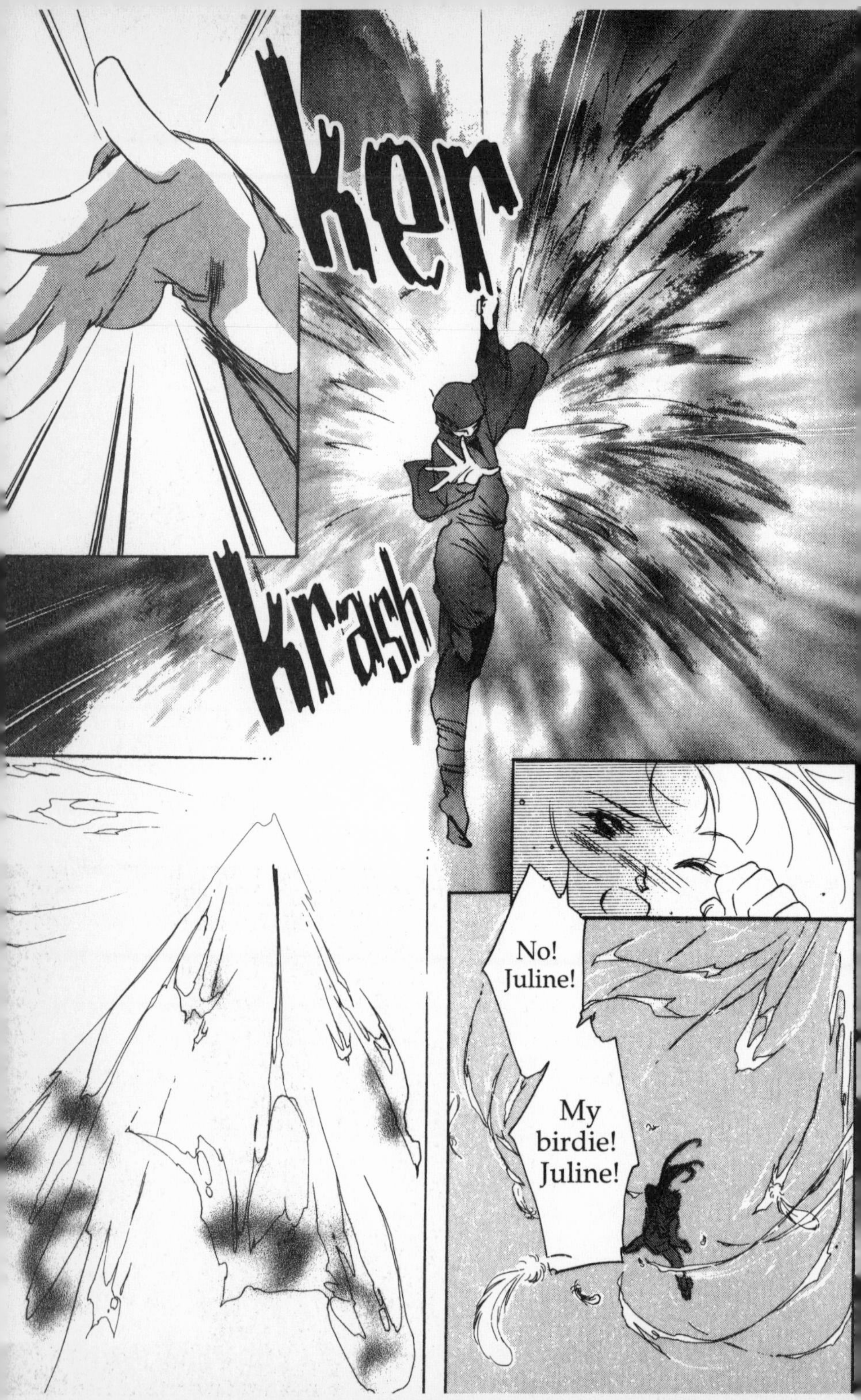
ker
Krash
No! Juline!
My birdie! Juline!

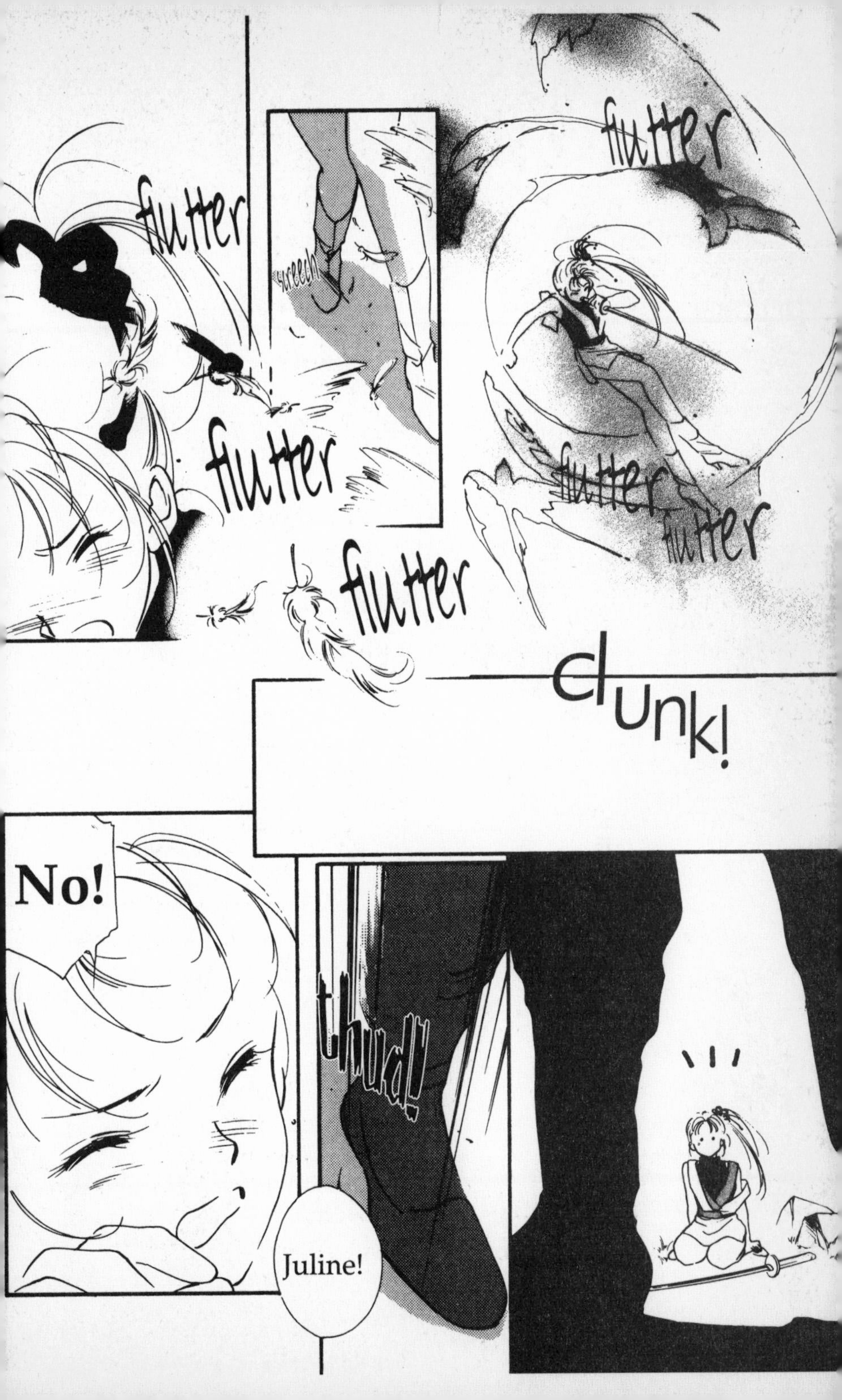

flutter
screech
flutter
flutter
flutter
flutter
flutter
clunk!
No!
thud!
Juline!

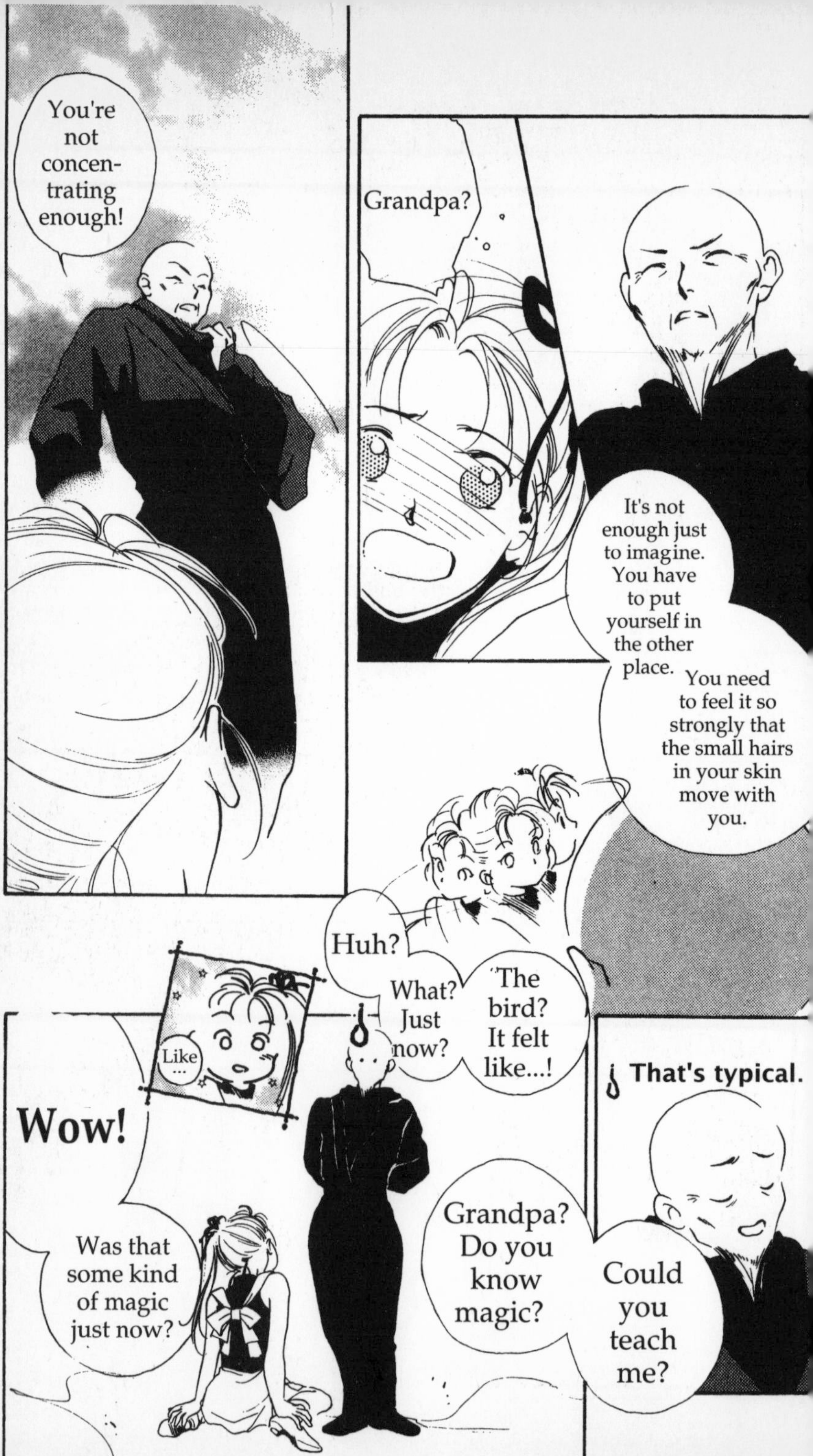
You're not concen-trating enough!
Grandpa?
It's not enough just to imagine. You have to put yourself in the other place.
You need to feel it so strongly that the small hairs in your skin move with you.
Huh?
What? Just now?
The bird? It felt like...!
Like ...
Wow!
Was that some kind of magic just now?
Grandpa? Do you know magic?
That's typical.
Could you teach me?

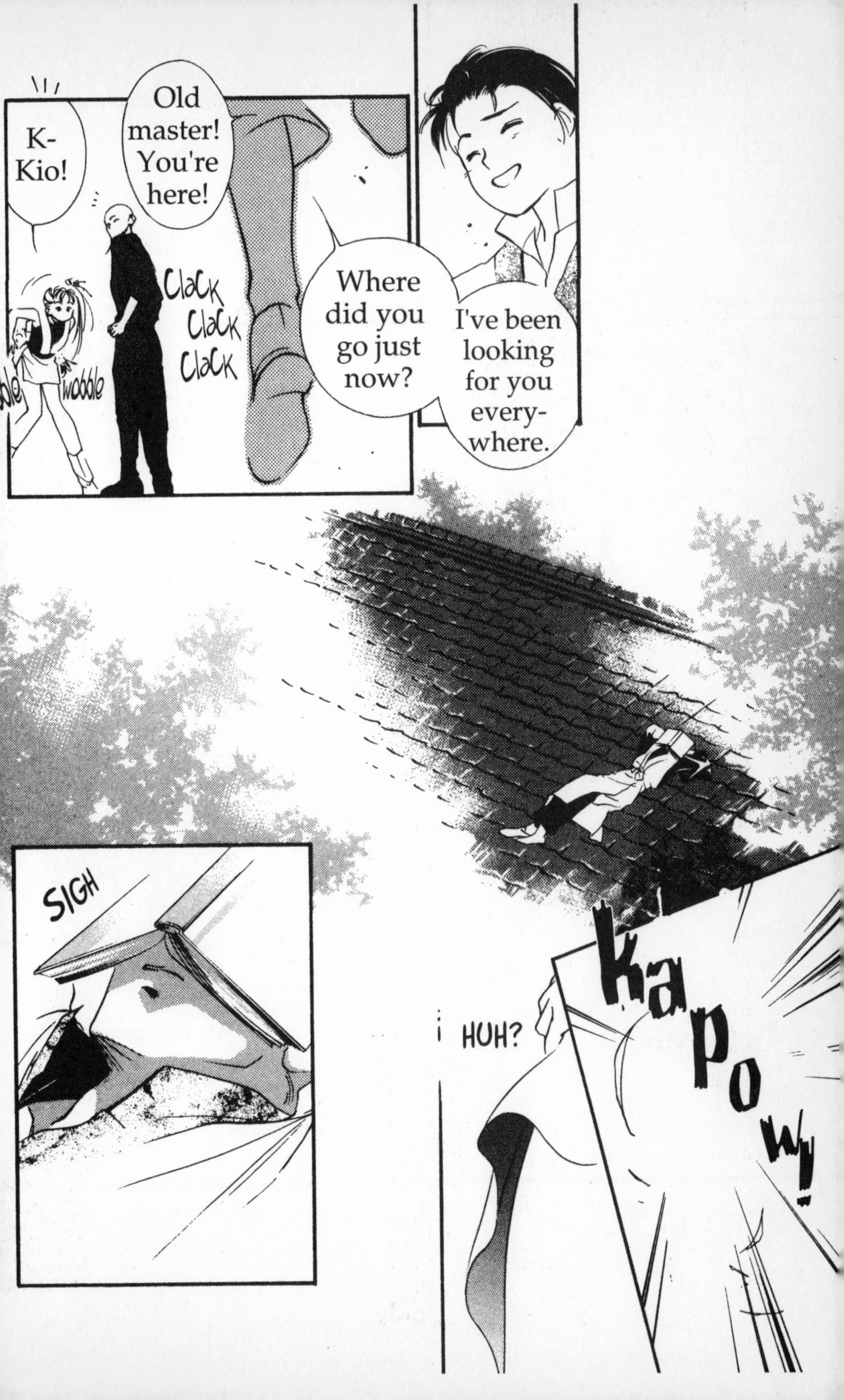
I've been looking for you every-where.
Where did you go just now?
Old master! You're here!
K-Kio!
CLACK CLACK CLACK
wobble
HUH?
KAPOW!
SIGH

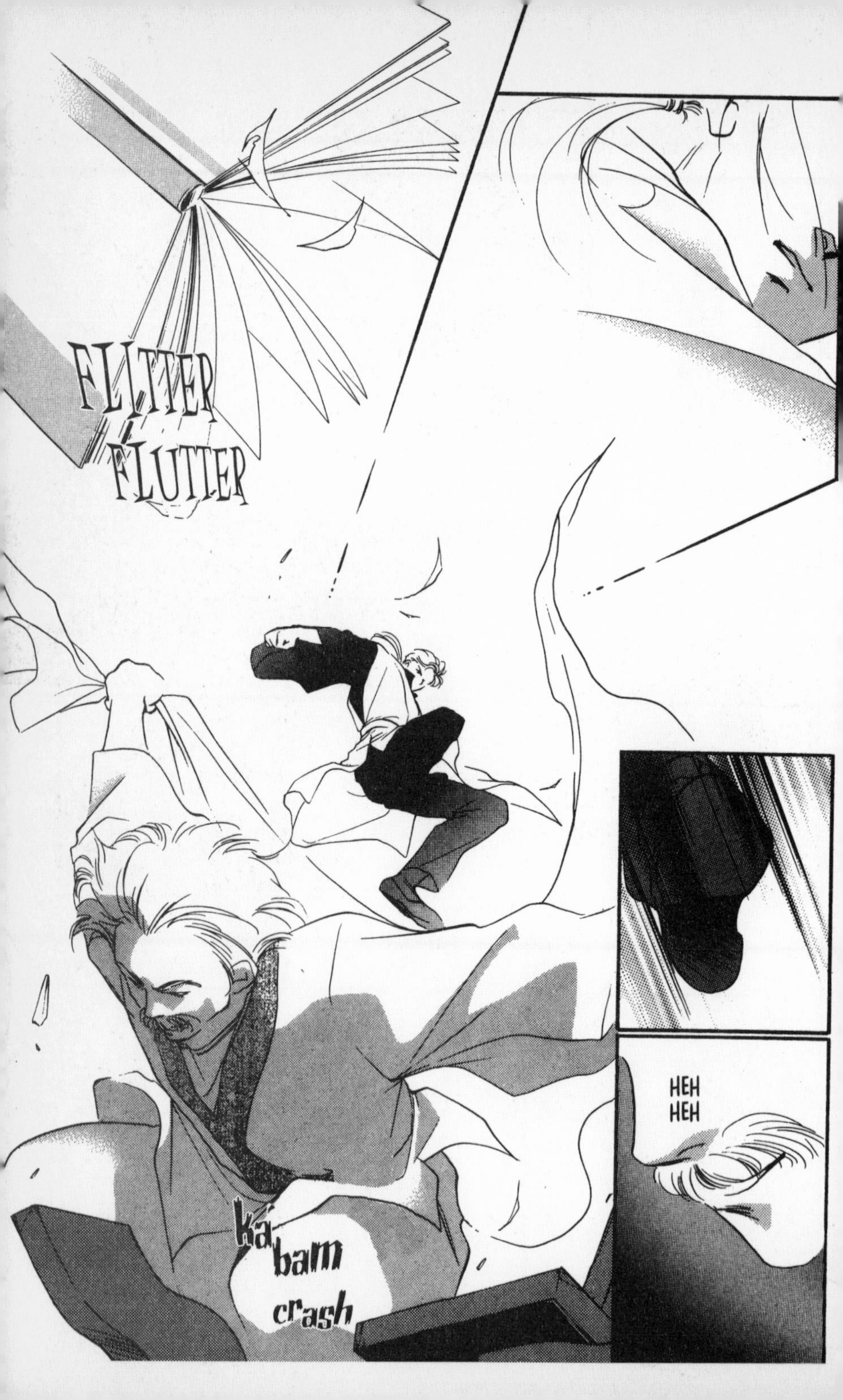
FLITTER FLUTTER
KA-BAM
CRASH
HEH HEH

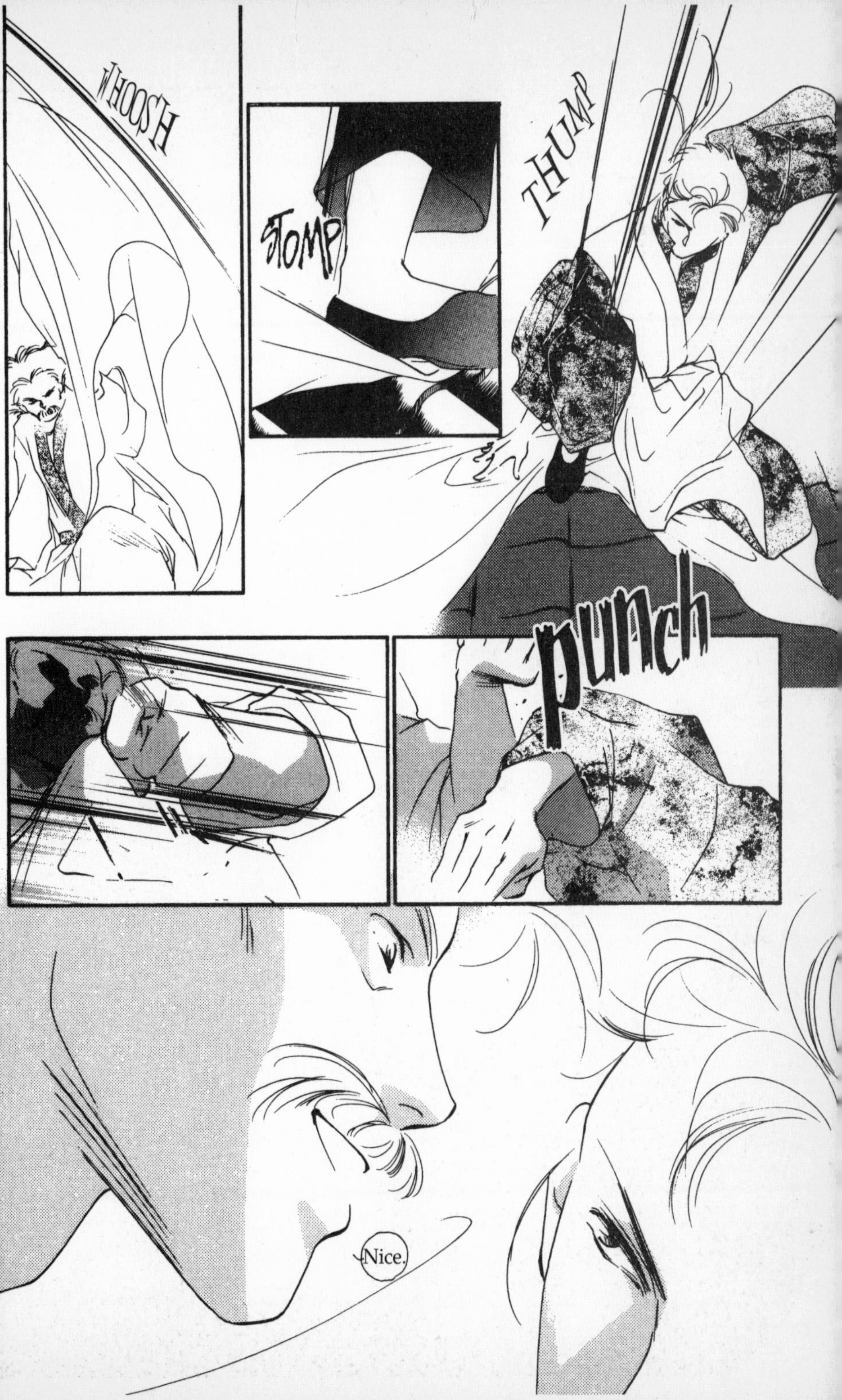
WHOOSH
STOMP
THUMP
punch
Nice.

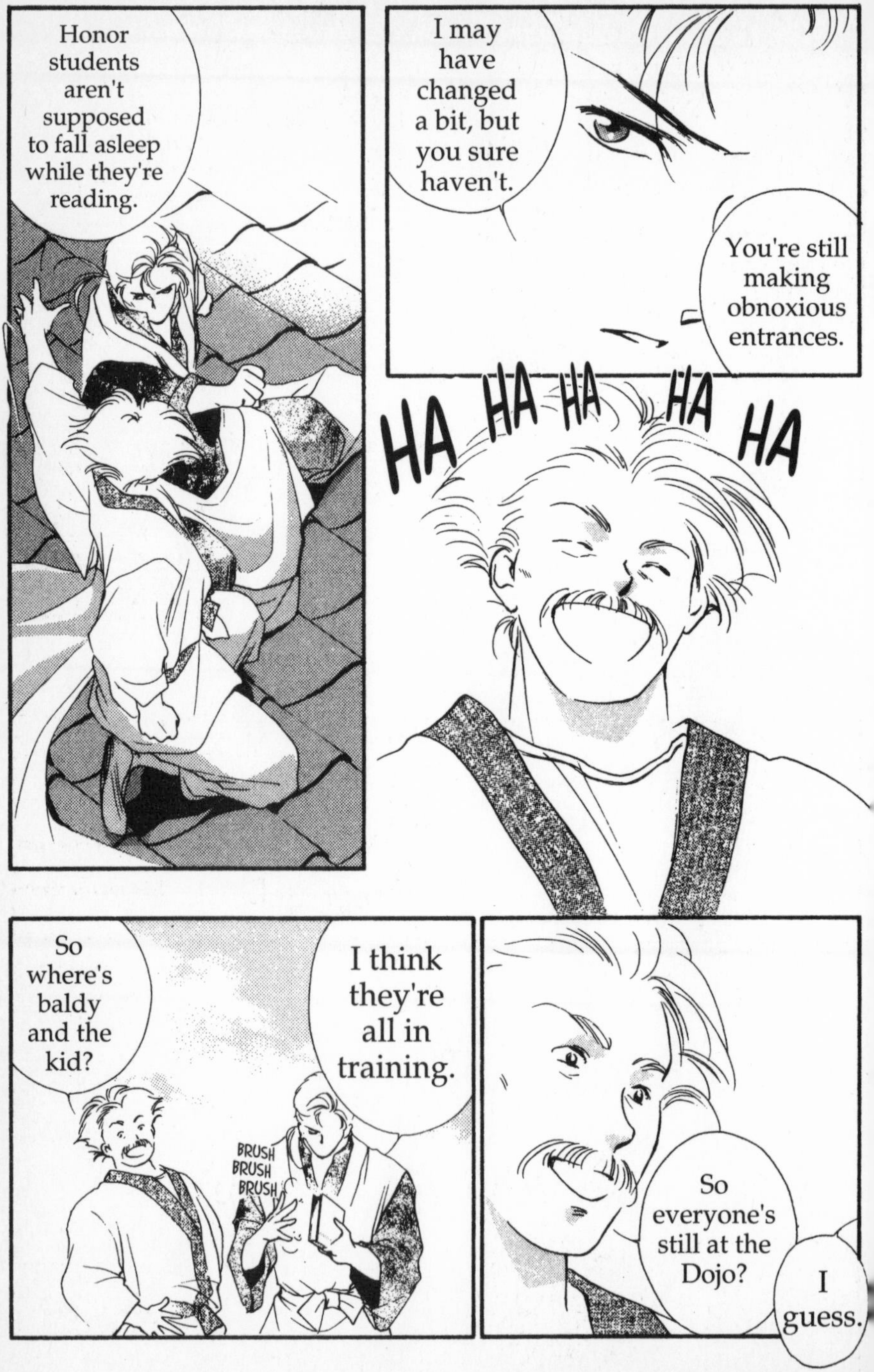
Honor students aren't supposed to fall asleep while they're reading.
I may have changed a bit, but you sure haven't.
You're still making obnoxious entrances.
HA HA HA HA HA
So where's baldy and the kid?
I think they're all in training.
BRUSH BRUSH BRUSH
So everyone's still at the Dojo?
I guess.

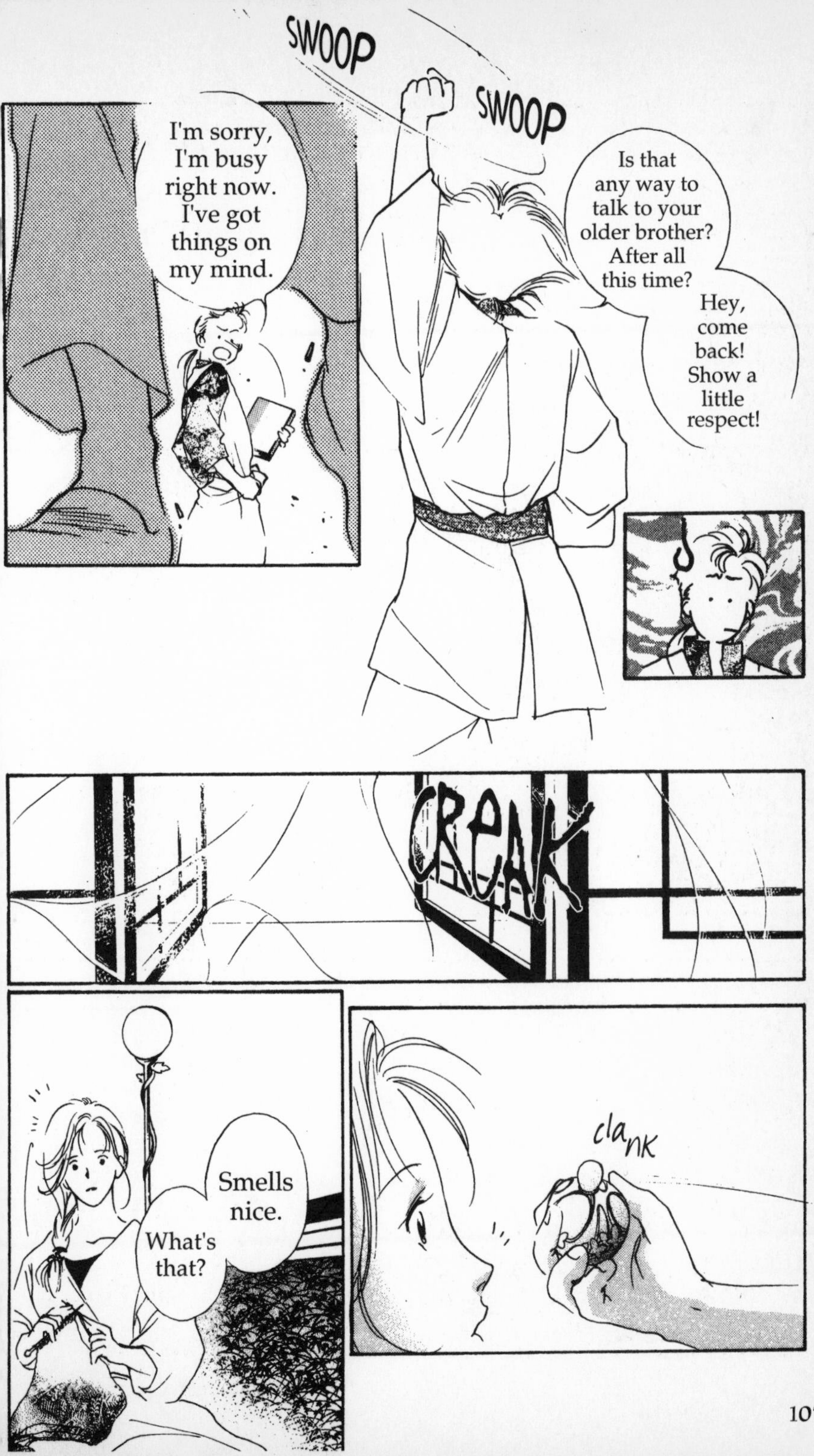
SWOOP
SWOOP
I'm sorry, I'm busy right now. I've got things on my mind.
Is that any way to talk to your older brother? After all this time?
Hey, come back! Show a little respect!
CREAK
Smells nice.
What's that?
clank

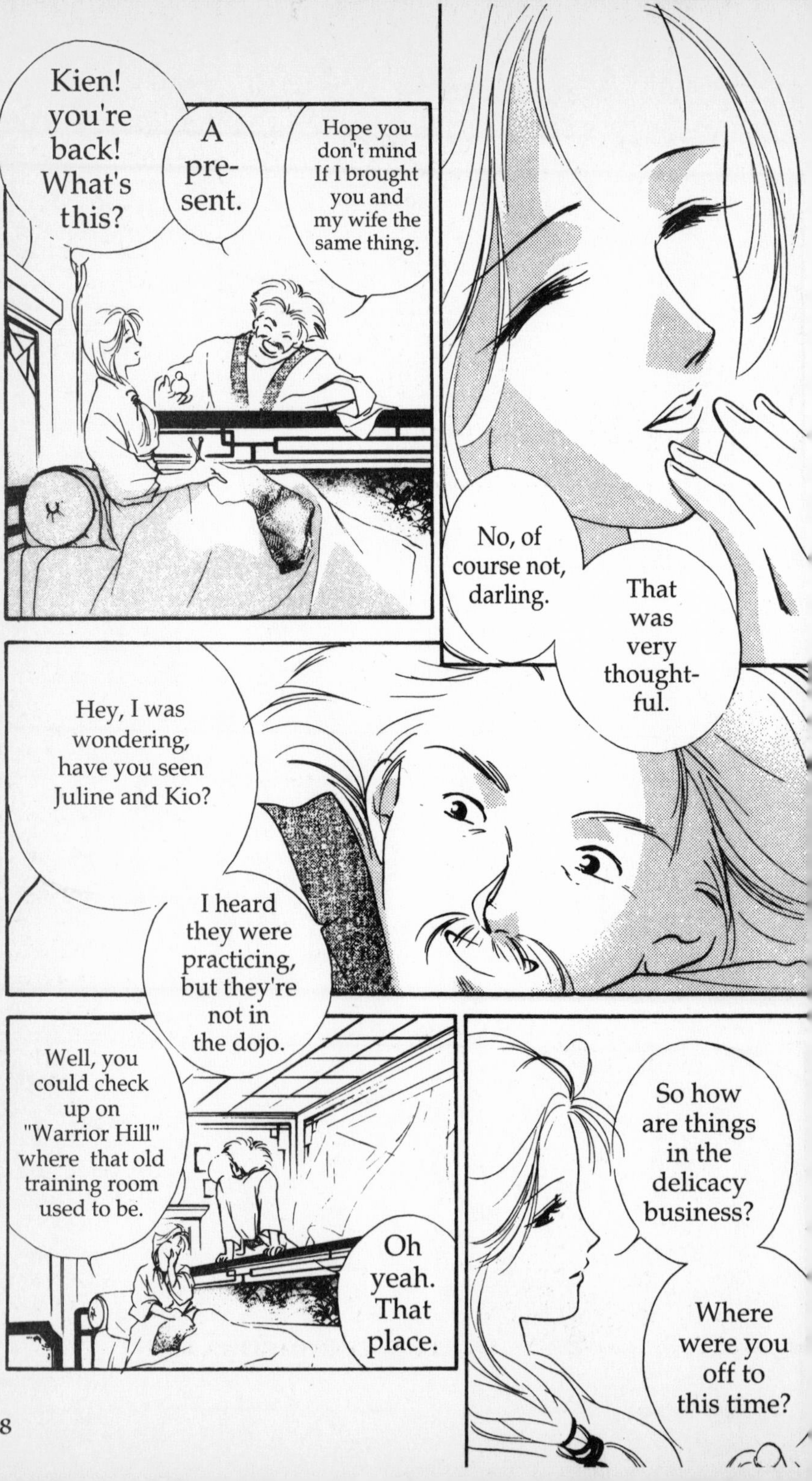

Kien! you're back! What's this?
A present.
Hope you don't mind If I brought you and my wife the same thing.
No, of course not, darling.
That was very thoughtful.
Hey, I was wondering, have you seen Juline and Kio?
I heard they were practicing, but they're not in the dojo.
Well, you could check up on "Warrior Hill" where that old training room used to be.
Oh yeah. That place.
So how are things in the delicacy business?
Where were you off to this time?

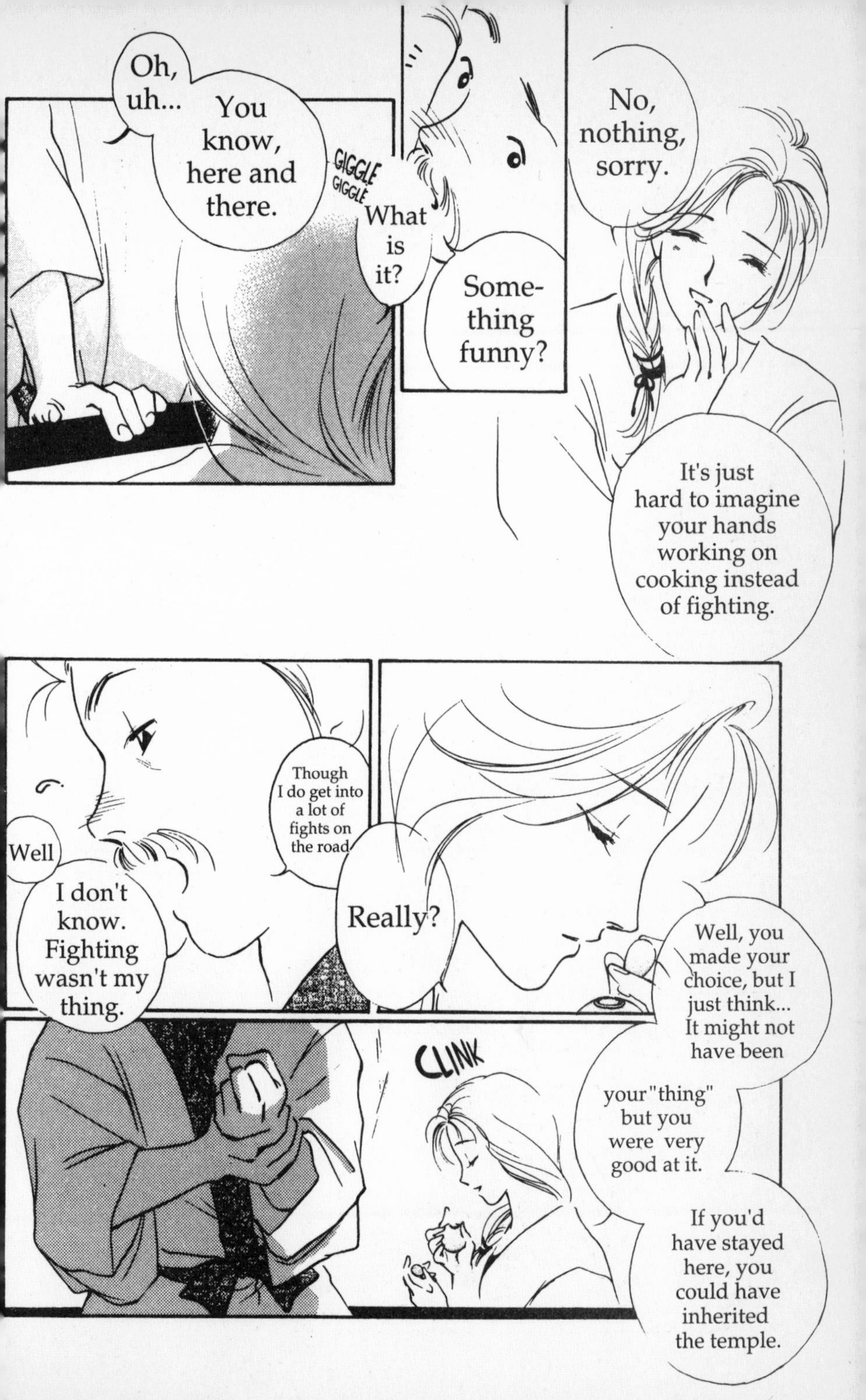
Oh, uh...
You know, here and there.
GIGGLE GIGGLE
What is it?
Something funny?
No, nothing, sorry.
It's just hard to imagine your hands working on cooking instead of fighting.
Well
I don't know. Fighting wasn't my thing.
Though I do get into a lot of fights on the road
Really?
Well, you made your choice, but I just think... It might not have been
CLINK
your "thing" but you were very good at it.
If you'd have stayed here, you could have inherited the temple.

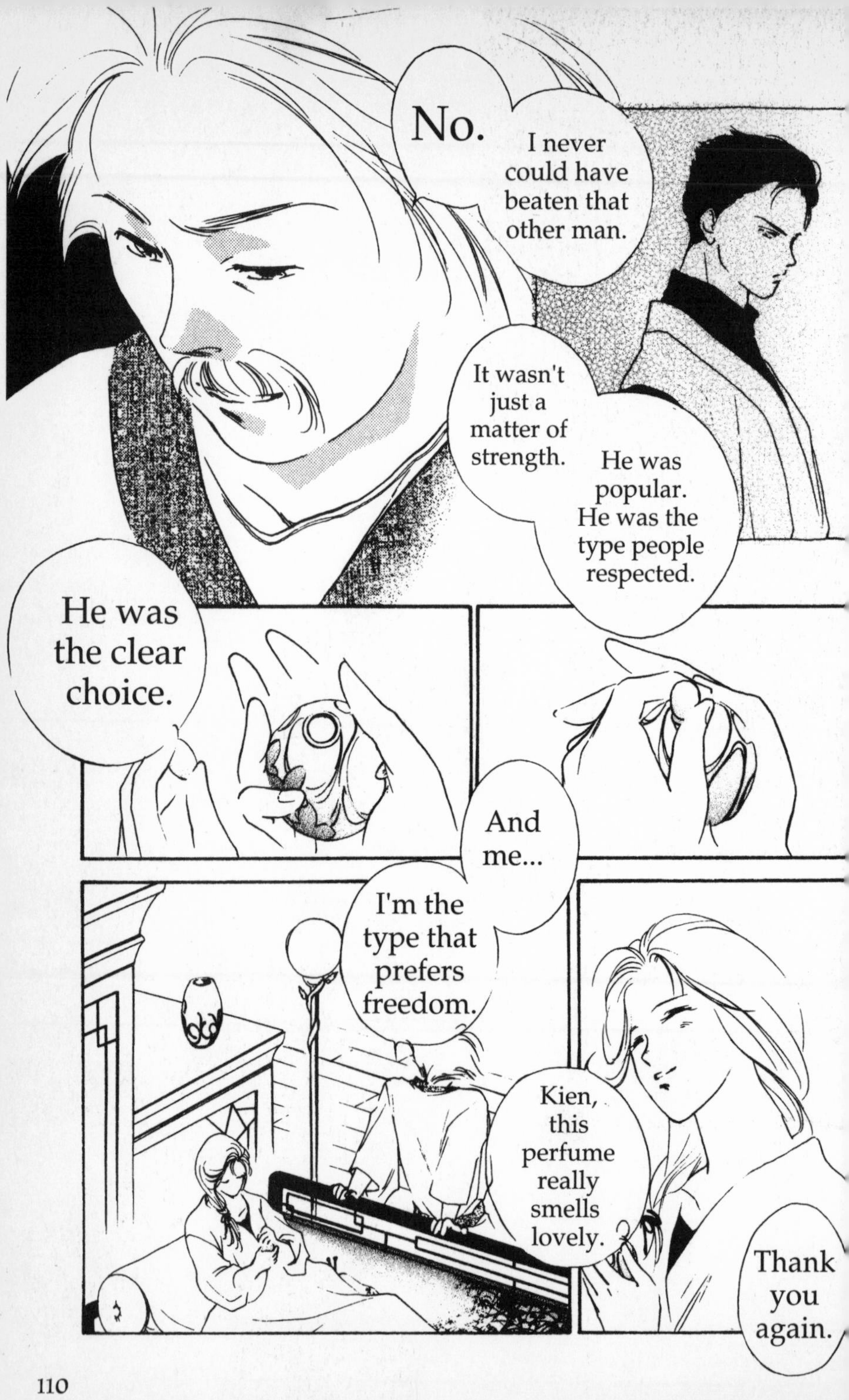
No.
I never could have beaten that other man.
It wasn't just a matter of strength.
He was popular. He was the type people respected.
He was the clear choice.
And me...
I'm the type that prefers freedom.
Kien, this perfume really smells lovely.
Thank you again.

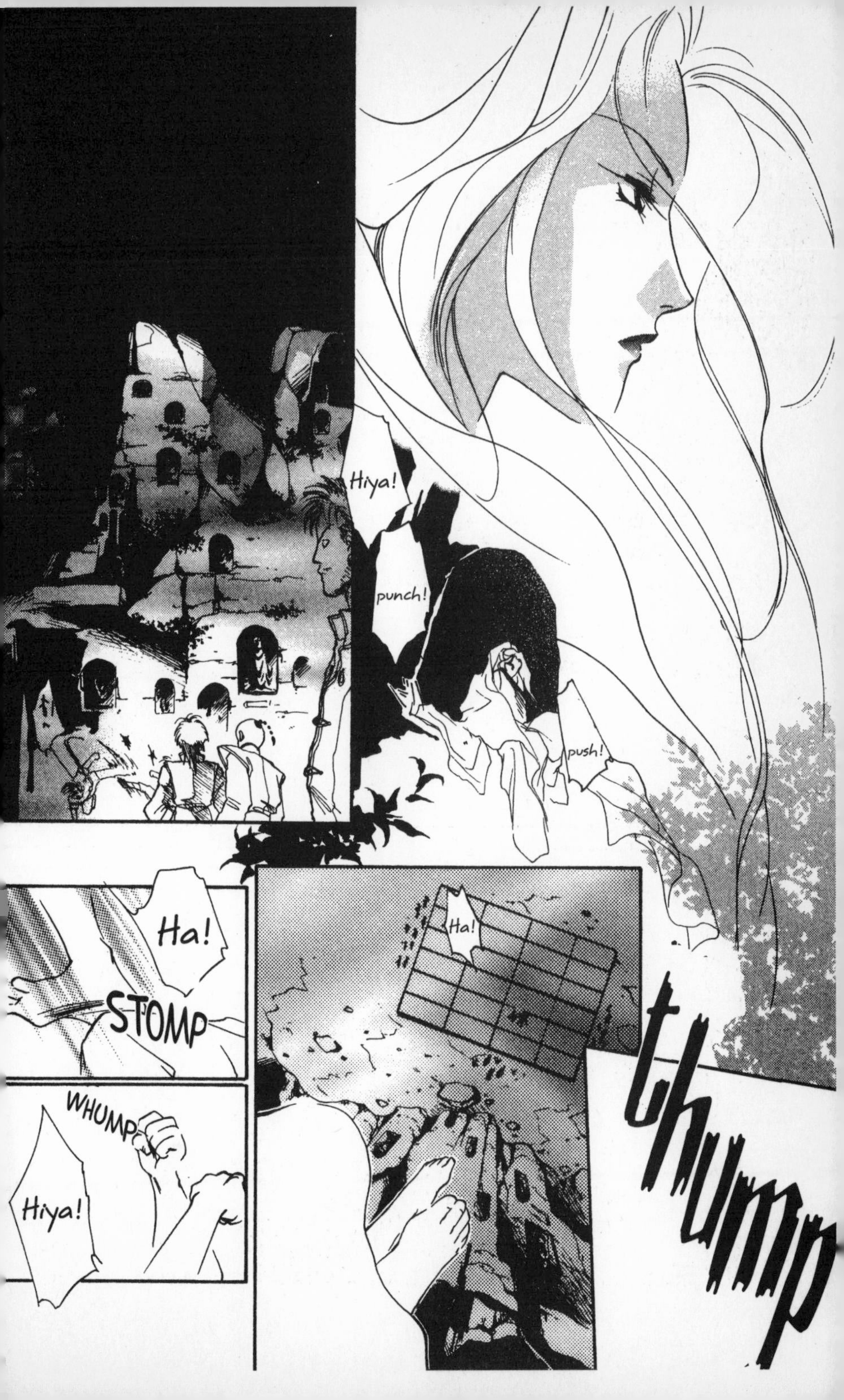
Hiya!
punch!
push!
Ha!
STOMP
WHUMP
Hiya!
Ha!
thump

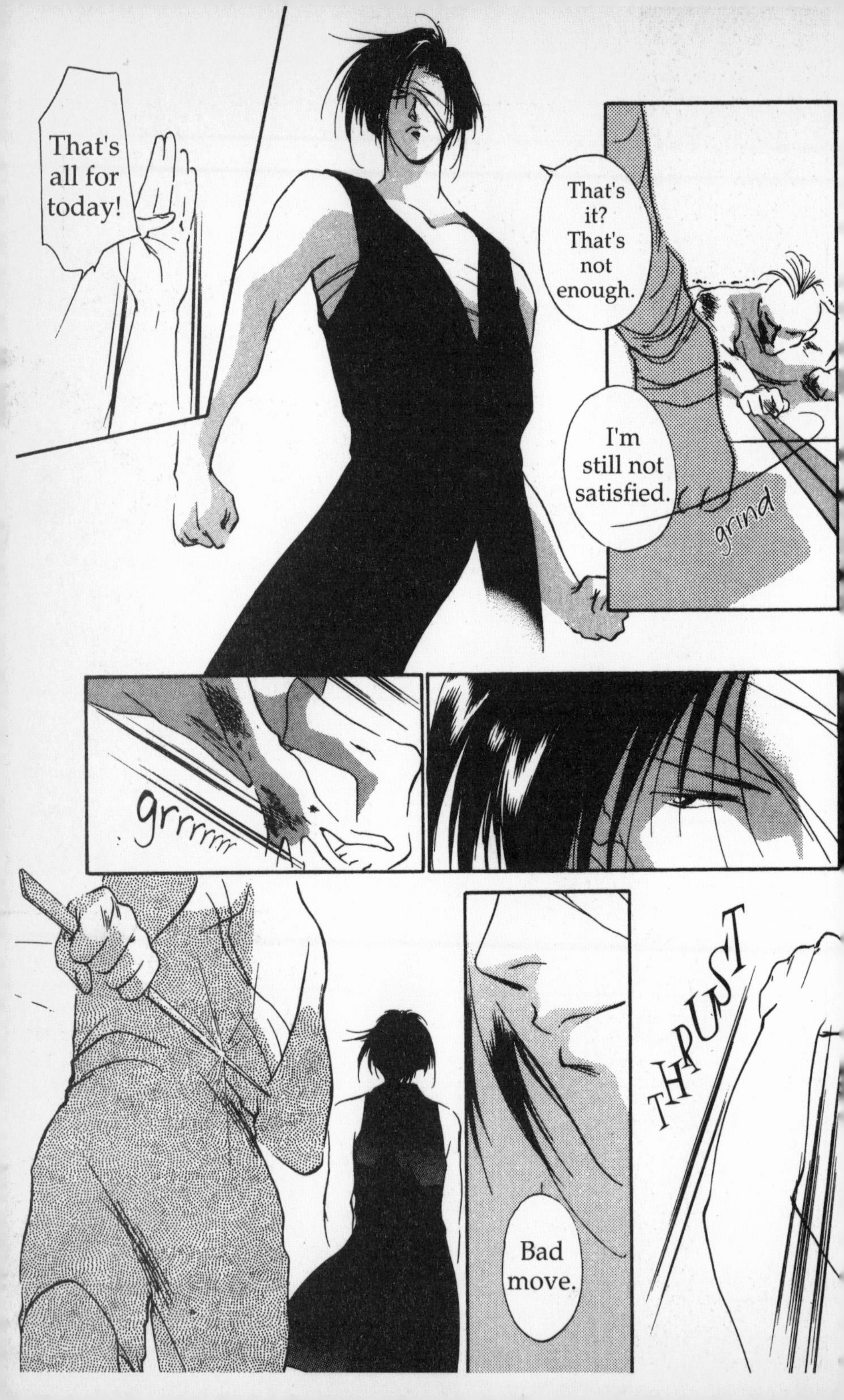
That's all for today!
That's it? That's not enough.
I'm still not satisfied.
grind
grrrrrrr
Bad move.
THRUST

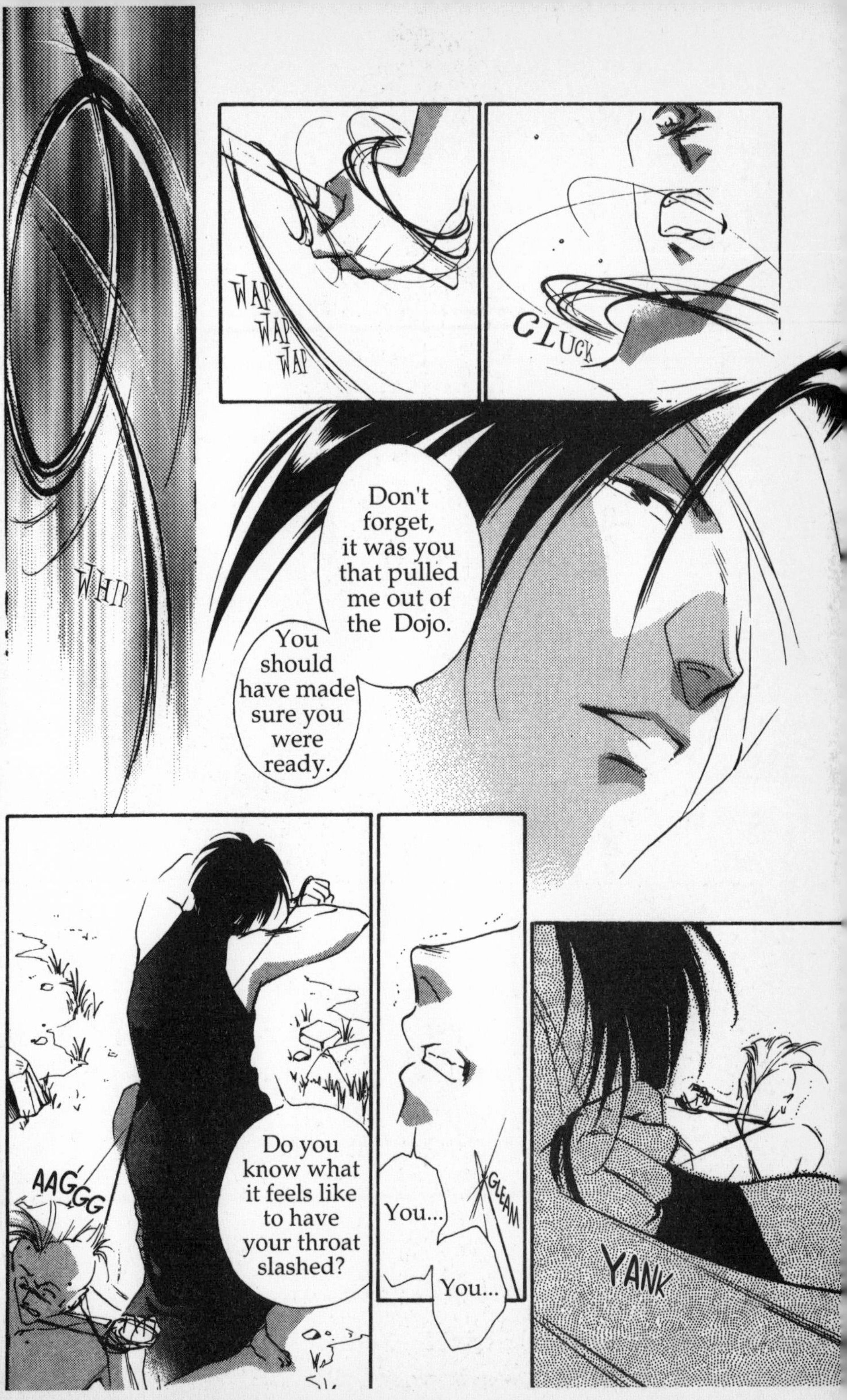
CLUCK
WAP WAP WAP
Don't forget, it was you that pulled me out of the Dojo.
You should have made sure you were ready.
WHIP
YANK
GLEAM
You...
You...
Do you know what it feels like to have your throat slashed?
AAGGG

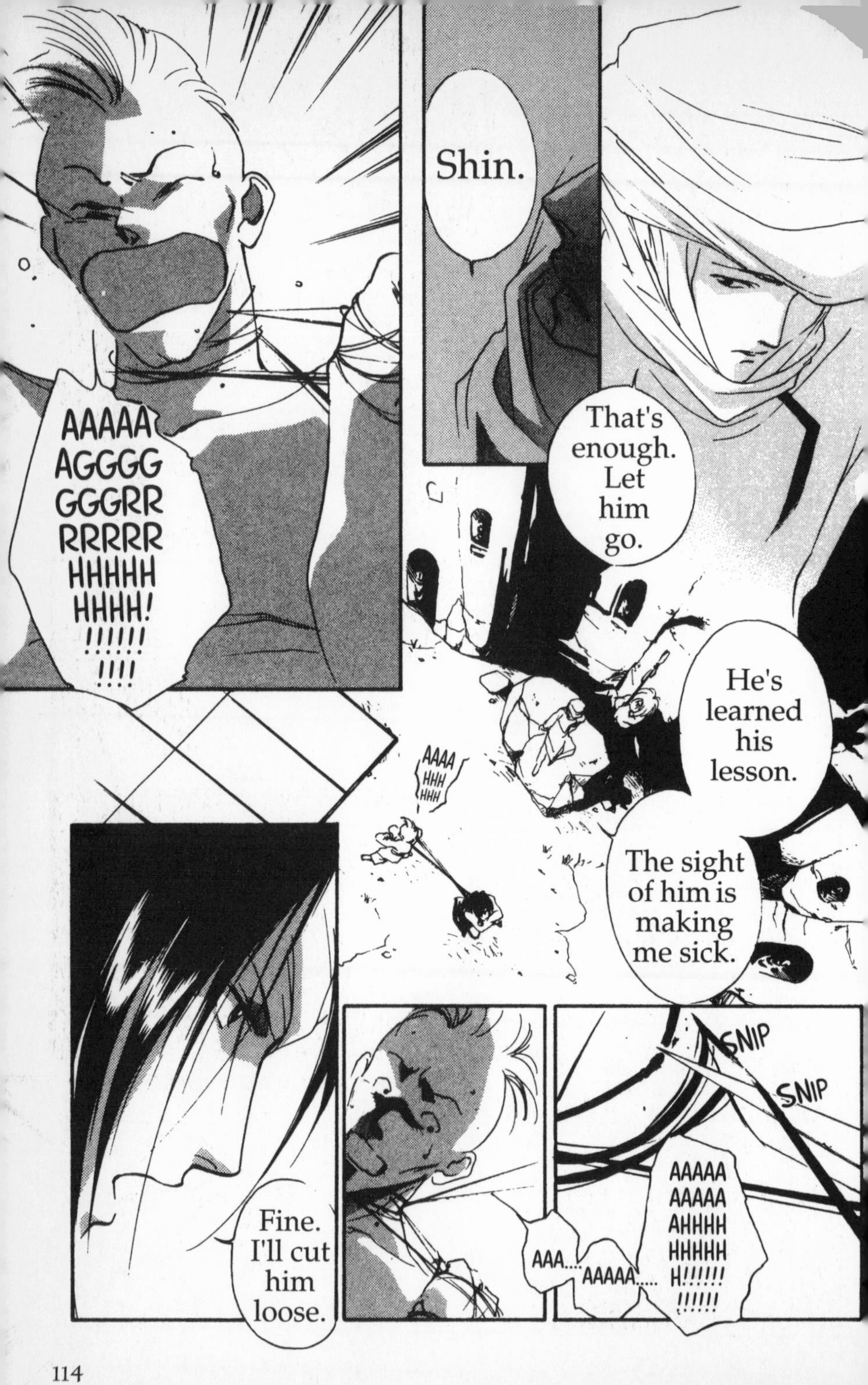

AAAAA AGGGG GGGRR RRRRR HHHHH HHHH! !!!!!! !!!!
Shin.
That's enough. Let him go.
AAAA HHH HHH
He's learned his lesson.
The sight of him is making me sick.
Fine. I'll cut him loose.
SNIP
SNIP
AAA.... AAAAA.....
AAAAA AAAAA AHHHH HHHHH H!!!!!! !!!!!!

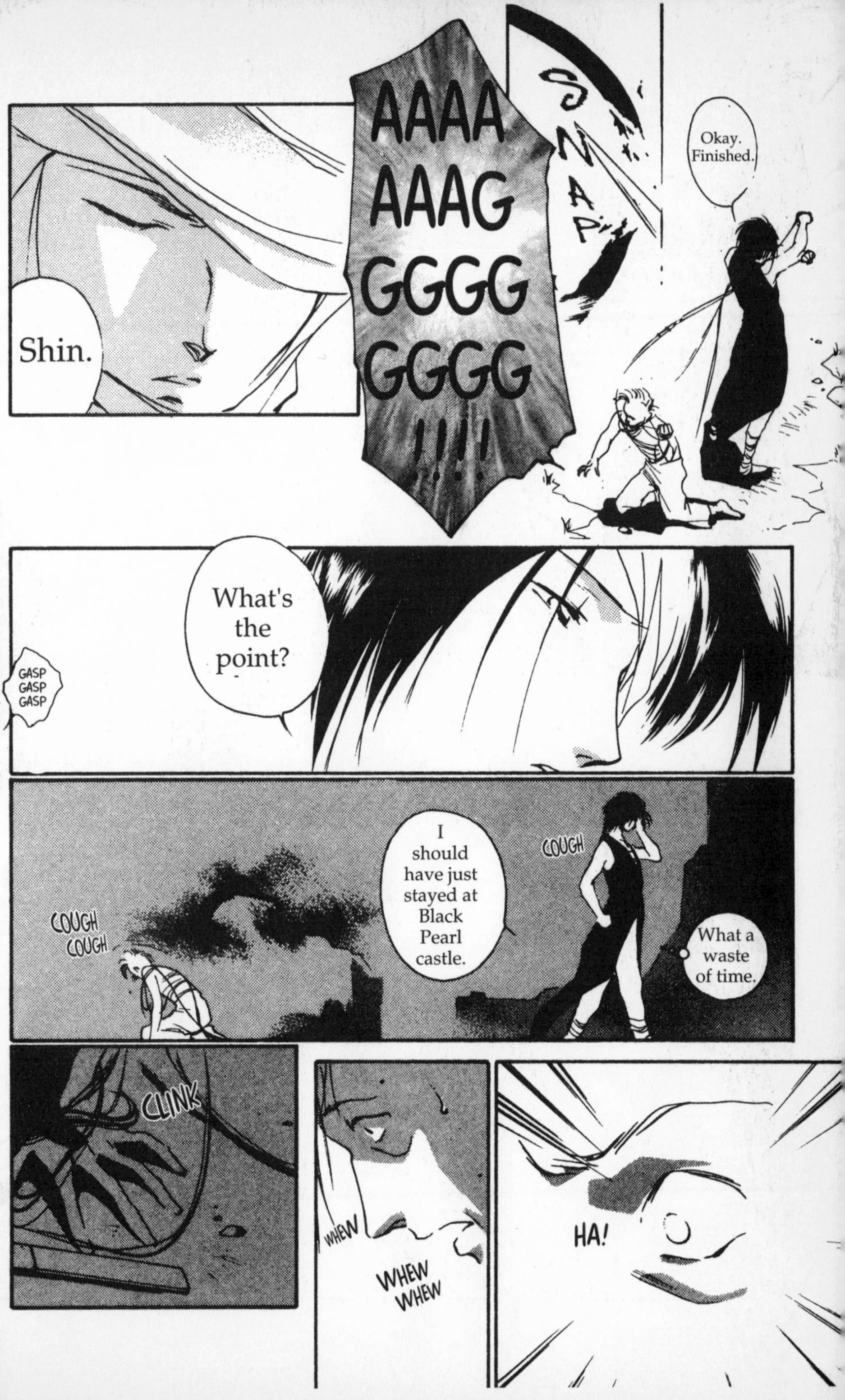
Shin.
AAAA AAAG GGGG GGGG !!!!
SNAP
Okay. Finished.
GASP GASP GASP
What's the point?
COUGH COUGH
I should have just stayed at Black Pearl castle.
COUGH
What a waste of time.
CLINK
WHEW
WHEW WHEW
HA!

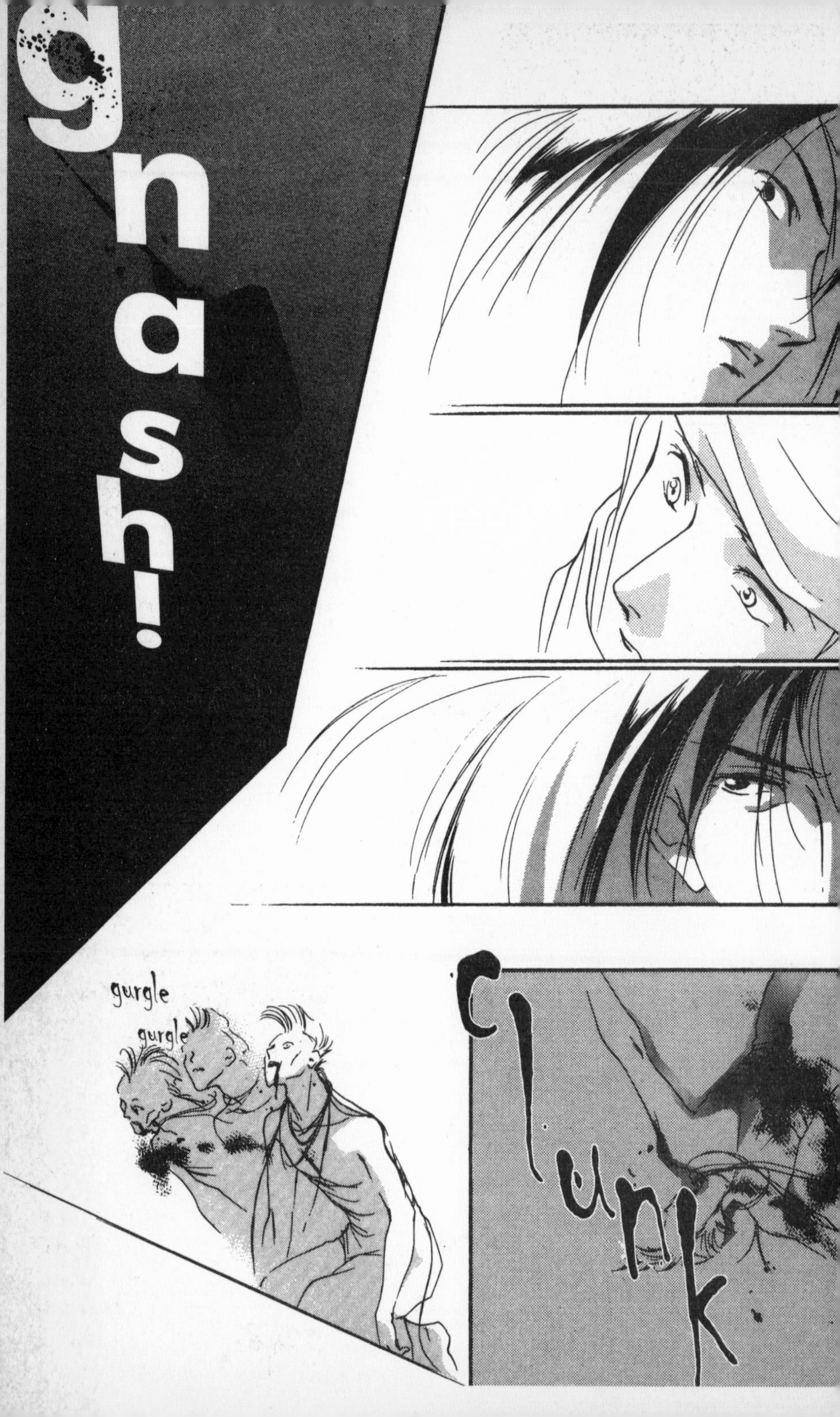
gnash!
gurgle
gurgle
Clunk

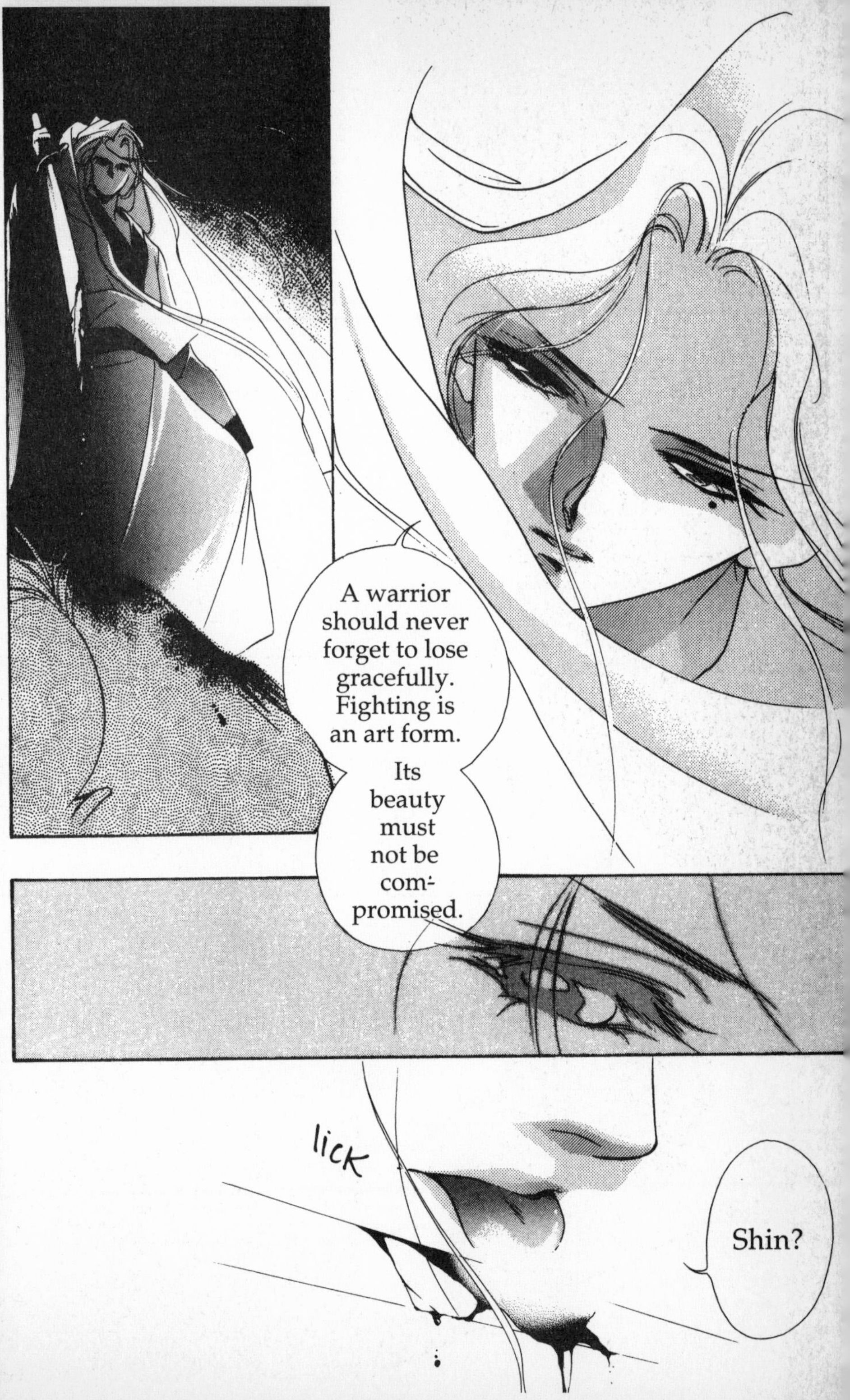
A warrior should never forget to lose gracefully. Fighting is an art form.
Its beauty must not be com-promised.
lick
Shin?

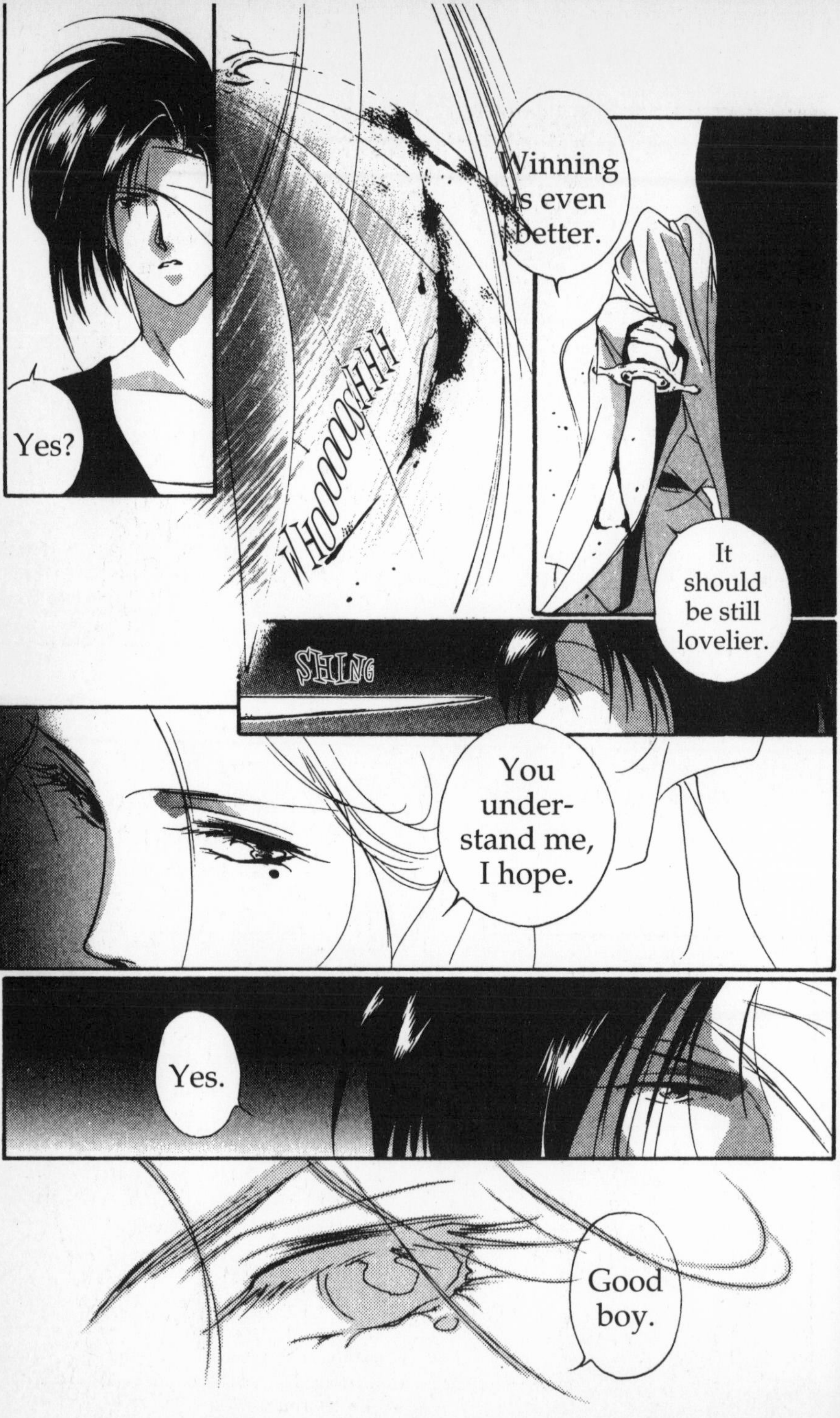
Yes?
WHOOOOOOSHHH
Winning is even better.
It should be still lovelier.
SHING
You under-stand me, I hope.
Yes.
Good boy.

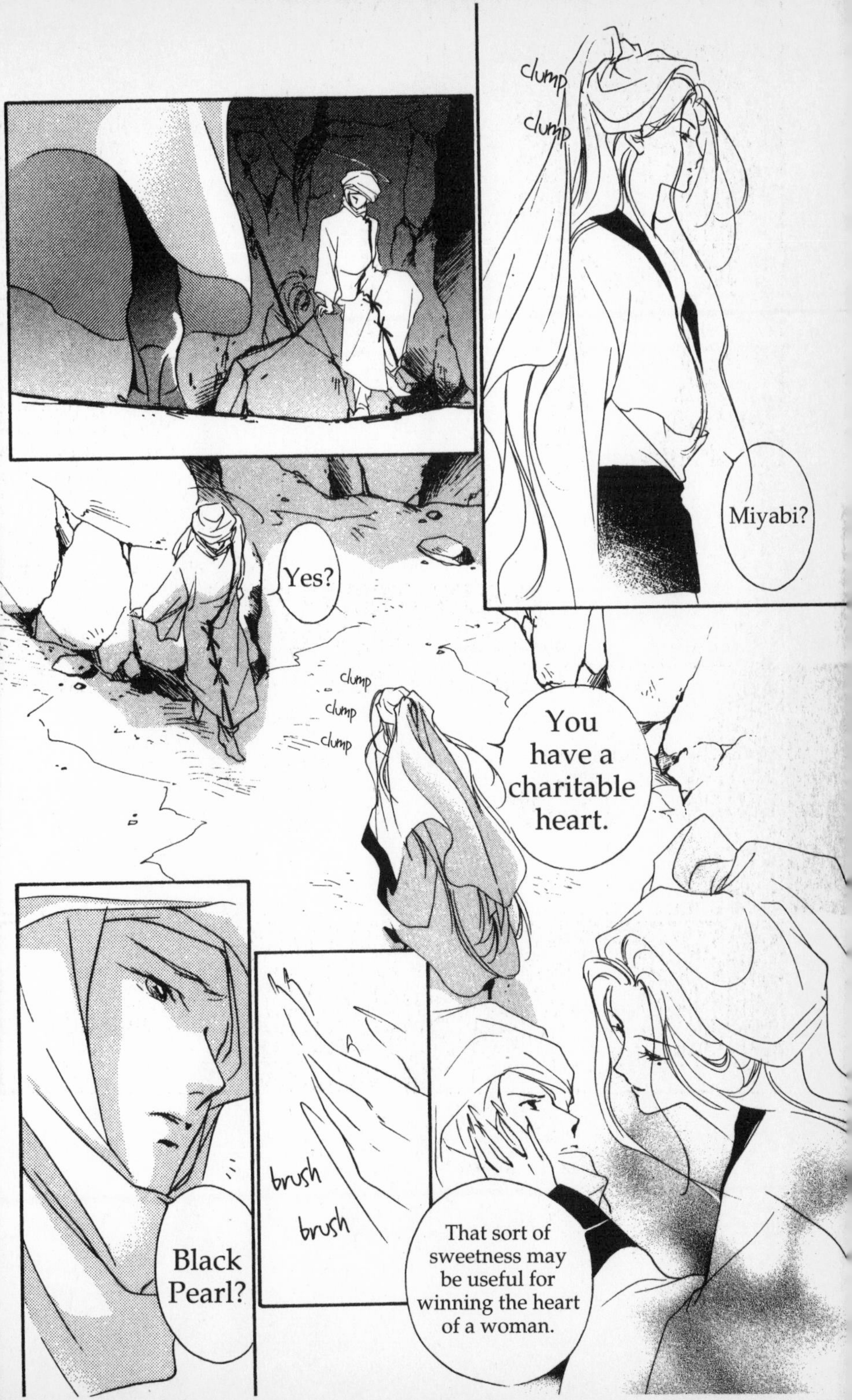
clump
clump
Miyabi?
Yes?
clump
clump
clump
You have a charitable heart.
Black Pearl?
brush
brush
That sort of sweetness may be useful for winning the heart of a woman.

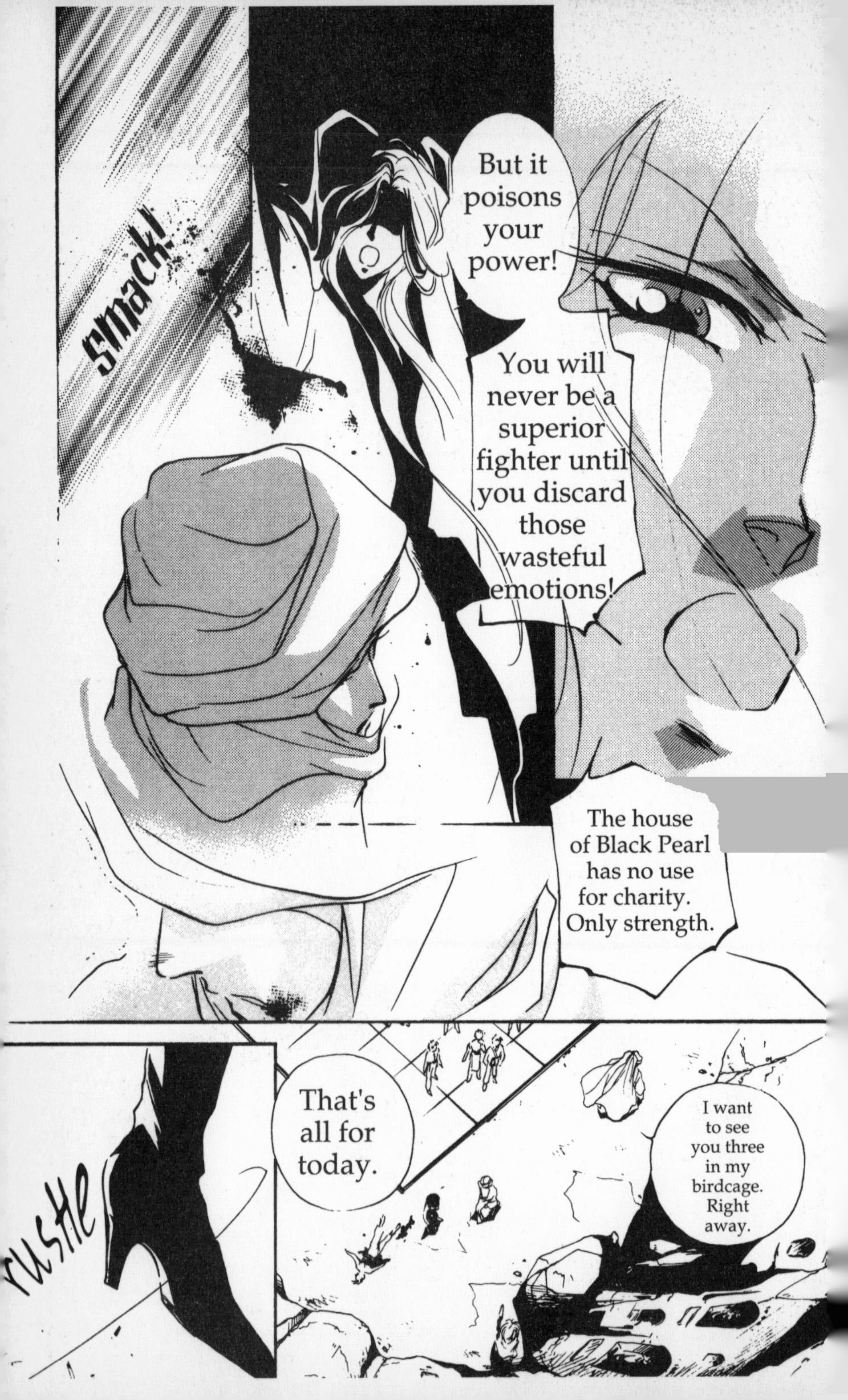
smack!
But it poisons your power!
You will never be a superior fighter until you discard those wasteful emotions!
The house of Black Pearl has no use for charity. Only strength.
rustle
That's all for today.
I want to see you three in my birdcage. Right away.

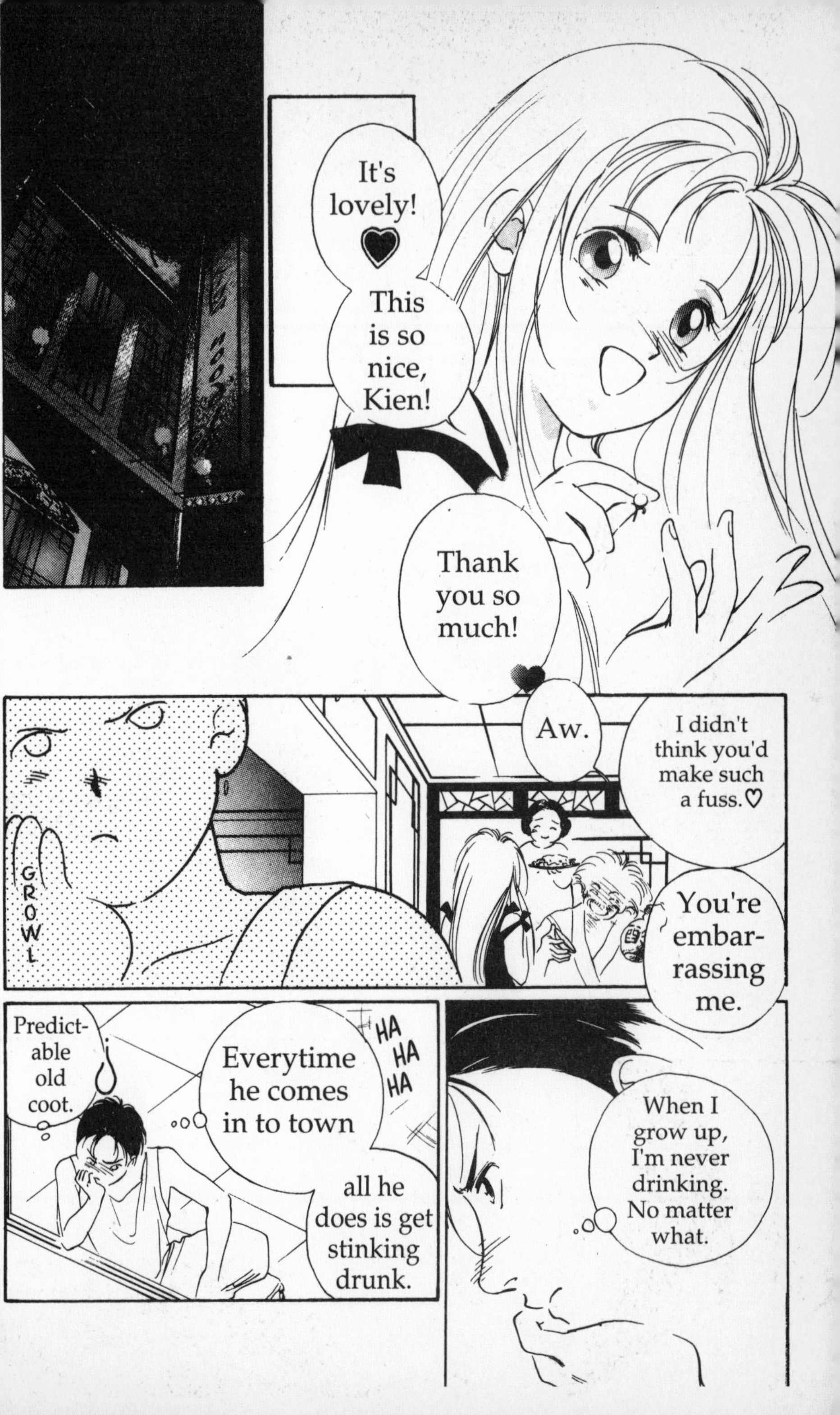
It's lovely! ♥
This is so nice, Kien!
Thank you so much!
GROWL
Aw.
I didn't think you'd make such a fuss.♡
You're embarrassing me.
Predictable old coot.
Everytime he comes in to town
HA HA HA
all he does is get stinking drunk.
When I grow up, I'm never drinking. No matter what.

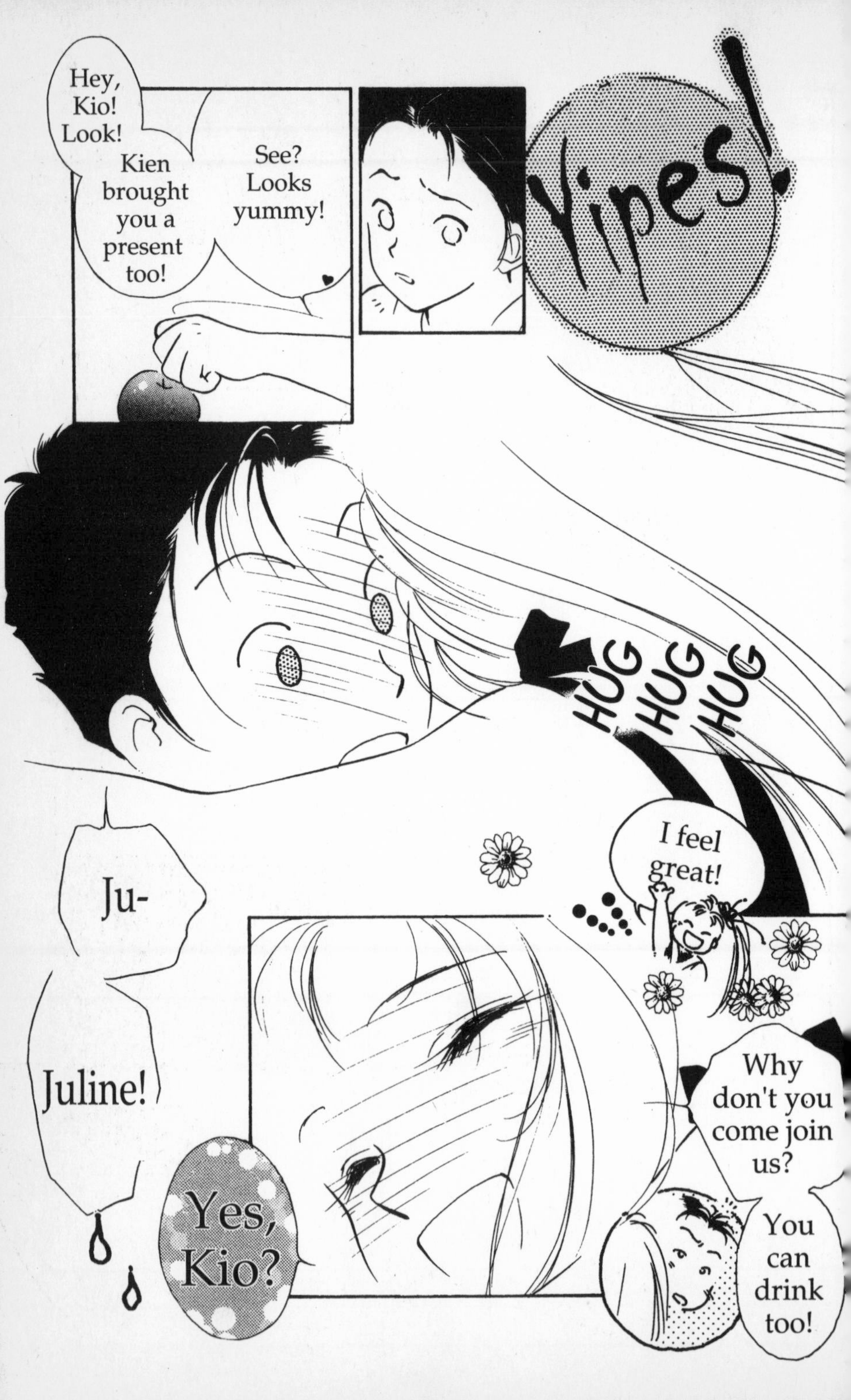
Hey, Kio! Look!
Kien brought you a present too!
See? Looks yummy!
Yipes!
HUG HUG HUG
I feel great!
Ju-
Juline!
Yes, Kio?
Why don't you come join us?
You can drink too!

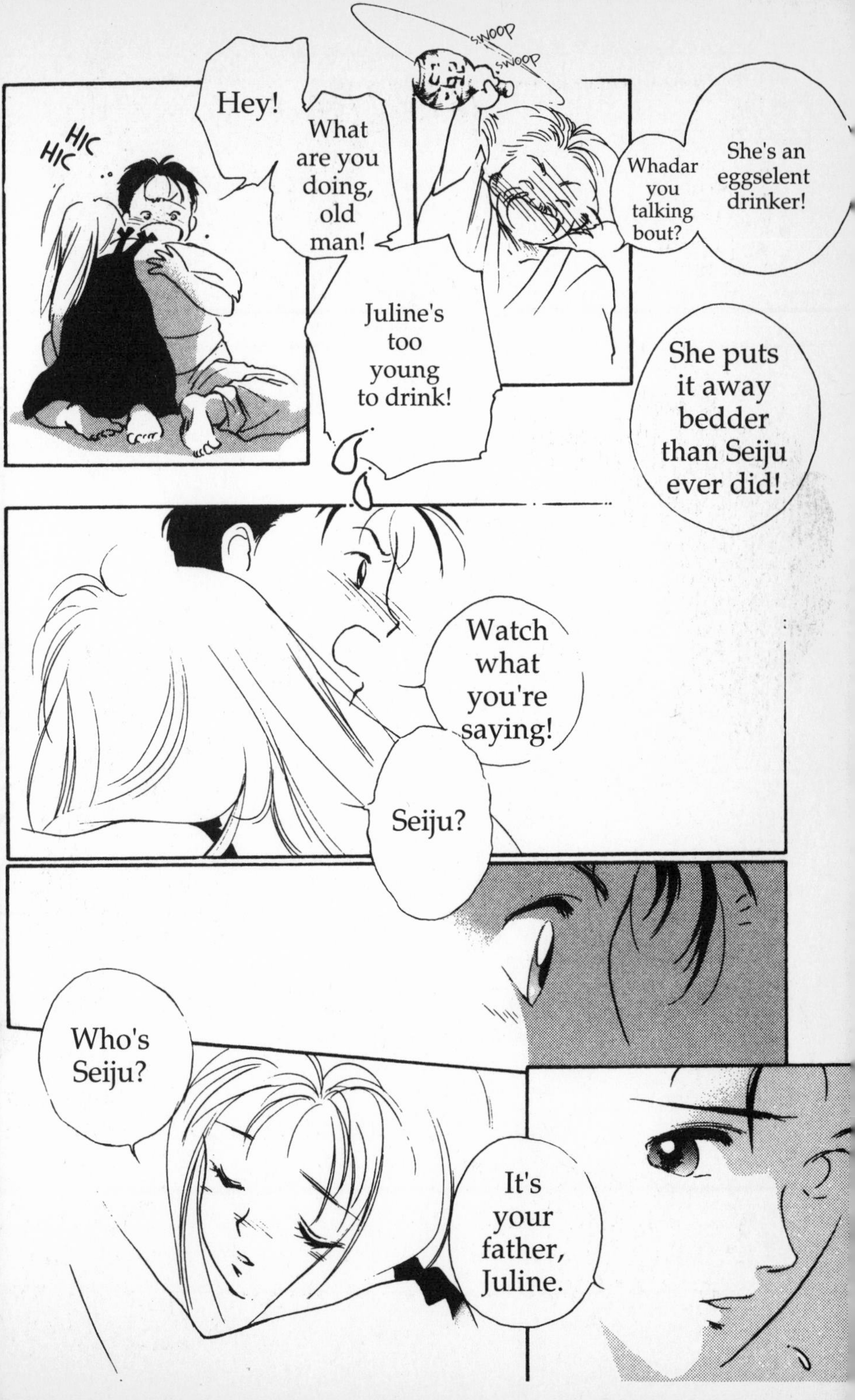
HIC HIC
Hey!
What are you doing, old man!
Juline's too young to drink!
SWOOP SWOOP
Whadar you talking bout?
She's an eggselent drinker!
She puts it away bedder than Seiju ever did!
Watch what you're saying!
Seiju?
Who's Seiju?
It's your father, Juline.

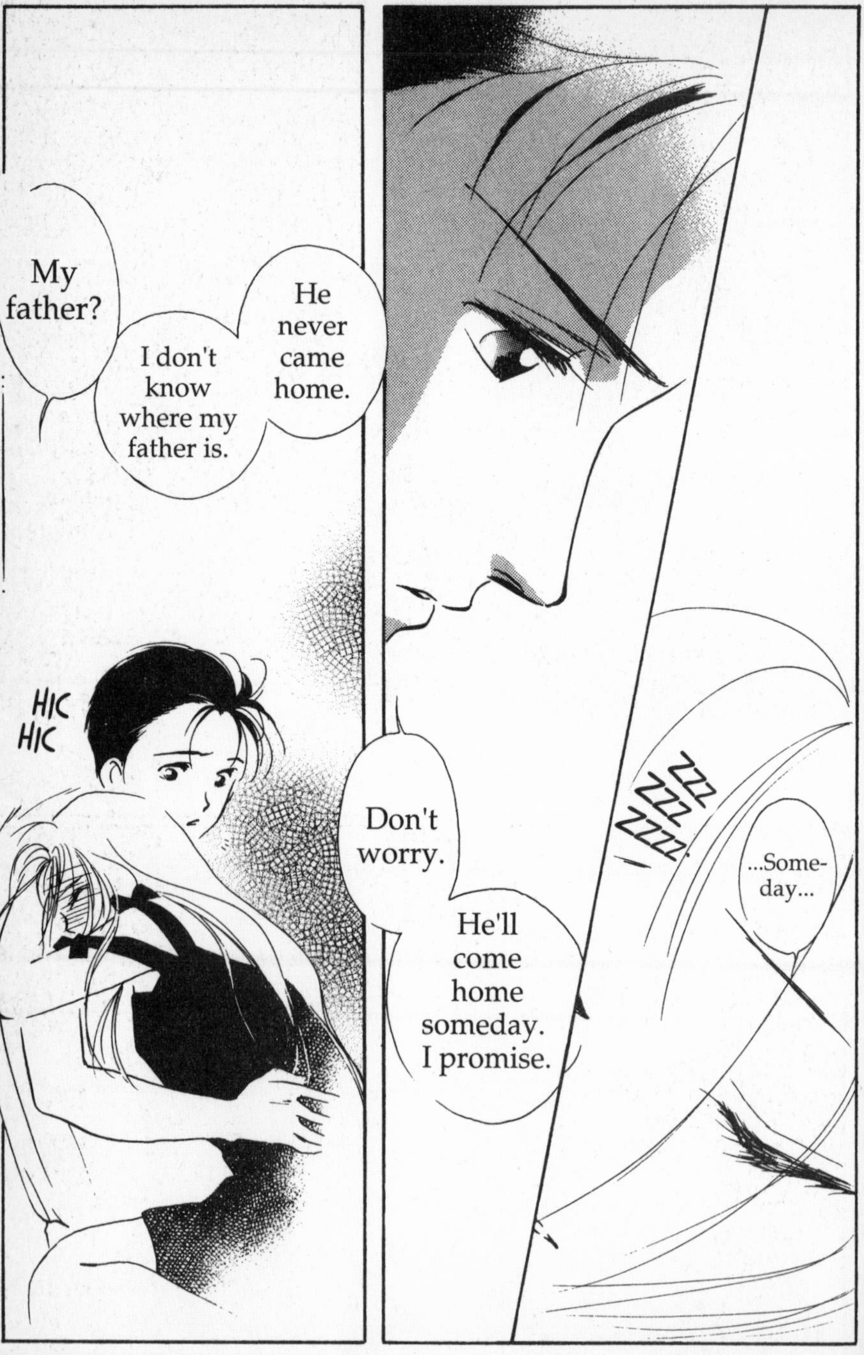
My father?
I don't know where my father is.
He never came home.
HIC HIC
Don't worry.
He'll come home someday. I promise.
ZZZ ZZZ ZZZZ
...Someday...

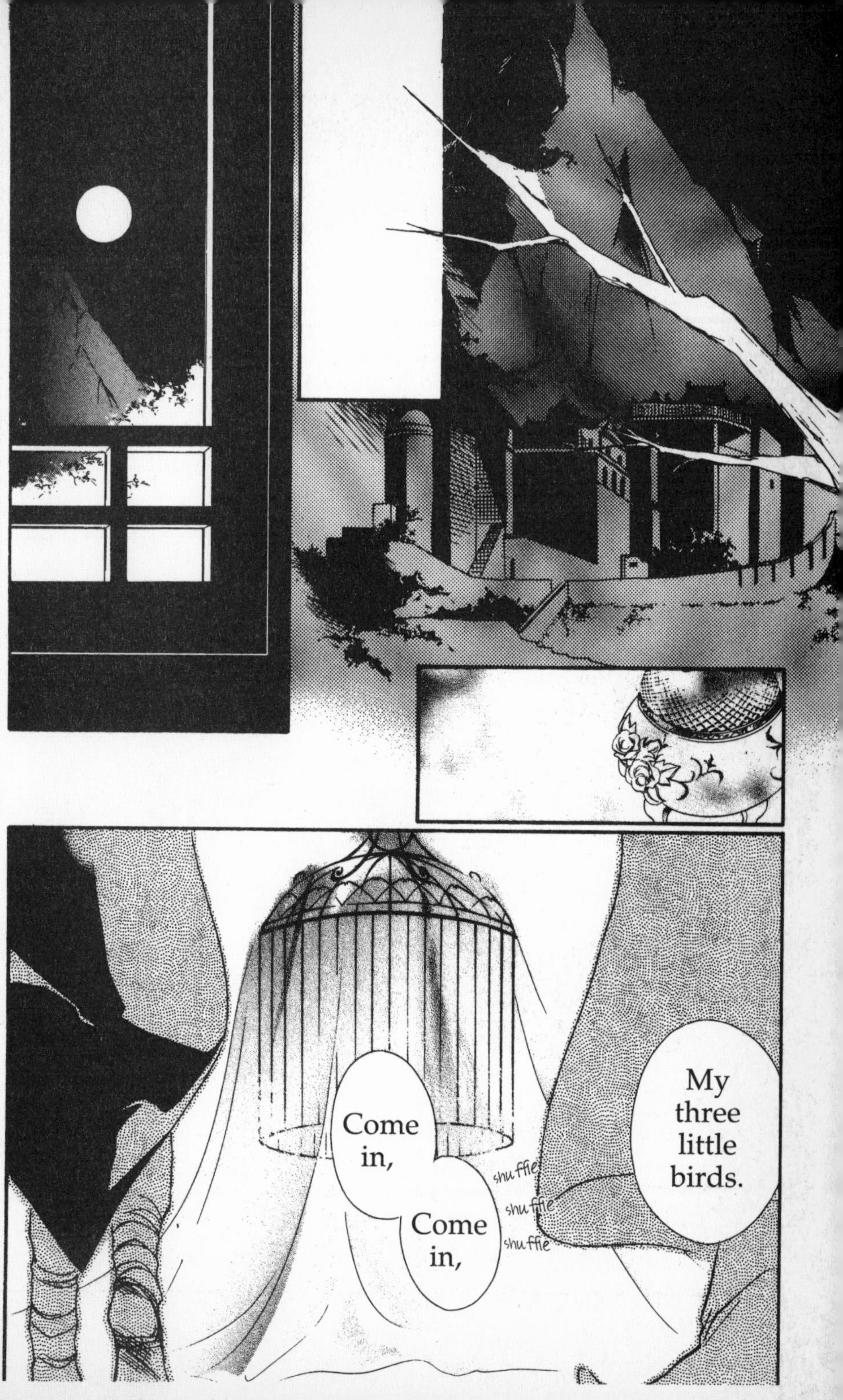
Come in,
Come in,
shuffle
shuffle
shuffle
My three little birds.

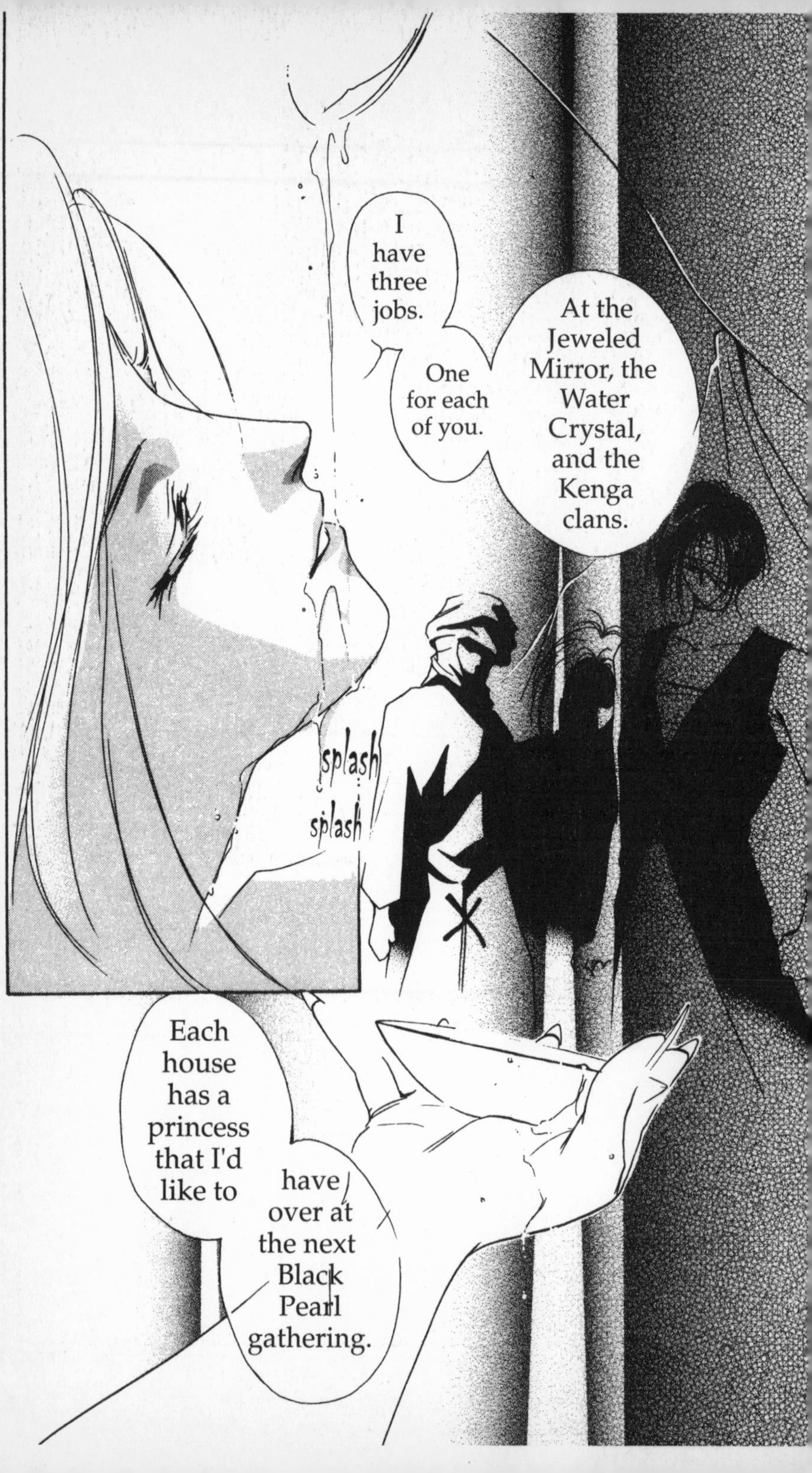
I have three jobs.
One for each of you.
At the Jeweled Mirror, the Water Crystal, and the Kenga clans.
splash
splash
Each house has a princess that I'd like to
have over at the next Black Pearl gathering.

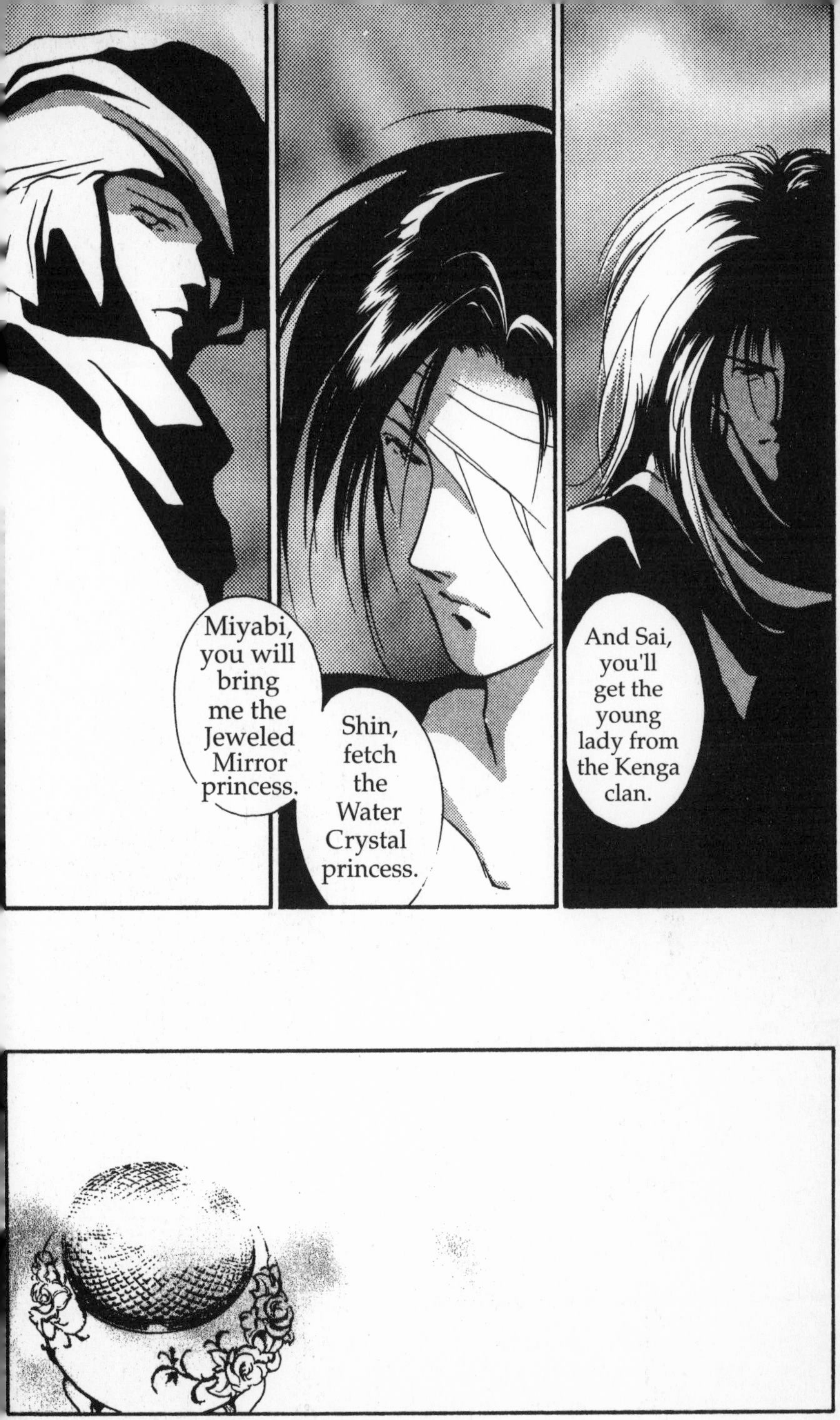
Miyabi, you will bring me the Jeweled Mirror princess.
Shin, fetch the Water Crystal princess.
And Sai, you'll get the young lady from the Kenga clan.

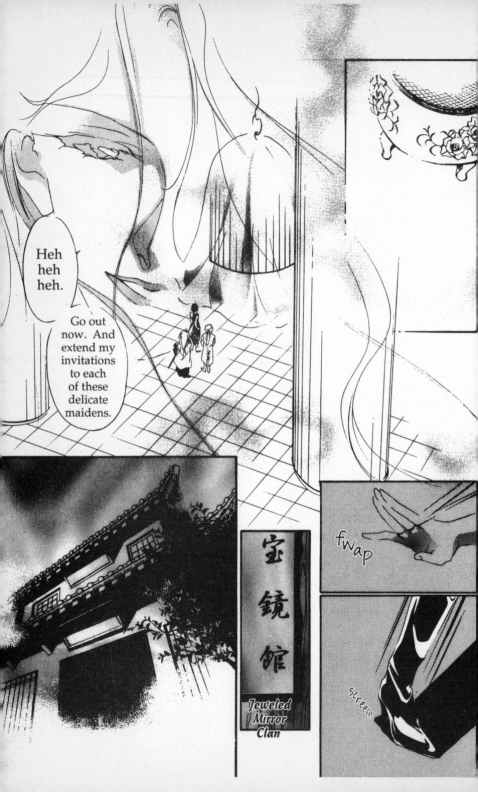

Heh heh heh.

Go out now. And extend my invitations to each of these delicate maidens.

宝鏡館

Jeweled Mirror Clan

fwap

screech

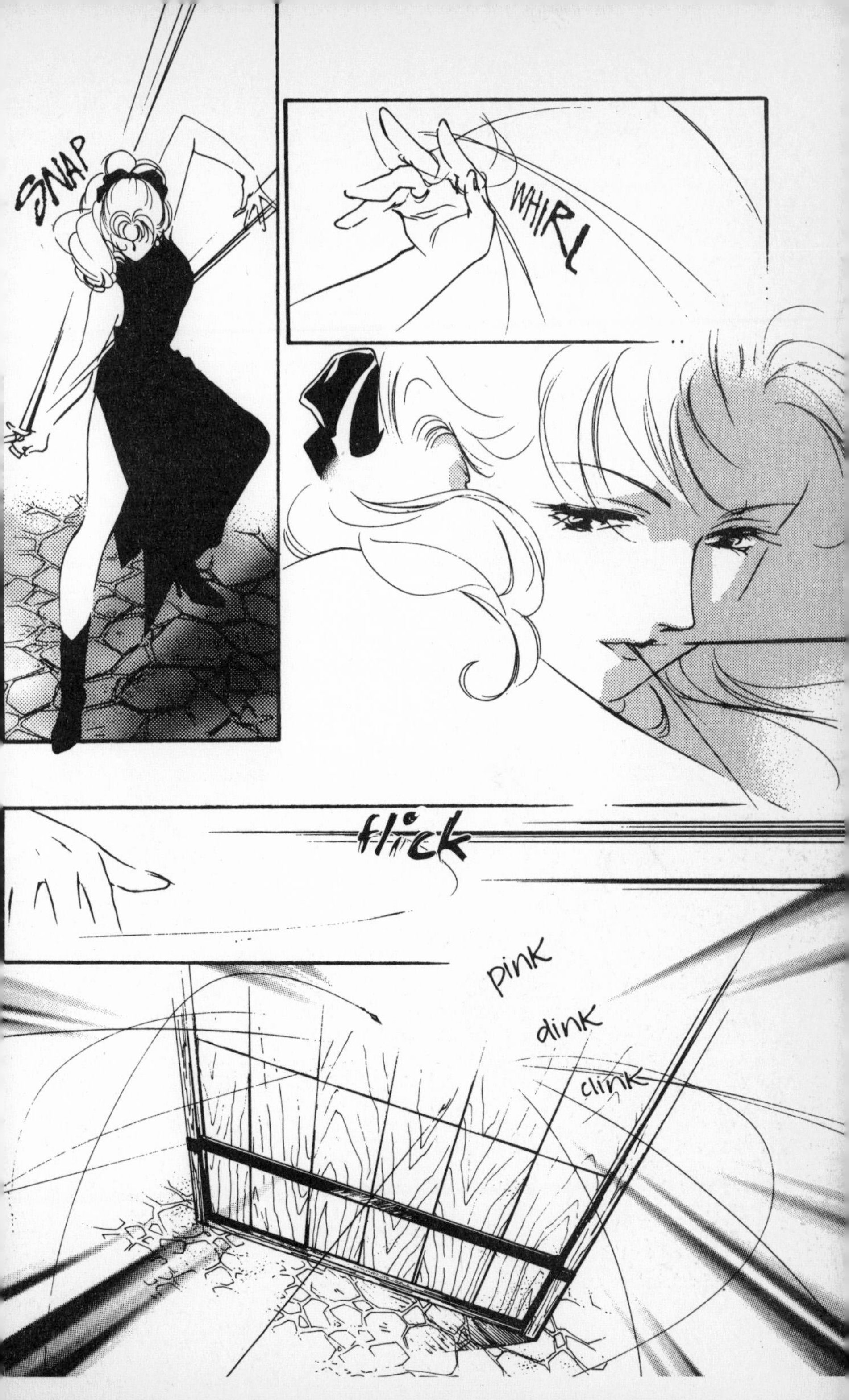
SNAP
WHIRL
flick
pink
dink
clink

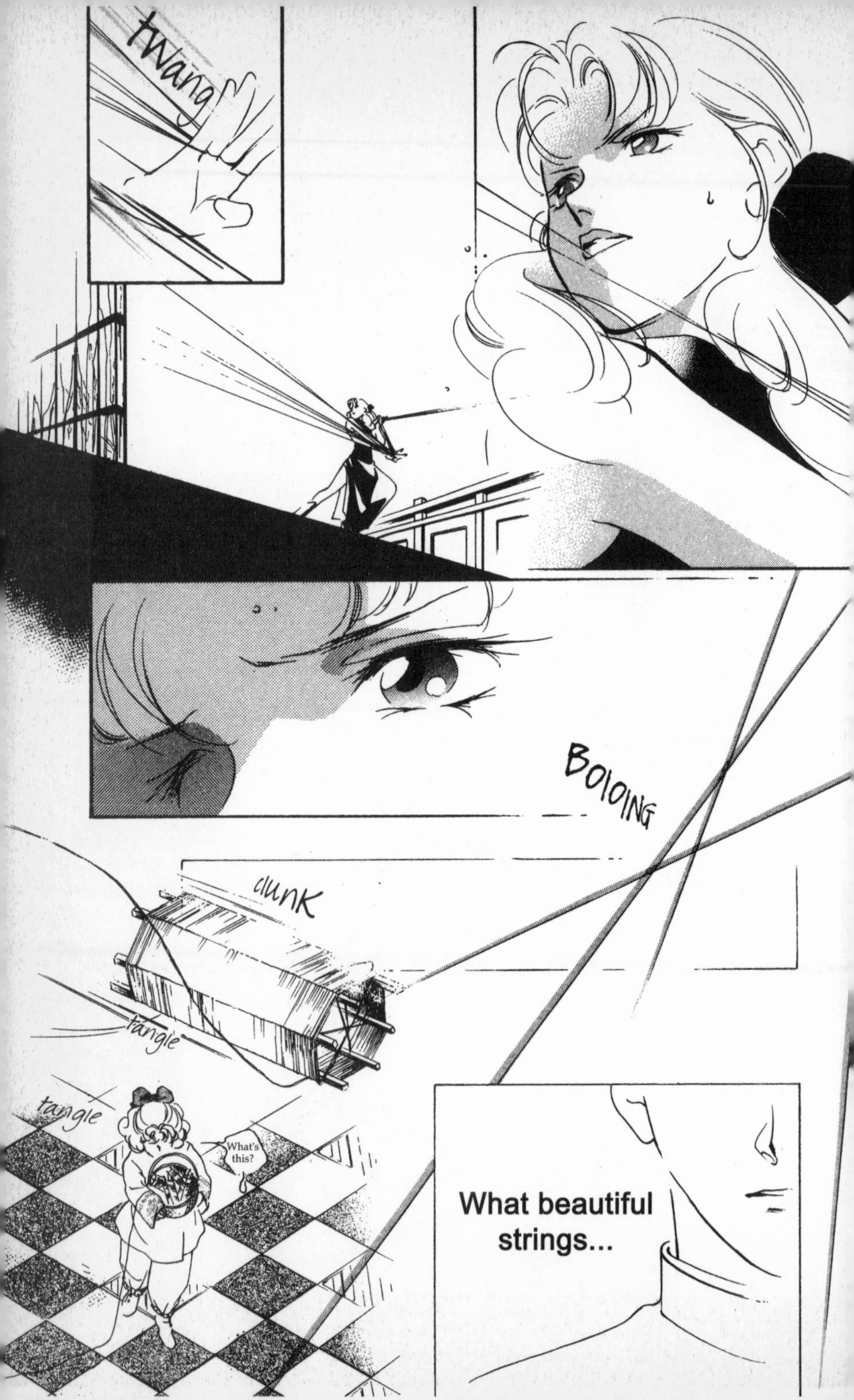
twang
Boioing
clunk
tangle
tangle
What's this?
What beautiful strings...

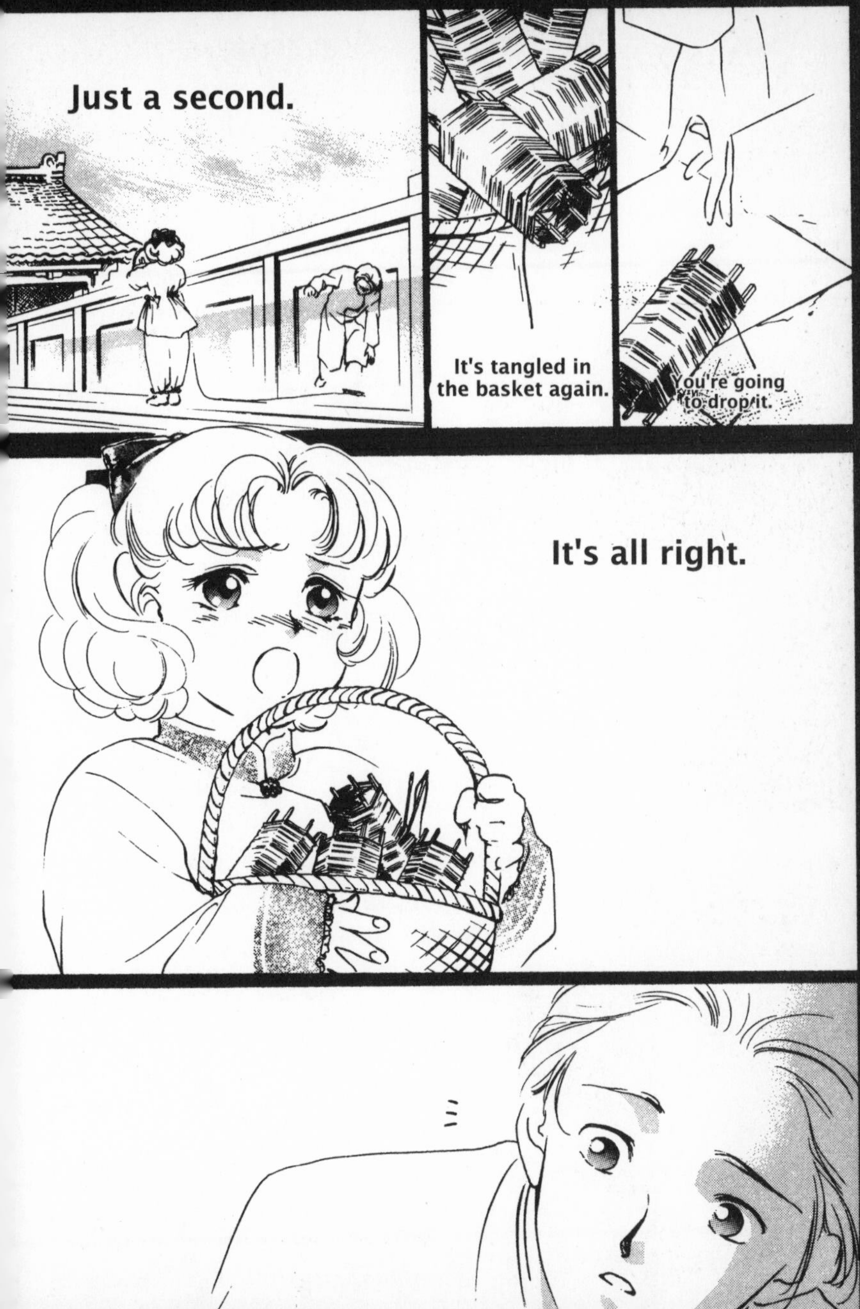
Just a second.
It's tangled in the basket again.
You're going to drop it.
It's all right.

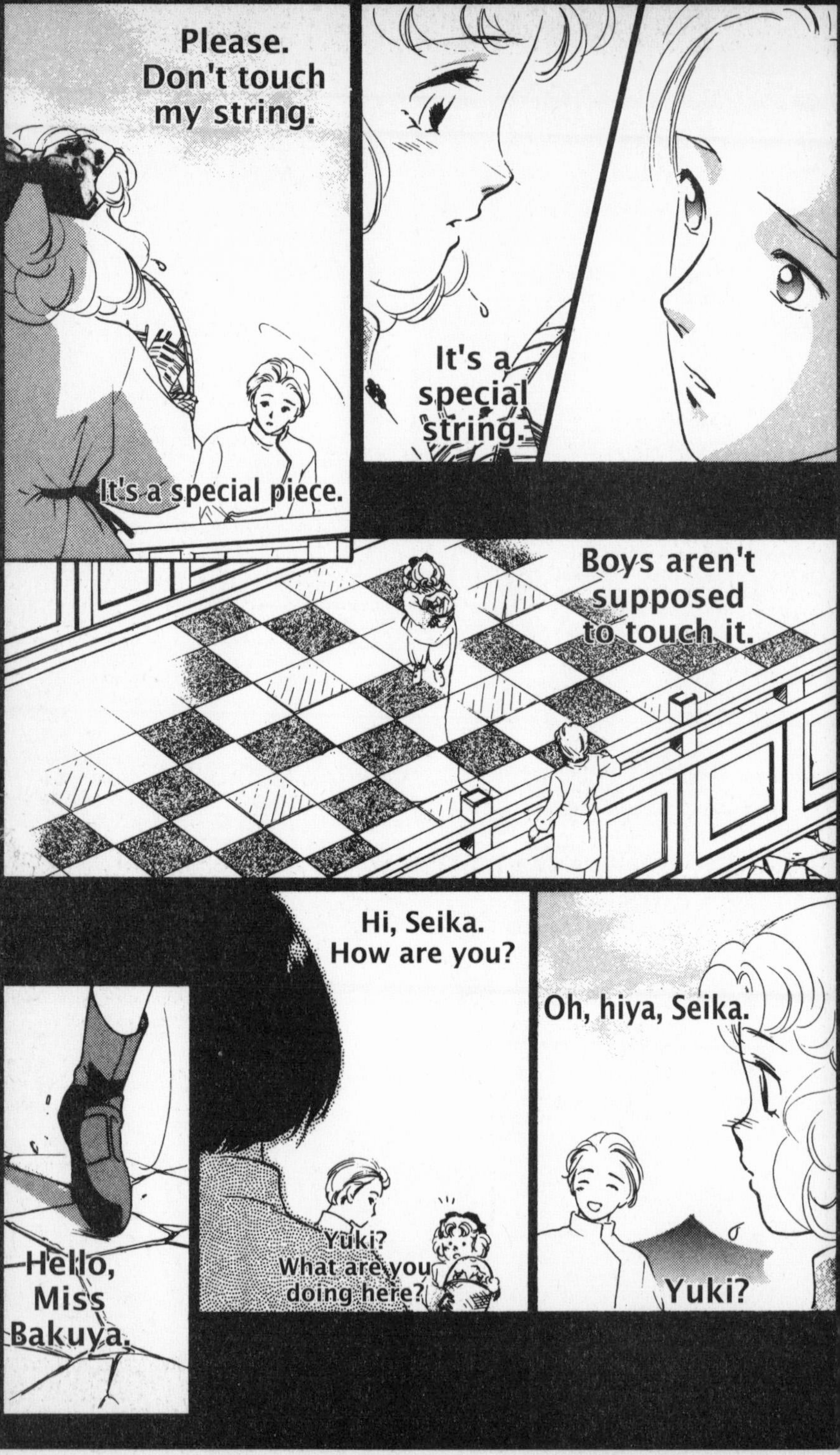

Please. Don't touch my string.
It's a special piece.
It's a special string.
Boys aren't supposed to touch it.
Hello, Miss Bakuya.
Hi, Seika. How are you?
Yuki? What are you doing here?
Oh, hiya, Seika.
Yuki?

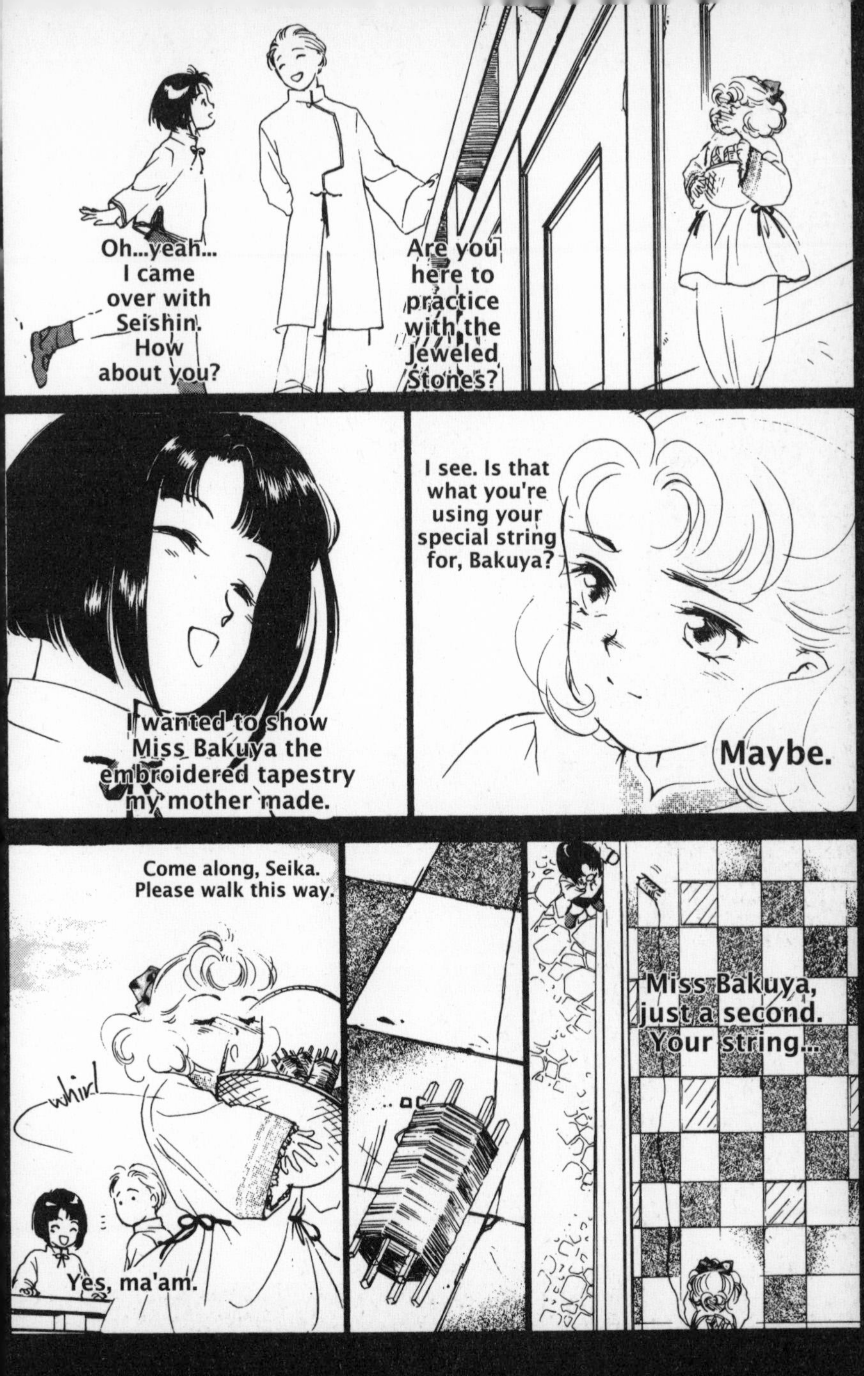
Oh...yeah...
I came over with Seishin. How about you?
Are you here to practice with the Jeweled Stones?
I wanted to show Miss Bakuya the embroidered tapestry my mother made.
I see. Is that what you're using your special string for, Bakuya?
Maybe.
Come along, Seika. Please walk this way.
whirl
Yes, ma'am.
...
Miss Bakuya, just a second. Your string...

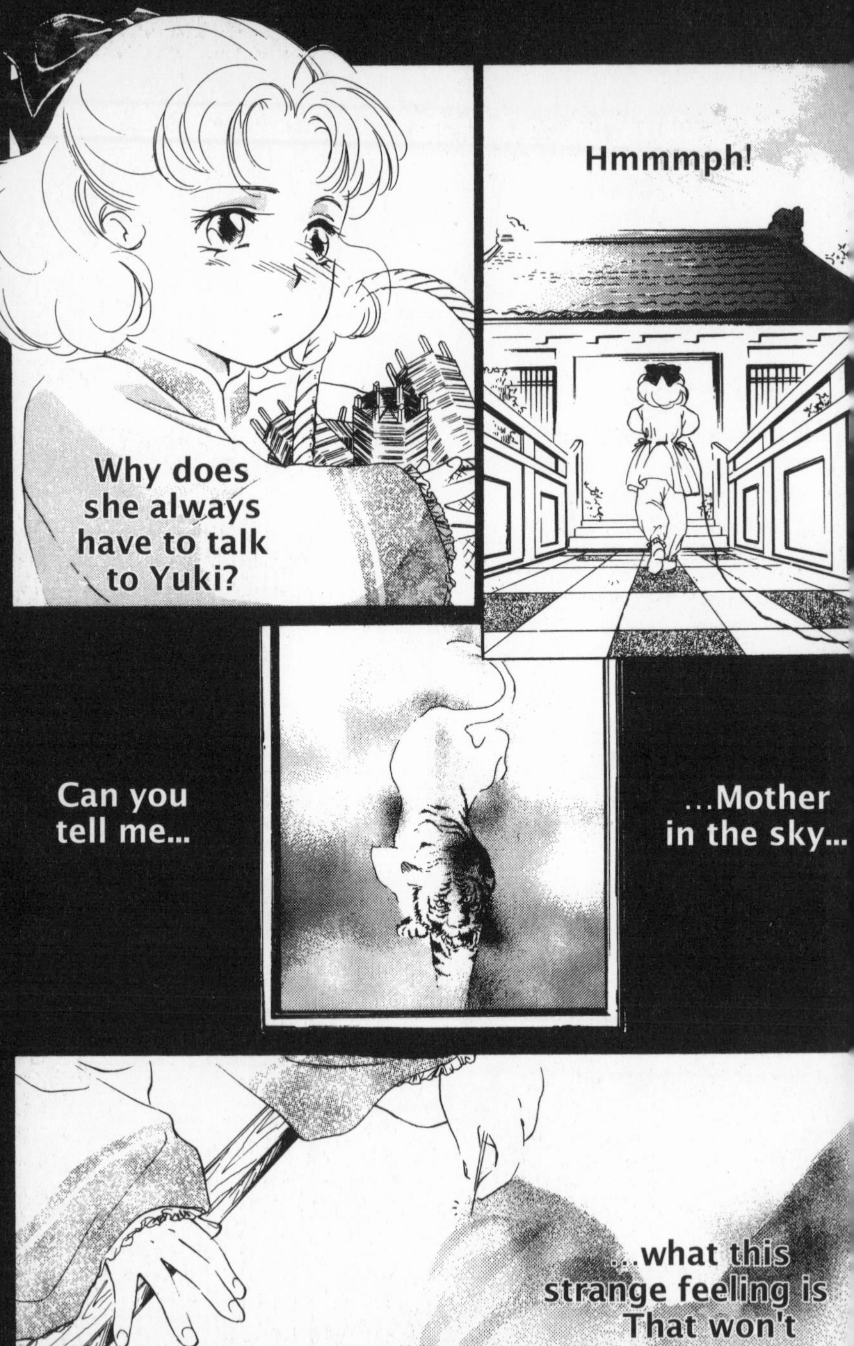
Why does she always have to talk to Yuki?
Hmmmph!
Can you tell me...
...Mother in the sky...
...what this strange feeling is That won't let me relax?

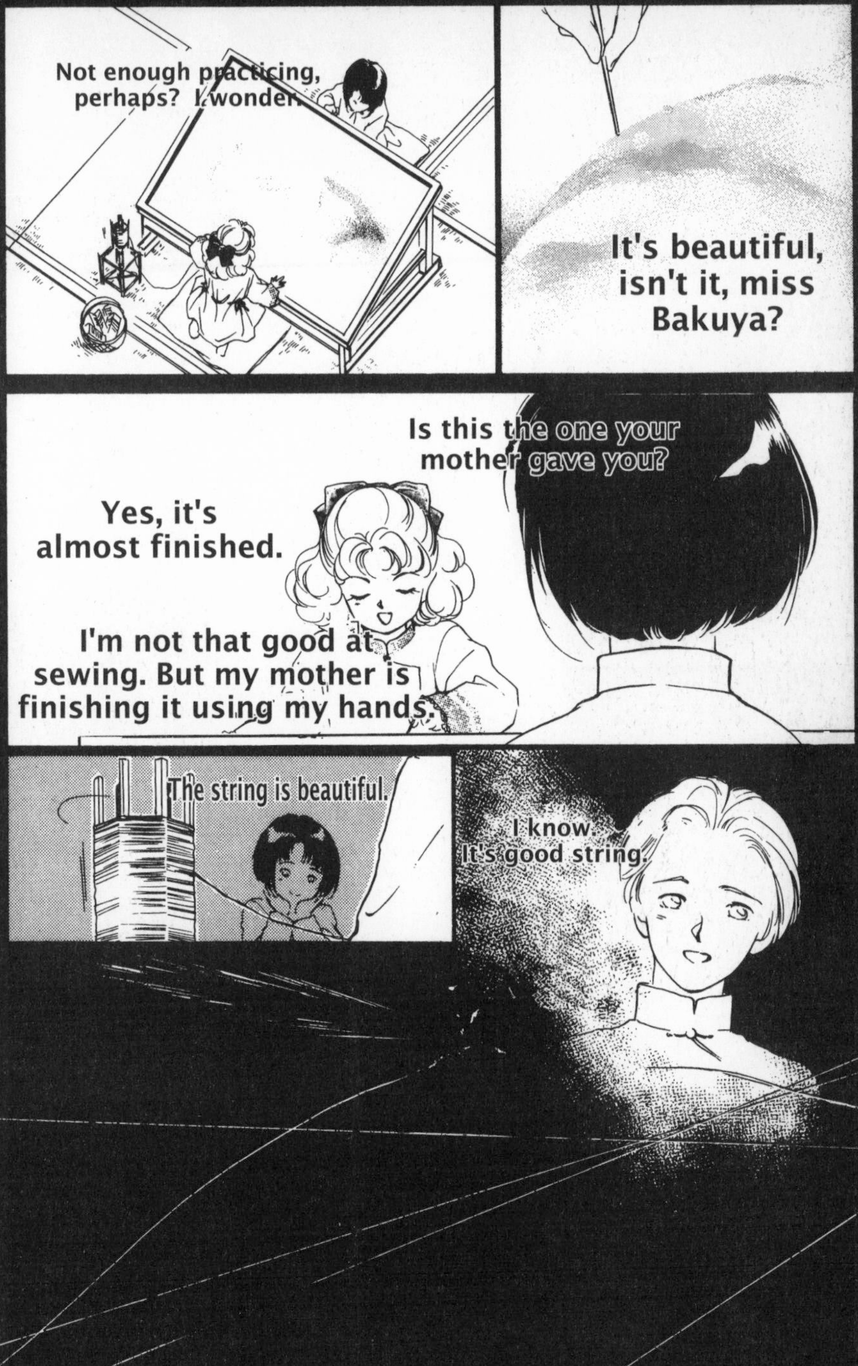
Not enough practicing, perhaps? I wonder.
It's beautiful, isn't it, miss Bakuya?
Is this the one your mother gave you?
Yes, it's almost finished.
I'm not that good at sewing. But my mother is finishing it using my hands.
The string is beautiful.
I know. It's good string.

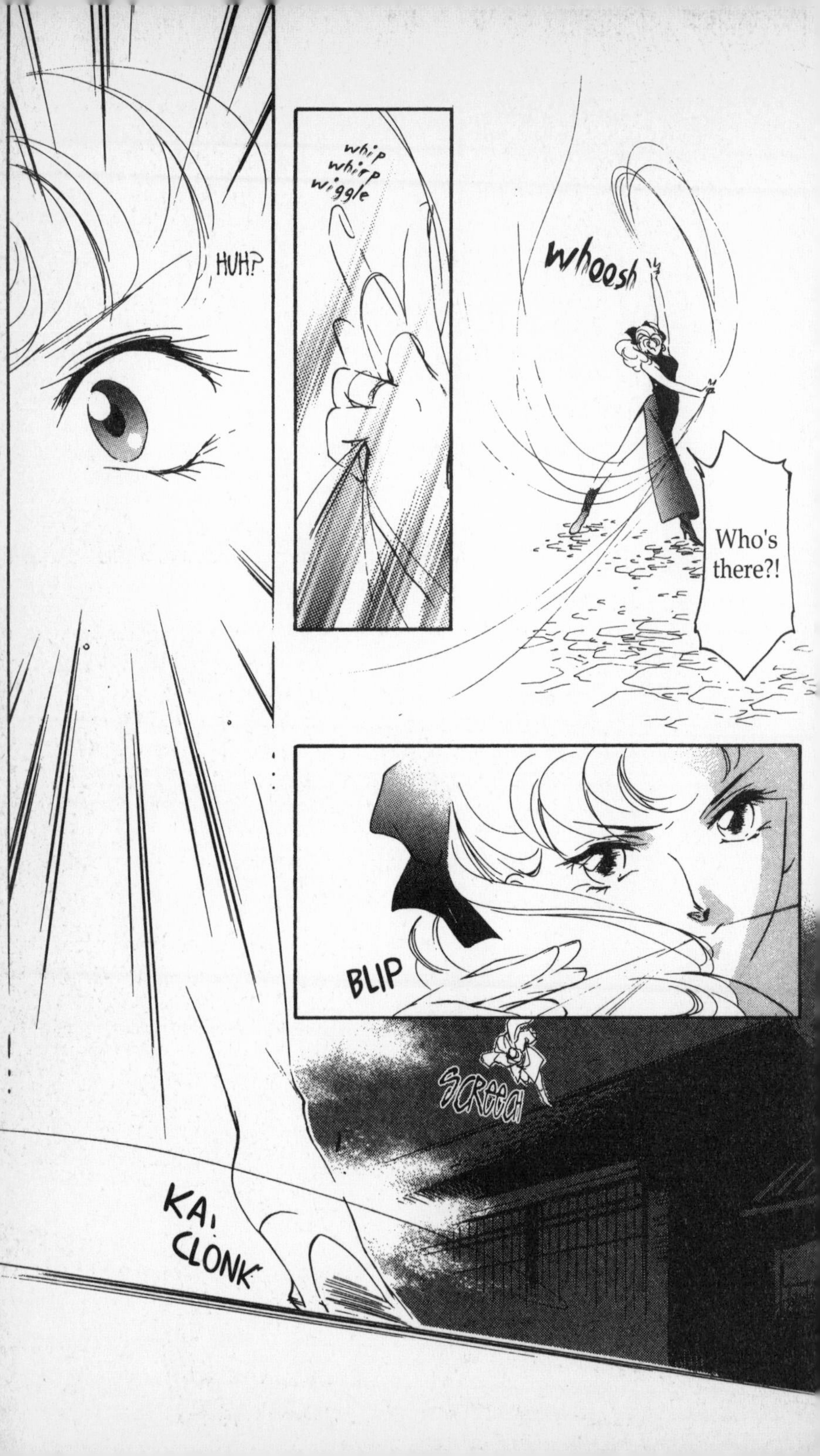
HUH?
whip
whirp
wiggle
whoosh
Who's there?!
BLIP
SCREECH
KA-
CLONK

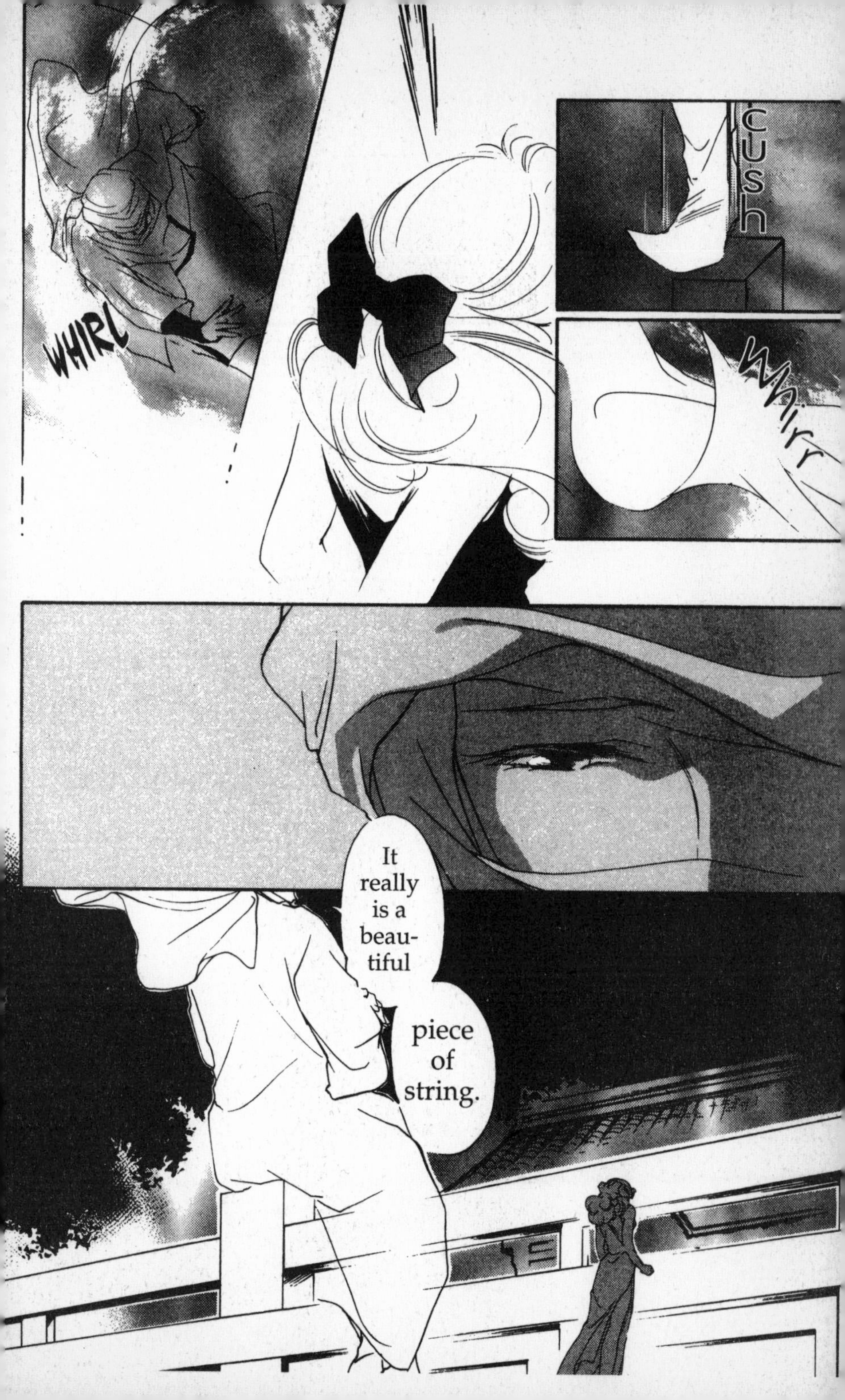
WHIRL
CUSH
Whirr
It really is a beau-tiful
piece of string.

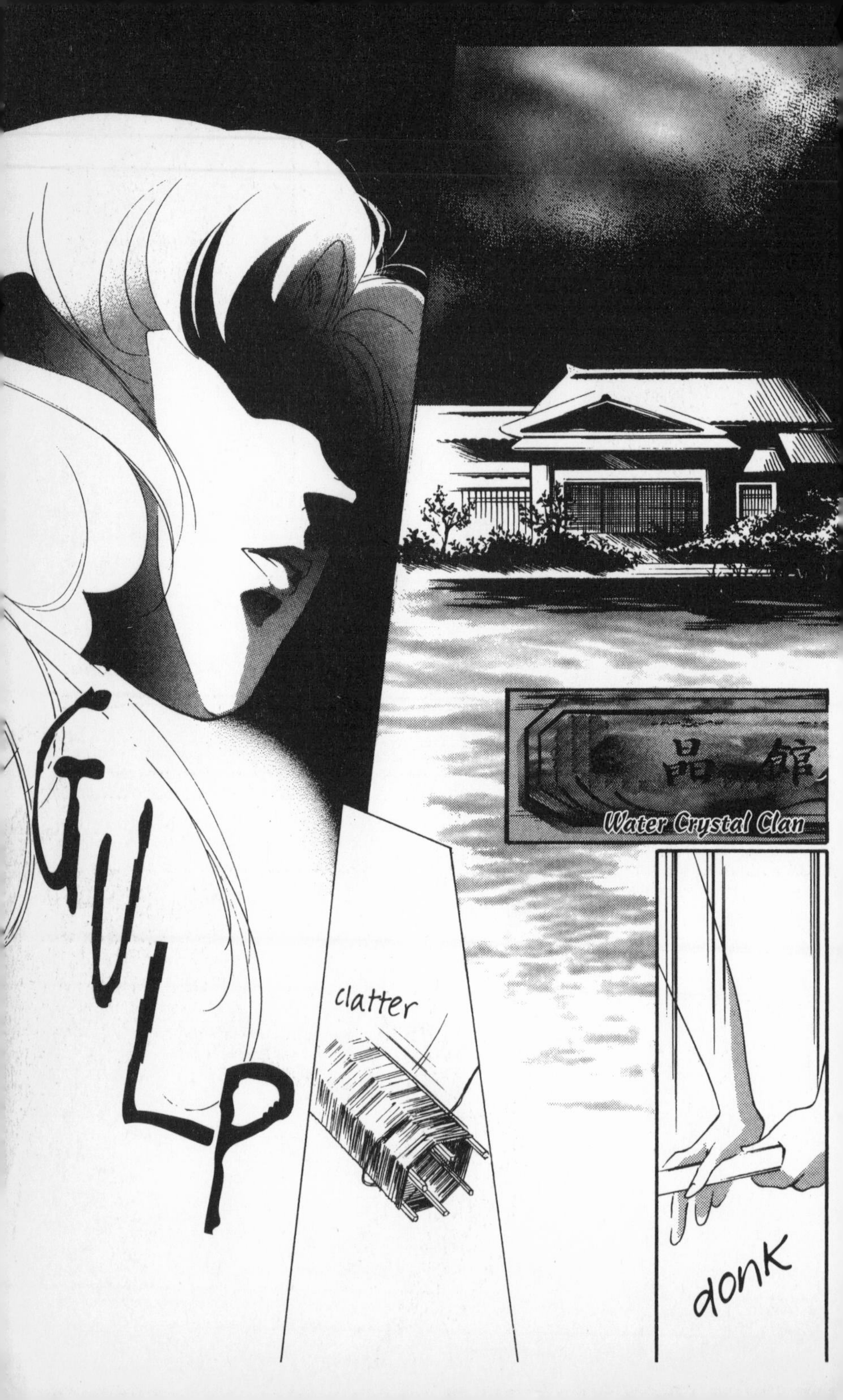
GULP
Water Crystal Clan
clatter
donk

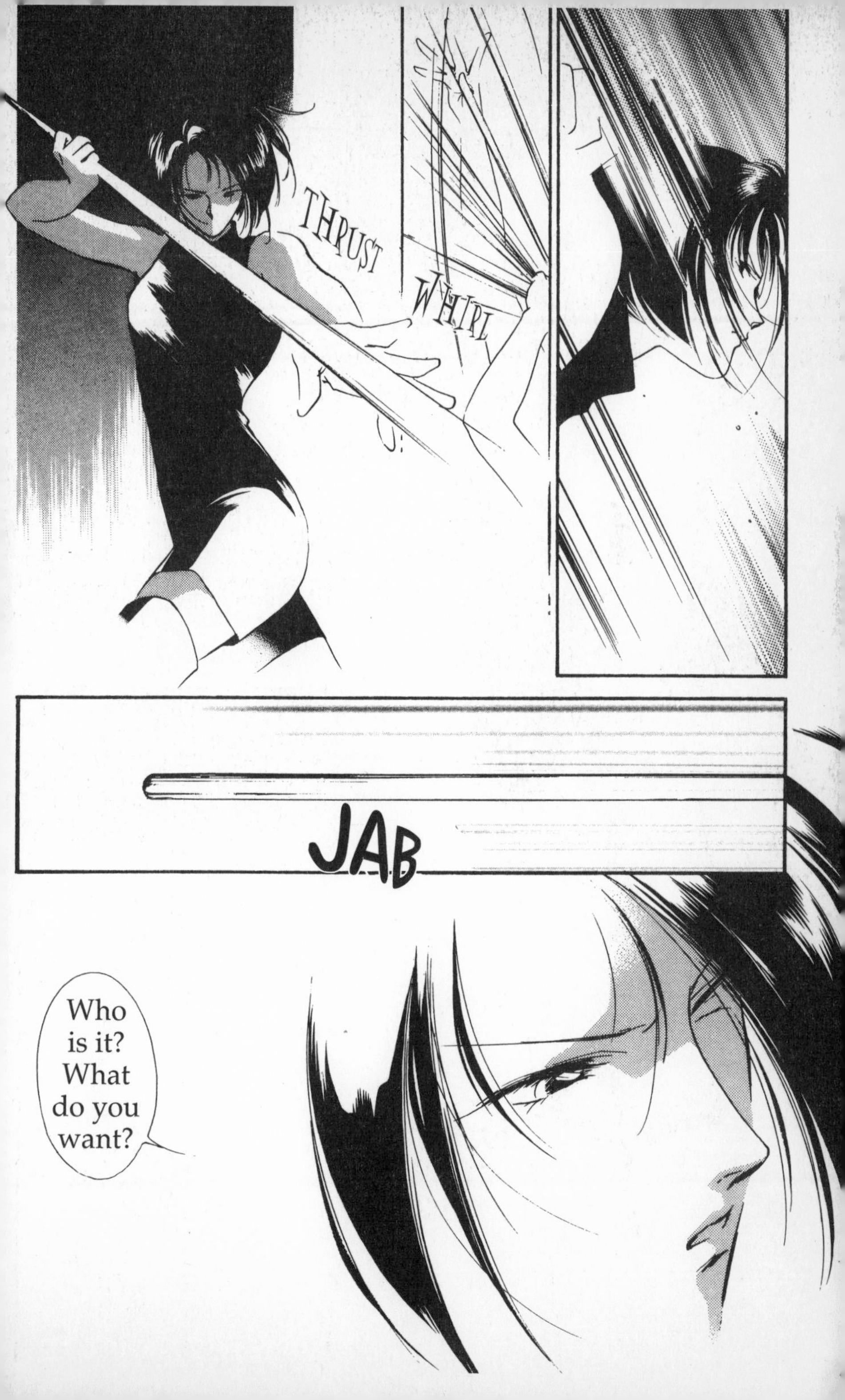
THRUST
WHIRL
JAB
Who is it? What do you want?

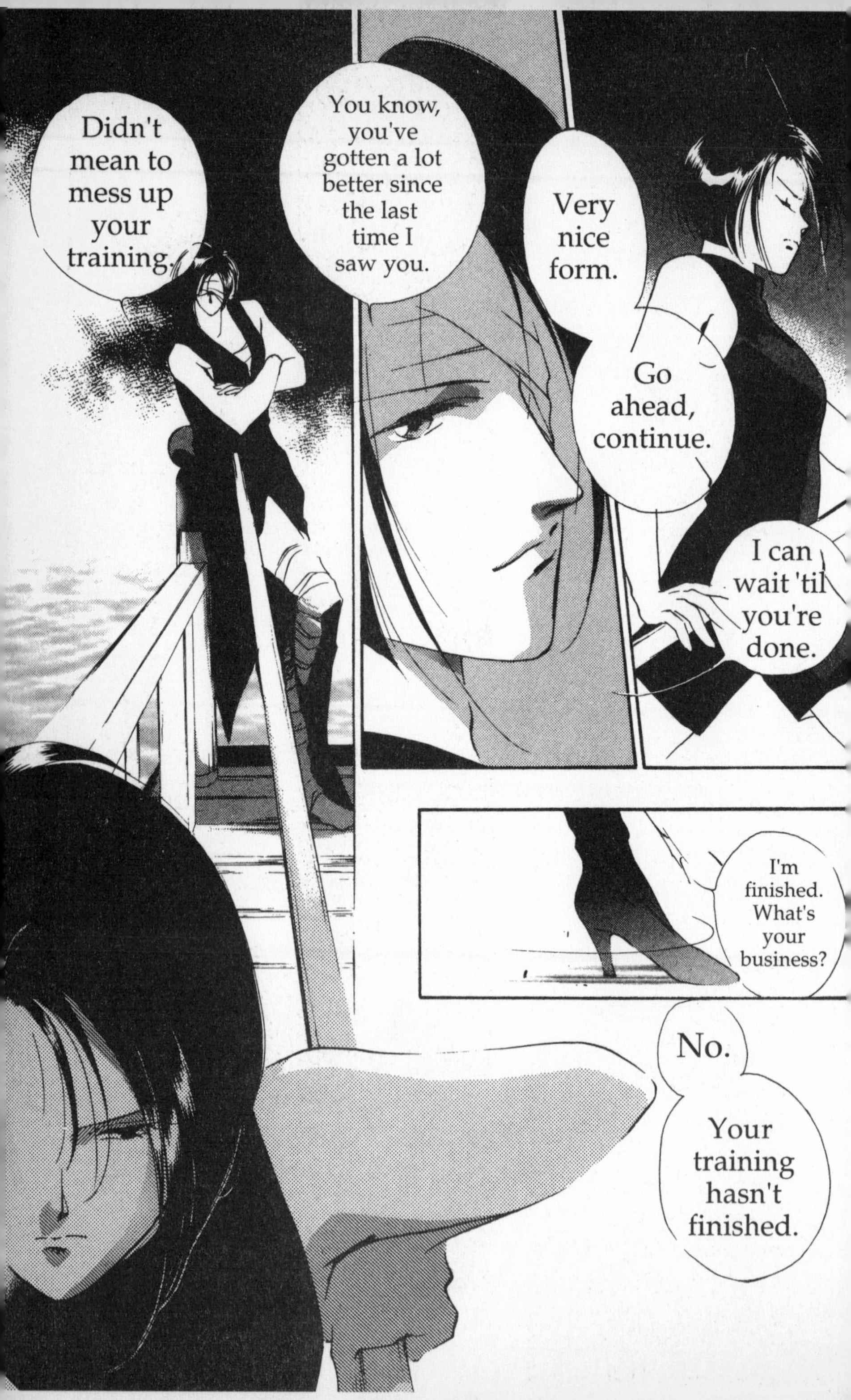
Didn't mean to mess up your training.
You know, you've gotten a lot better since the last time I saw you.
Very nice form.
Go ahead, continue.
I can wait 'til you're done.
I'm finished. What's your business?
No.
Your training hasn't finished.

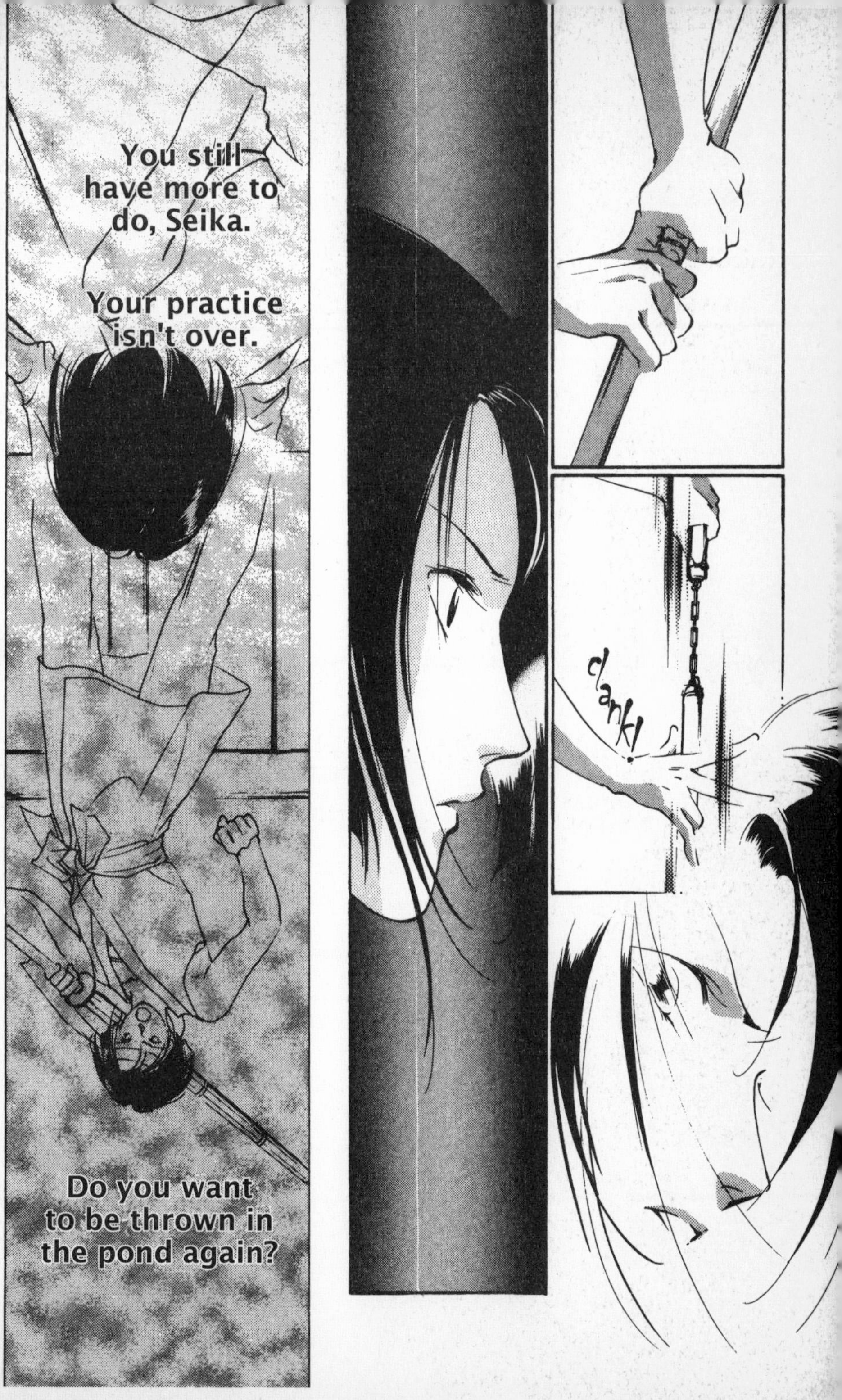
You still have more to do, Seika.
Your practice isn't over.
Do you want to be thrown in the pond again?
clank!

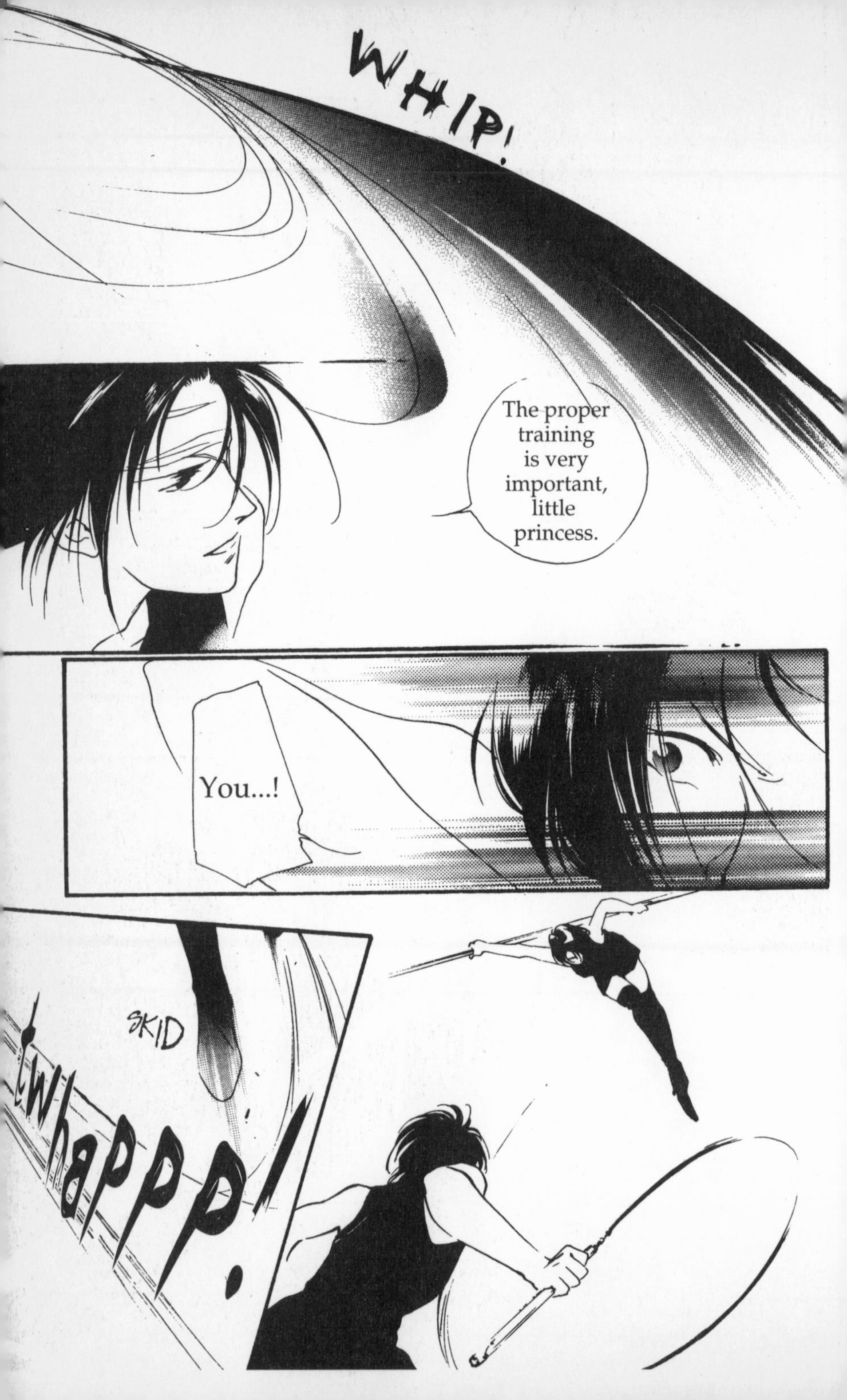
WHIP!
The proper training is very important, little princess.
You...!
SKID
twhappp!

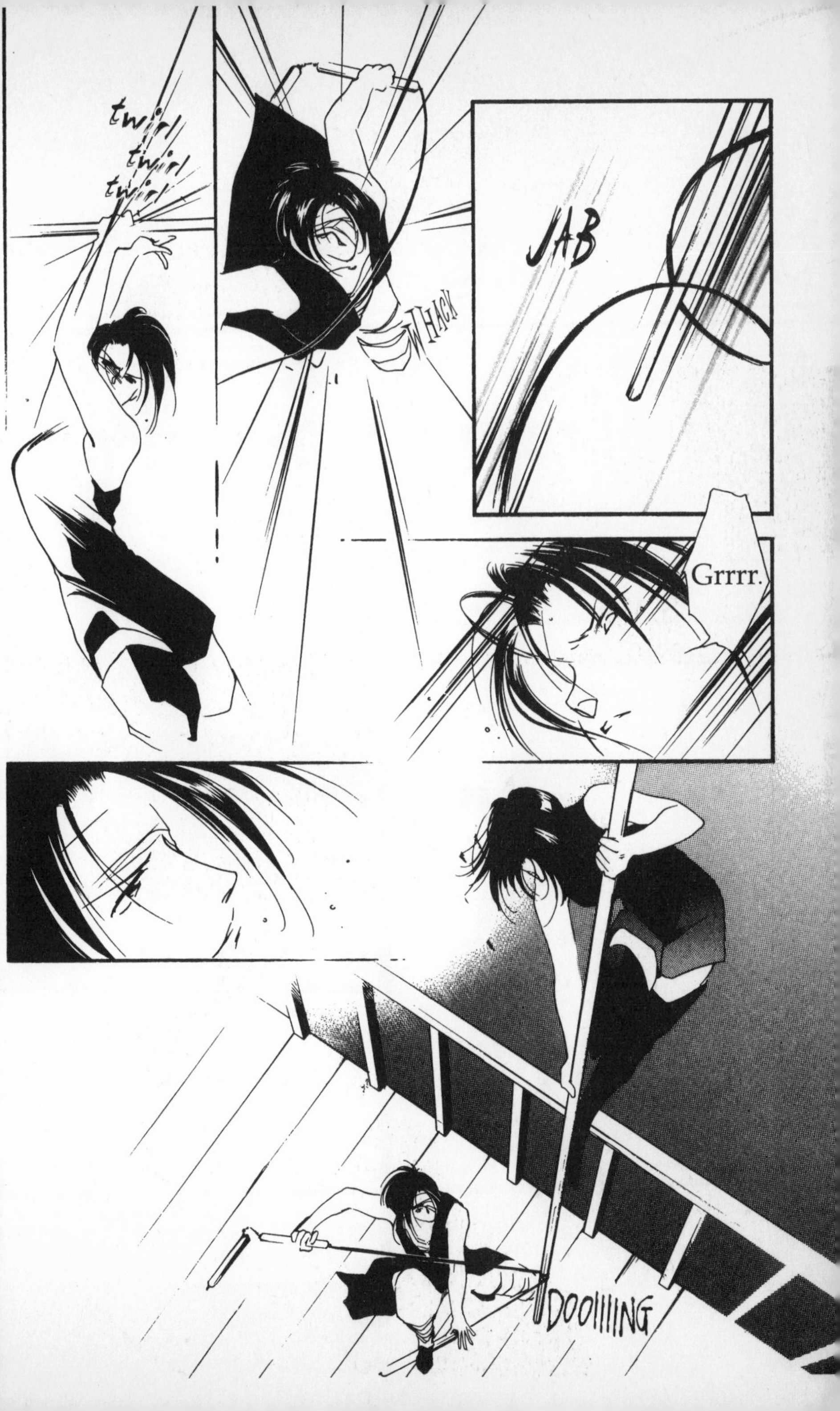
twirl
twirl
twirl
WHACK
JAB
Grrrr.
DOOIIIING

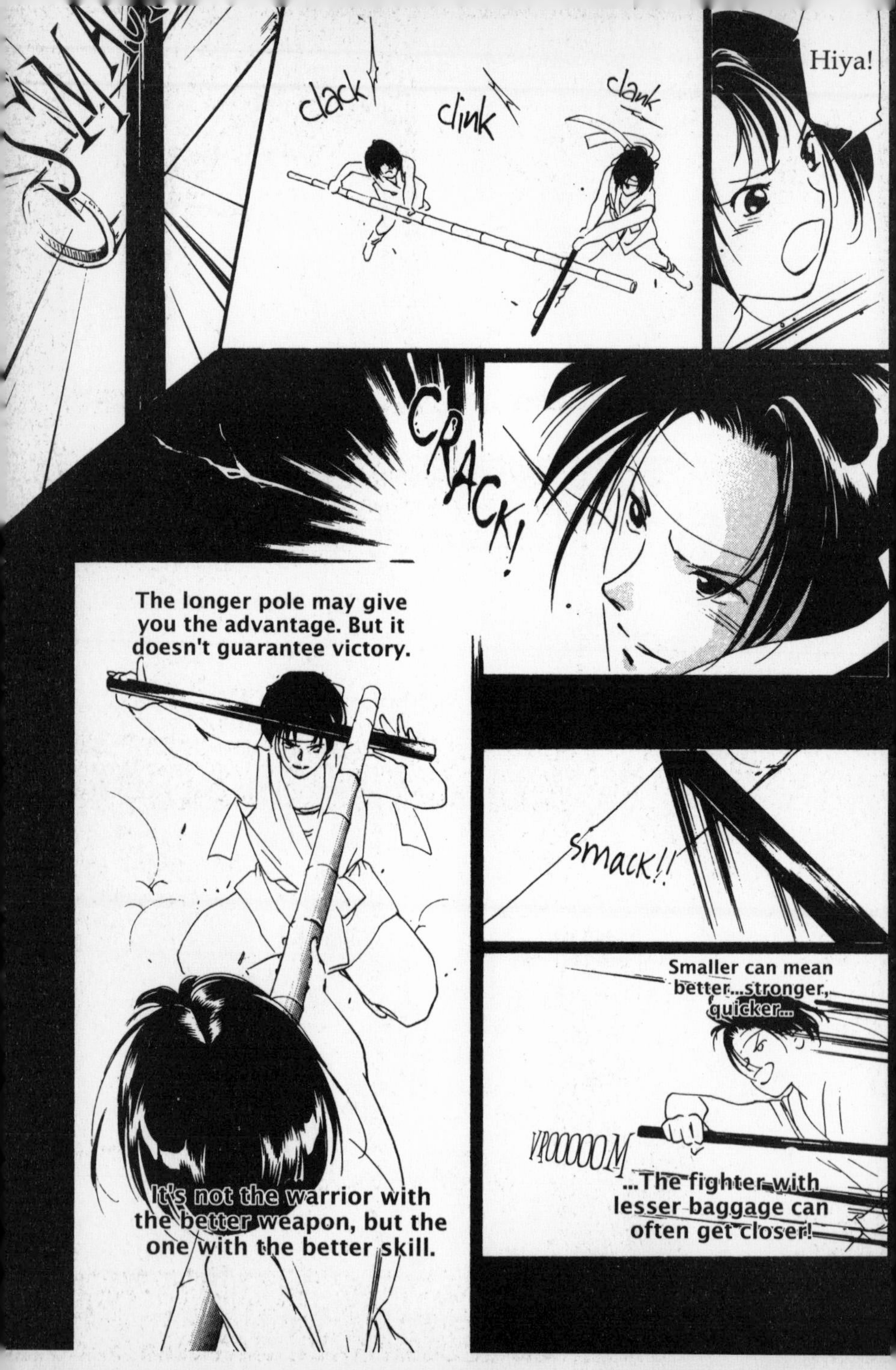
SMACK
clack
clink
clank
Hiya!
CRACK!
The longer pole may give you the advantage. But it doesn't guarantee victory.
It's not the warrior with the better weapon, but the one with the better skill.
SMACK!!
Smaller can mean better...stronger, quicker...
VROOOOOM
...The fighter with lesser baggage can often get closer!

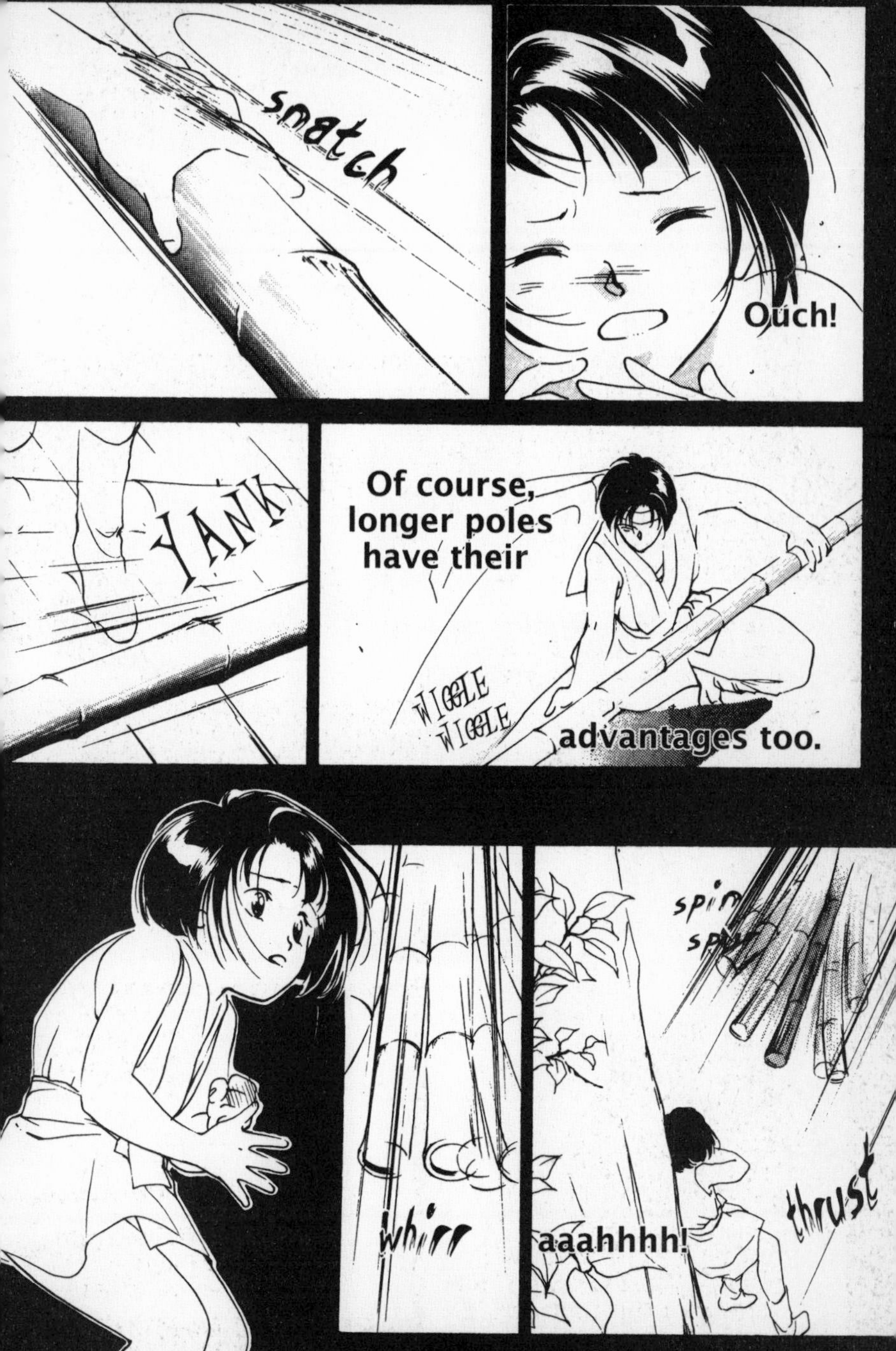
snatch
Ouch!
YANK
Of course, longer poles have their
WIGGLE WIGGLE
advantages too.
whirr
aaahhhh!
spin
thrust

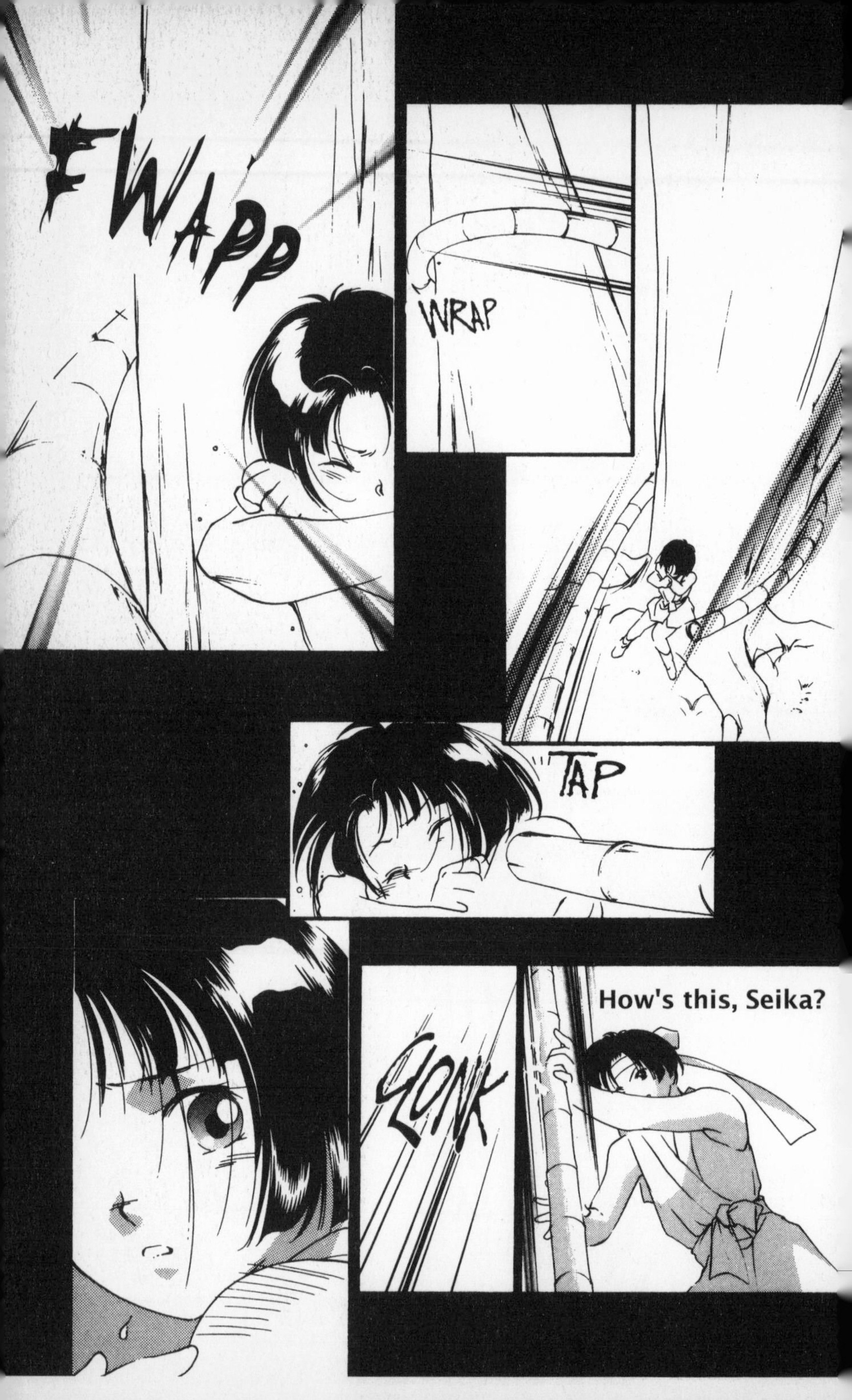
FWAPP
WRAP
TAP
CLONK
How's this, Seika?

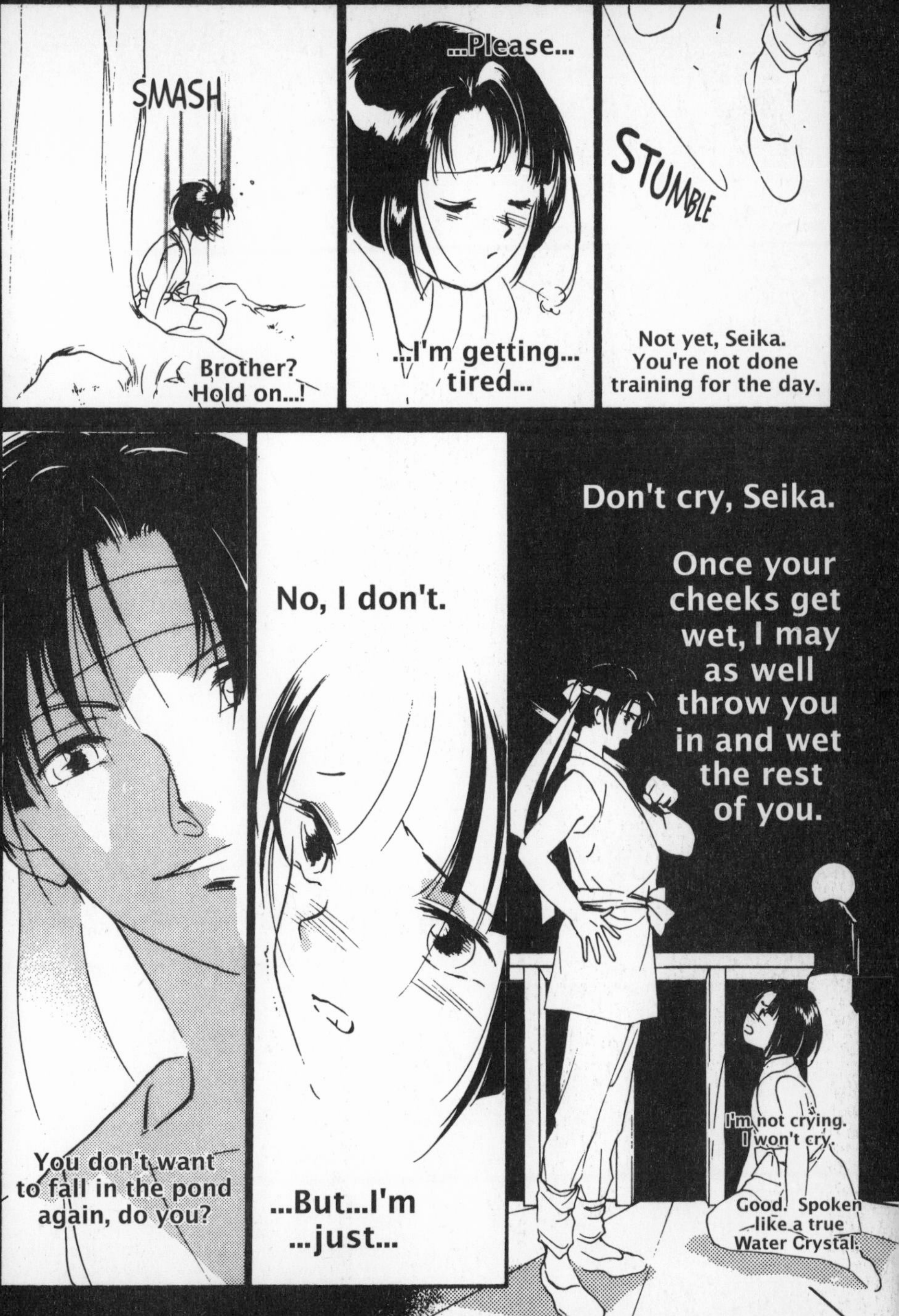
SMASH
Brother? Hold on...!
...Please...
...I'm getting... tired...
STUMBLE
Not yet, Seika. You're not done training for the day.
You don't want to fall in the pond again, do you?
No, I don't.
...But...I'm ...just...
Don't cry, Seika.
Once your cheeks get wet, I may as well throw you in and wet the rest of you.
I'm not crying. I won't cry.
Good. Spoken like a true Water Crystal.

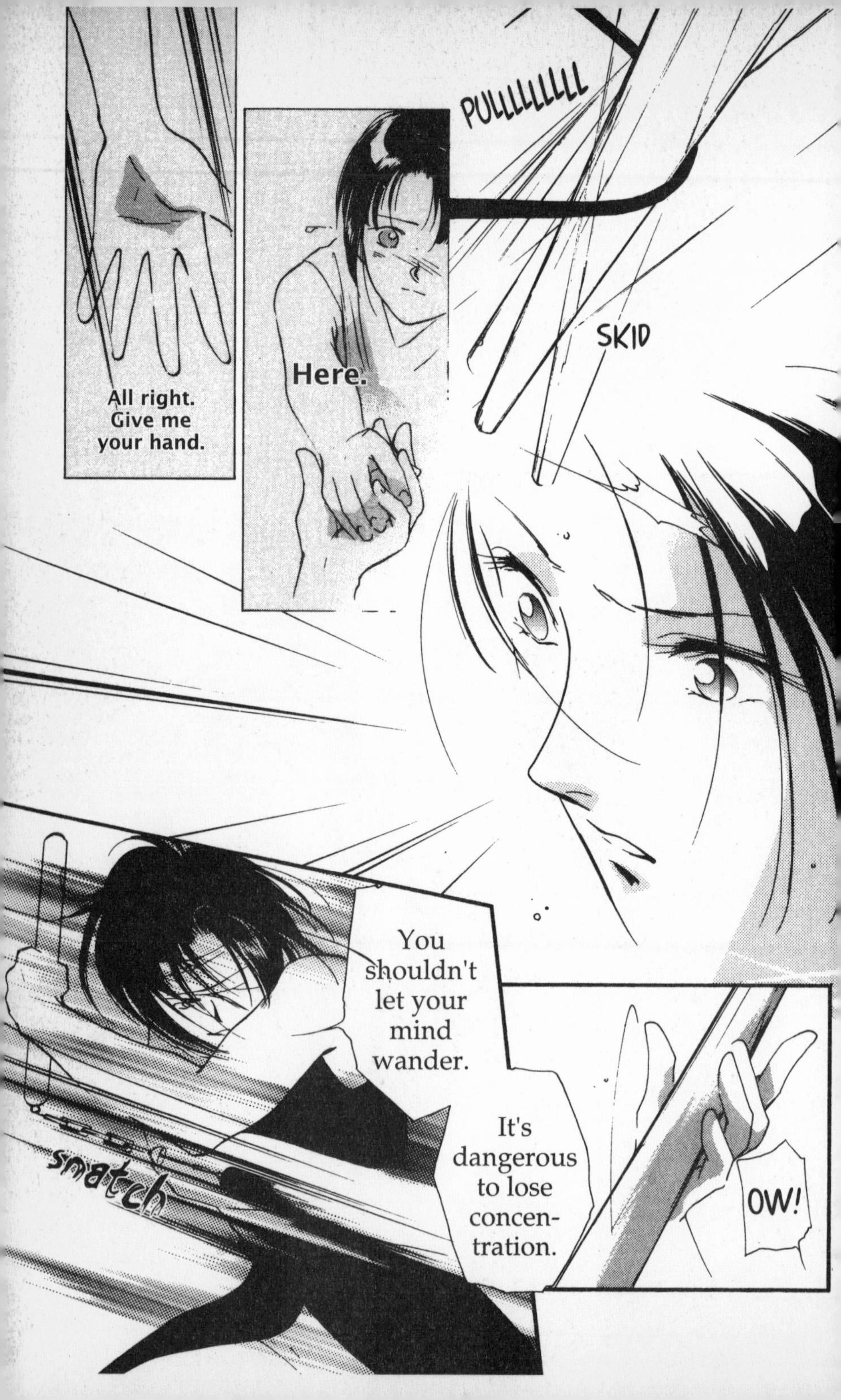
All right. Give me your hand.
Here.
PULLLLLLLLL
SKID
snatch
You shouldn't let your mind wander.
It's dangerous to lose concentration.
OW!

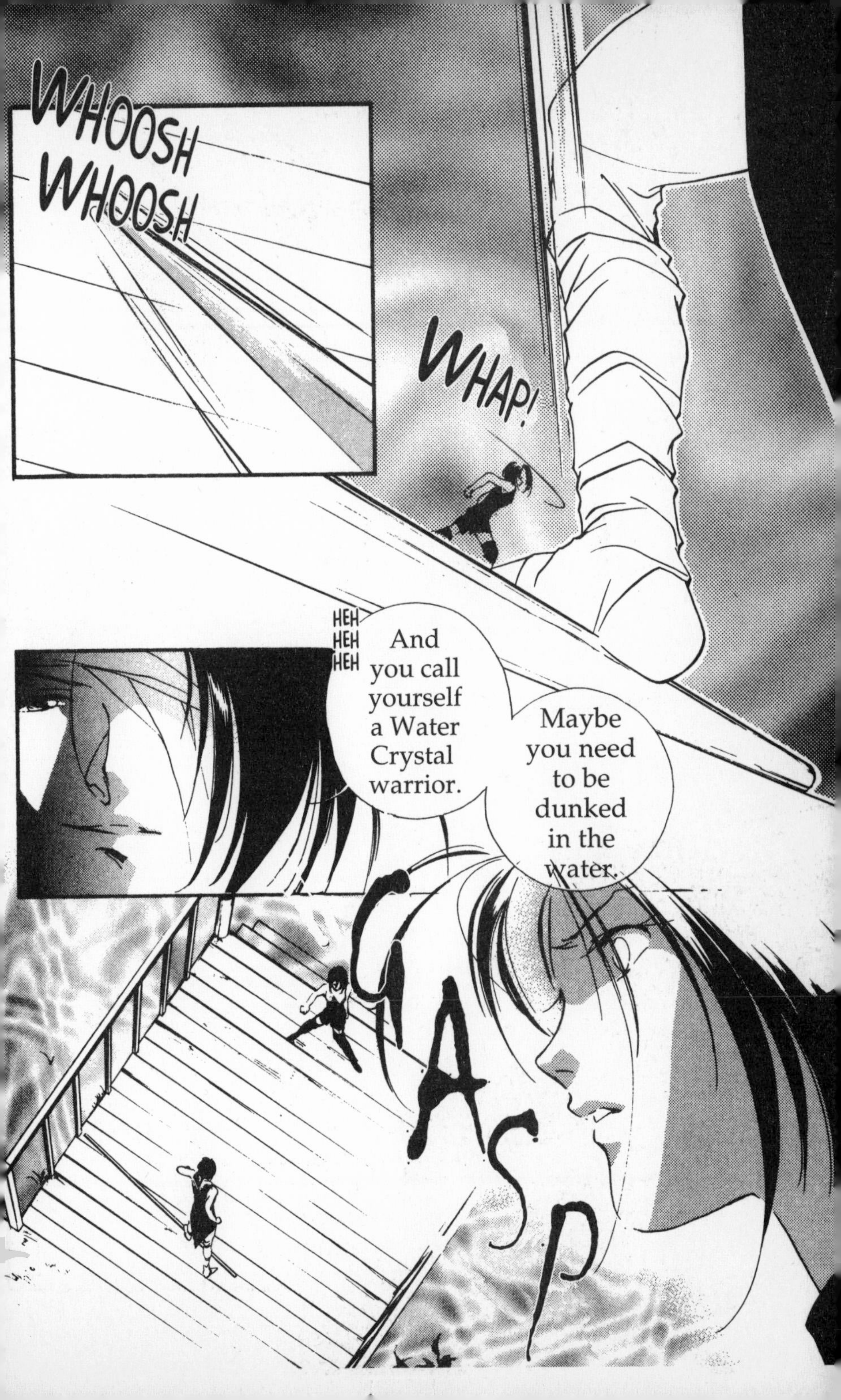

WHOOSH
WHOOSH
WHAP!
HEH HEH HEH
And you call yourself a Water Crystal warrior.
Maybe you need to be dunked in the water.
GASP

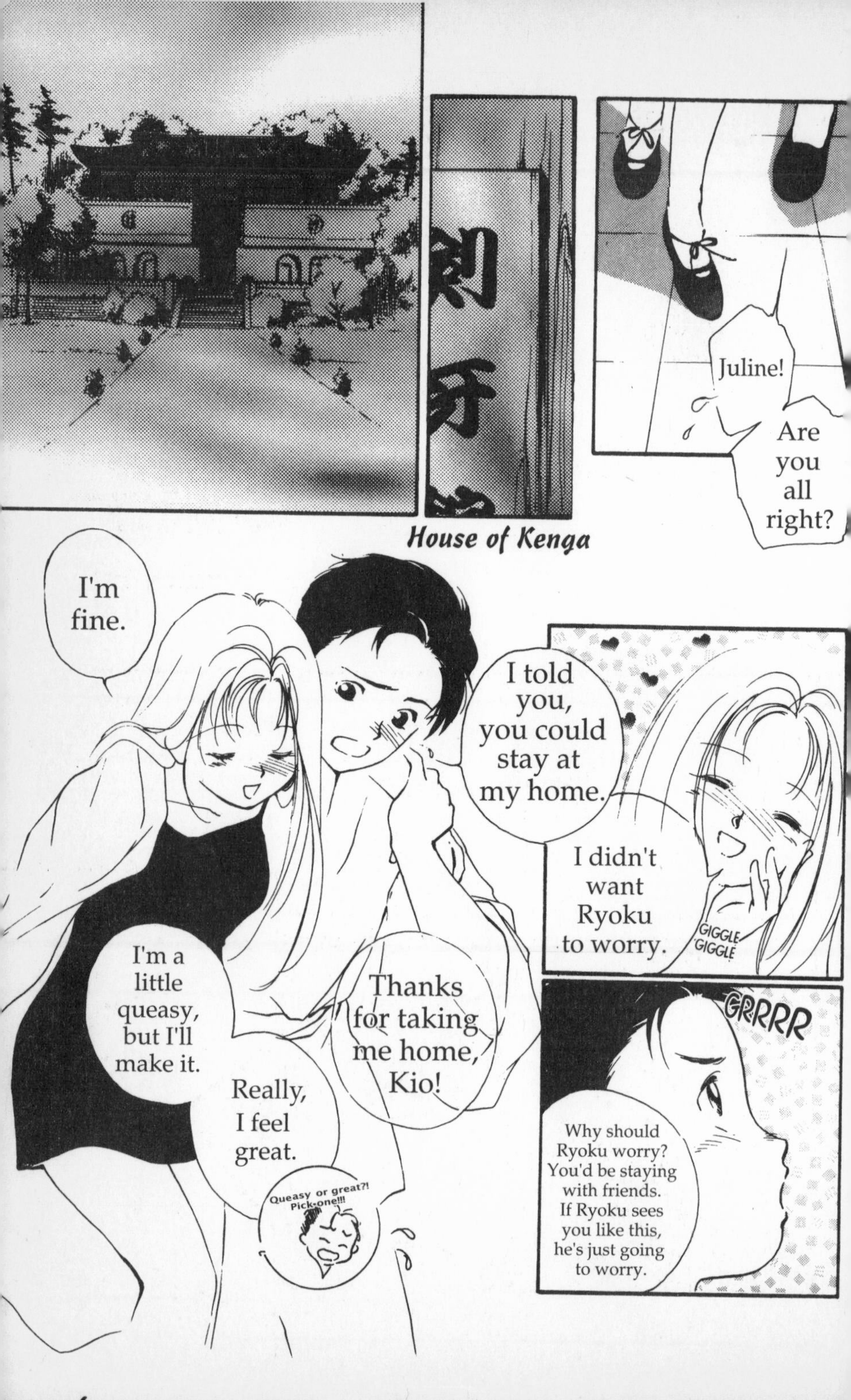
Juline!
Are you all right?
House of Kenga
I'm fine.
I'm a little queasy, but I'll make it.
Thanks for taking me home, Kio!
Really, I feel great.
Queasy or great?! Pick one!!!
I told you, you could stay at my home.
I didn't want Ryoku to worry.
GIGGLE GIGGLE
GRRRR
Why should Ryoku worry? You'd be staying with friends. If Ryoku sees you like this, he's just going to worry.

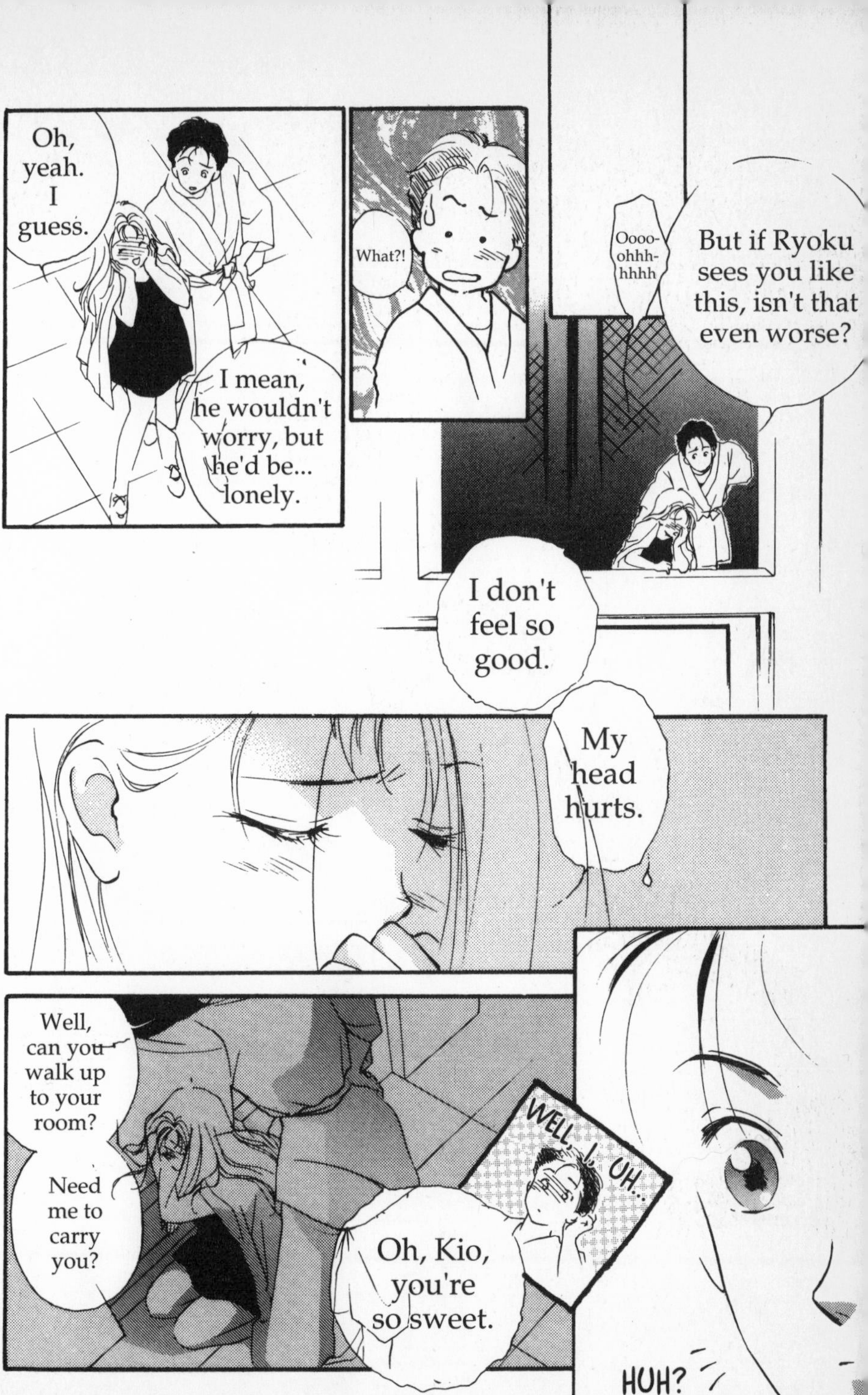
Oh, yeah. I guess.
I mean, he wouldn't worry, but he'd be... lonely.
What?!
Oooo-ohhh-hhhh
But if Ryoku sees you like this, isn't that even worse?
I don't feel so good.
My head hurts.
Well, can you walk up to your room?
Need me to carry you?
Oh, Kio, you're so sweet.
WELL, I, UH...
HUH?

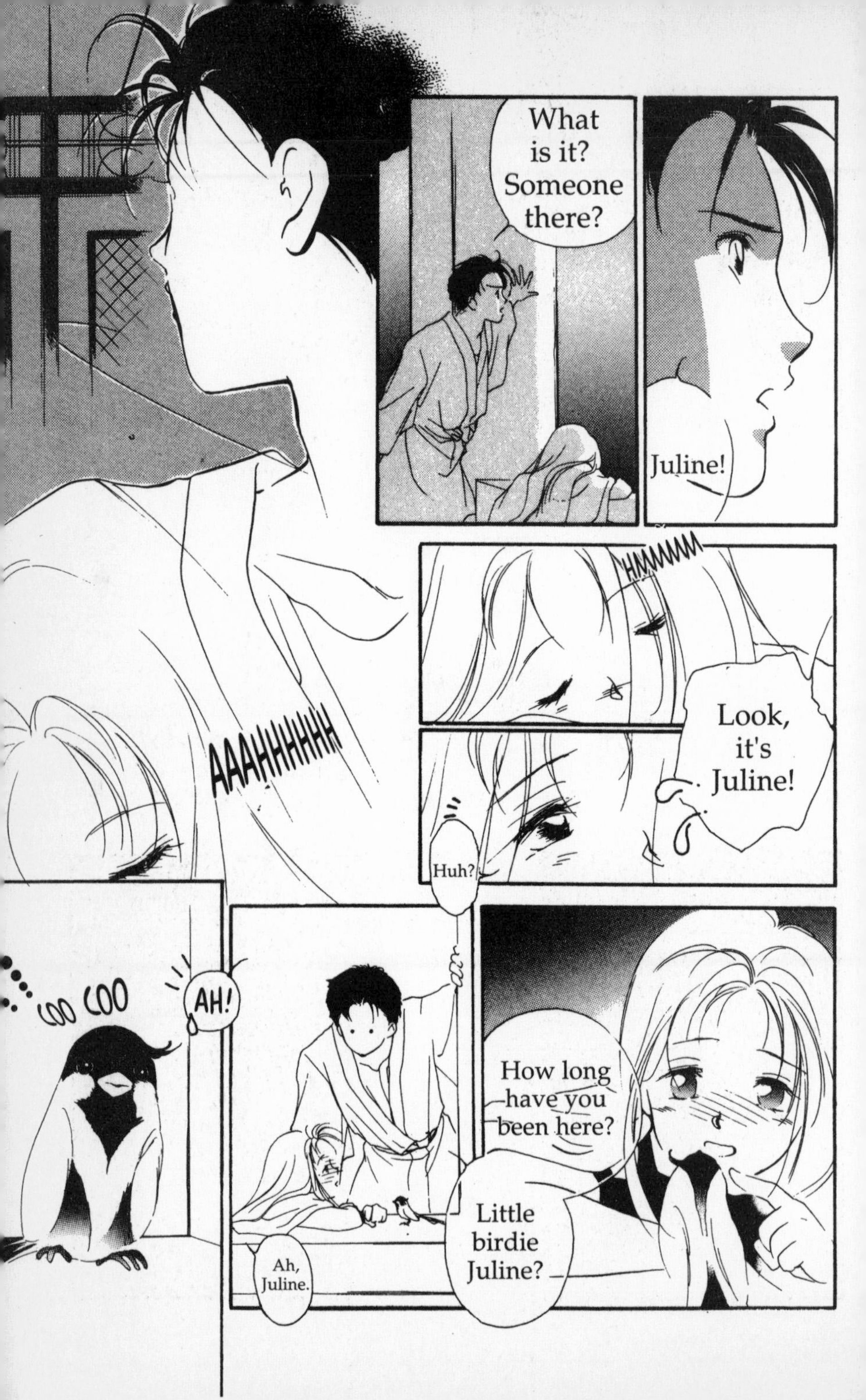
AAAHHHHHH
What is it? Someone there?
Juline!
HMMMMM
Look, it's Juline!
Huh?
...COO COO
AH!
Ah, Juline.
How long have you been here?
Little birdie Juline?

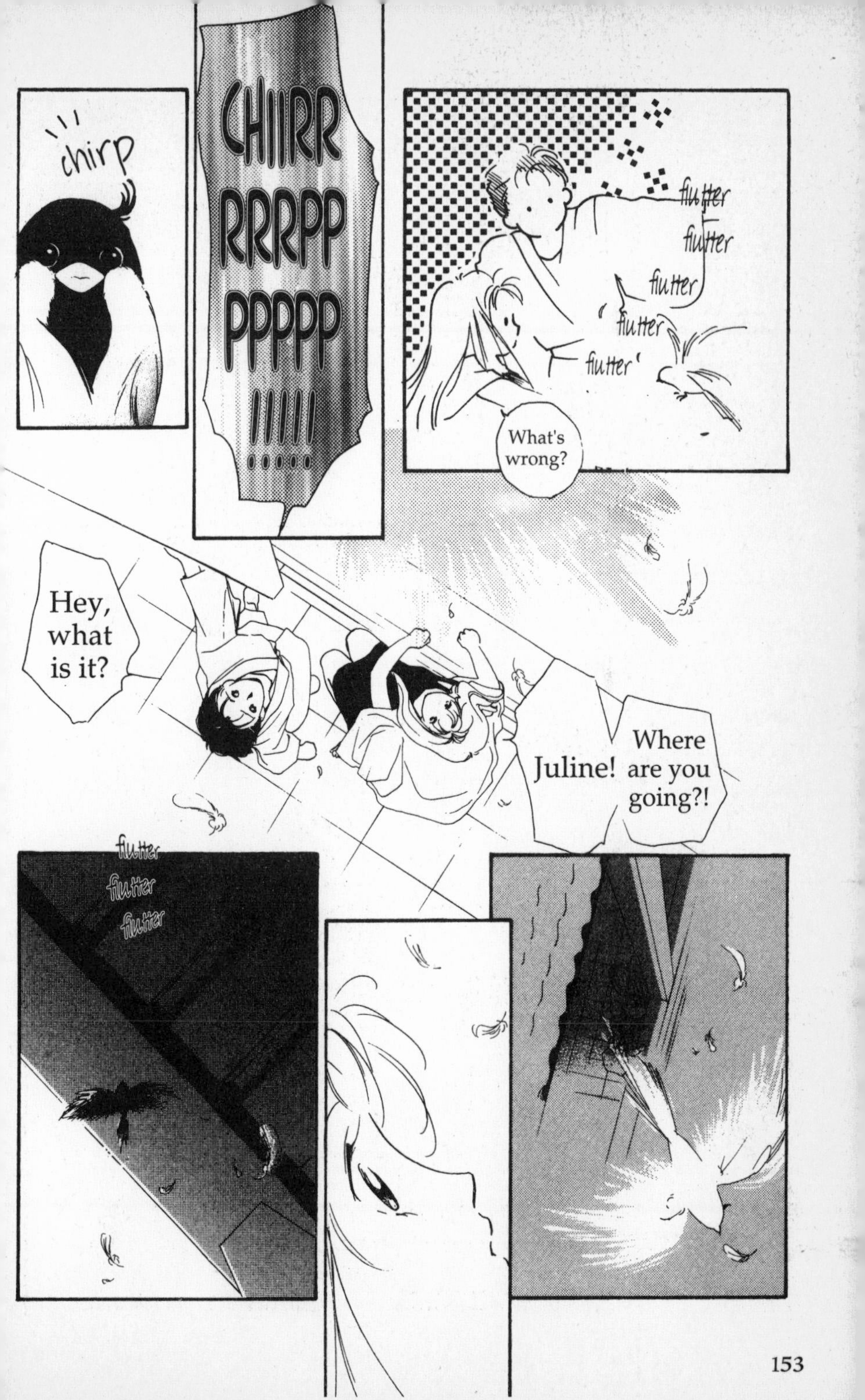

chirp
CHIRR RRRPP PPPPP !!!!!
flutter
flutter
flutter
flutter
flutter
What's wrong?
Hey, what is it?
Juline!
Where are you going?!
flutter
flutter
flutter

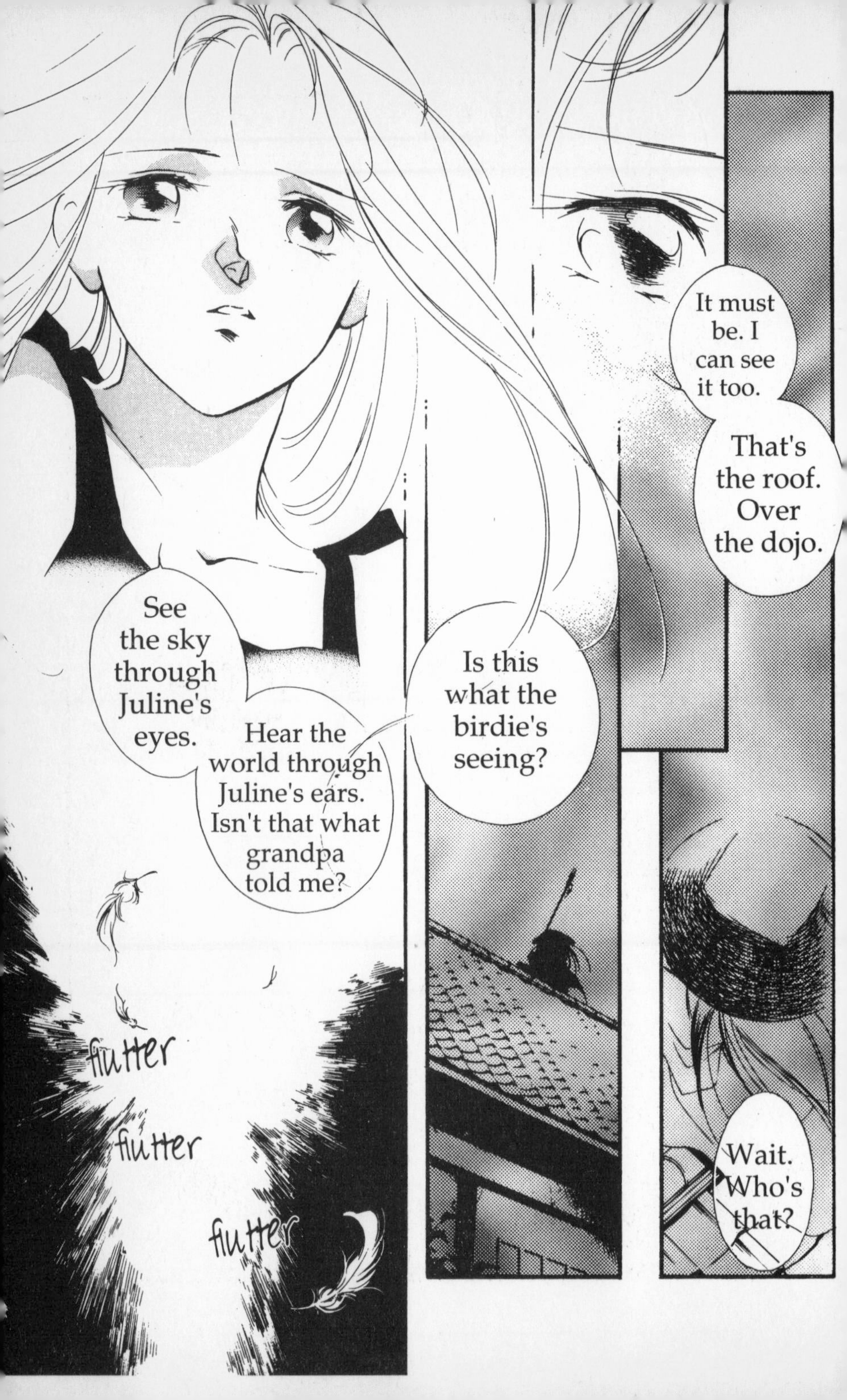
See the sky through Juline's eyes.
Hear the world through Juline's ears. Isn't that what grandpa told me?
flutter
flutter
flutter
Is this what the birdie's seeing?
It must be. I can see it too.
That's the roof. Over the dojo.
Wait. Who's that?

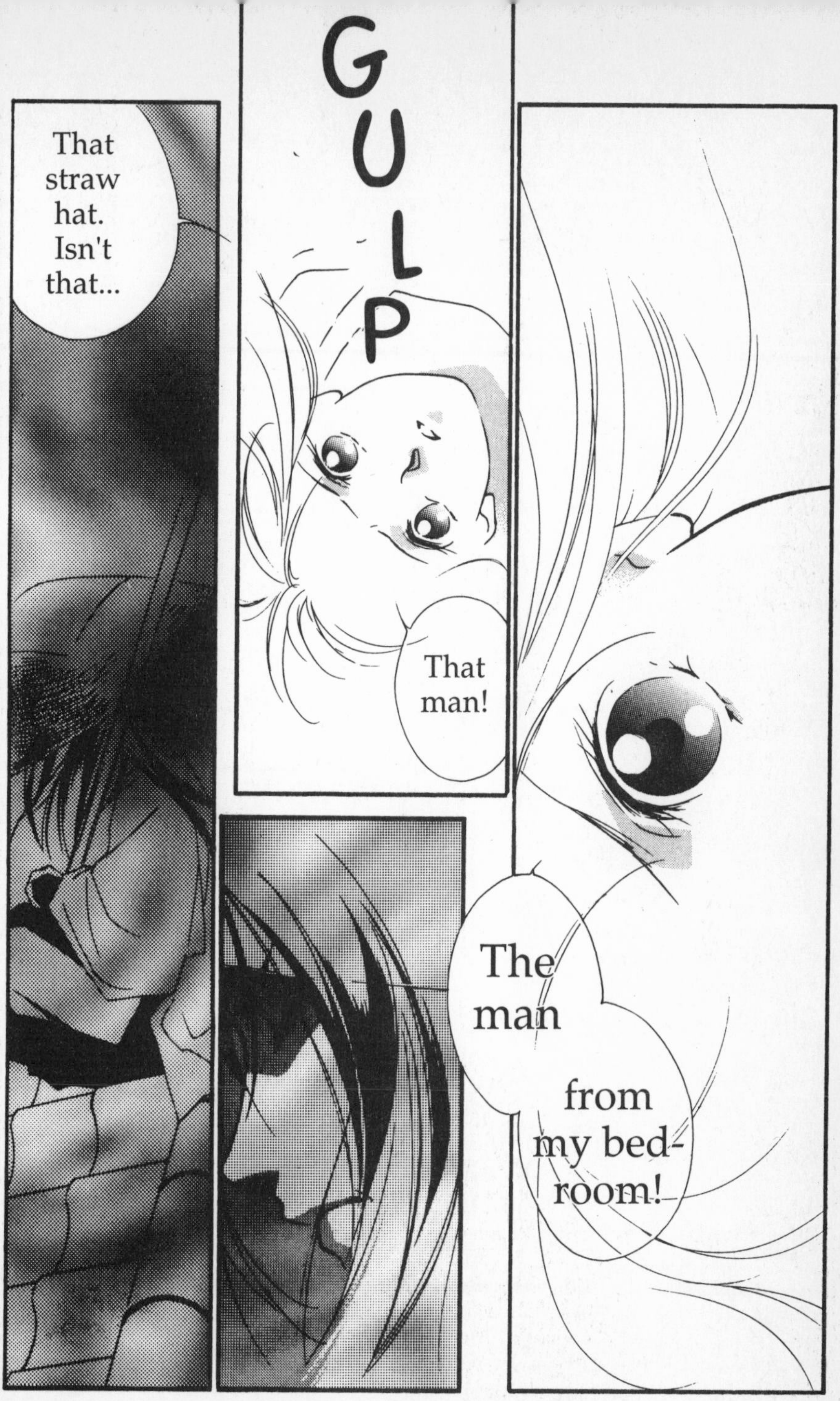
That straw hat. Isn't that...
GULP
That man!
The man
from my bed-room!

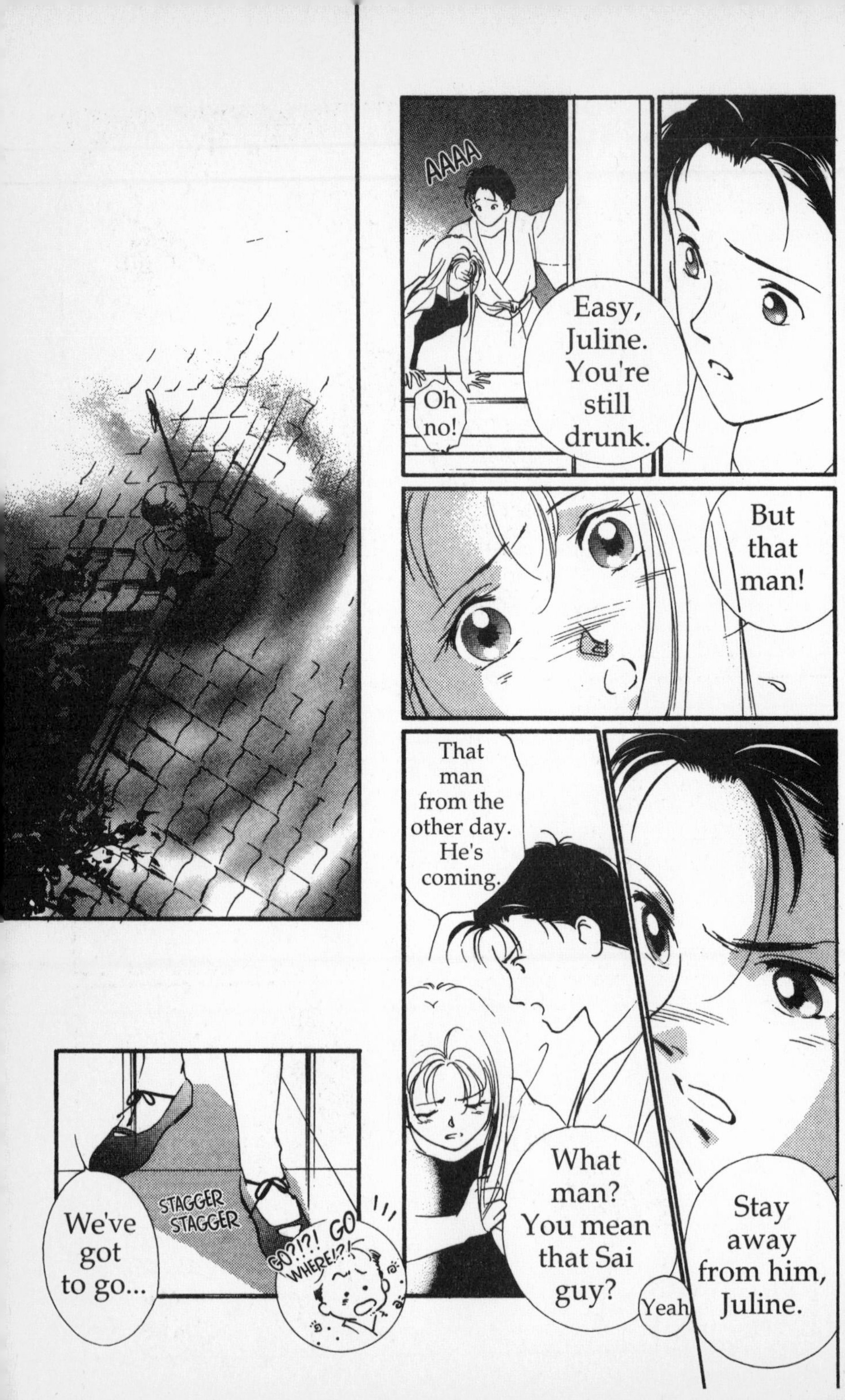
AAAA
Oh no!
Easy, Juline. You're still drunk.
But that man!
That man from the other day. He's coming.
What man? You mean that Sai guy?
Yeah
Stay away from him, Juline.
We've got to go...
STAGGER STAGGER
GO?!?! GO WHERE!?!

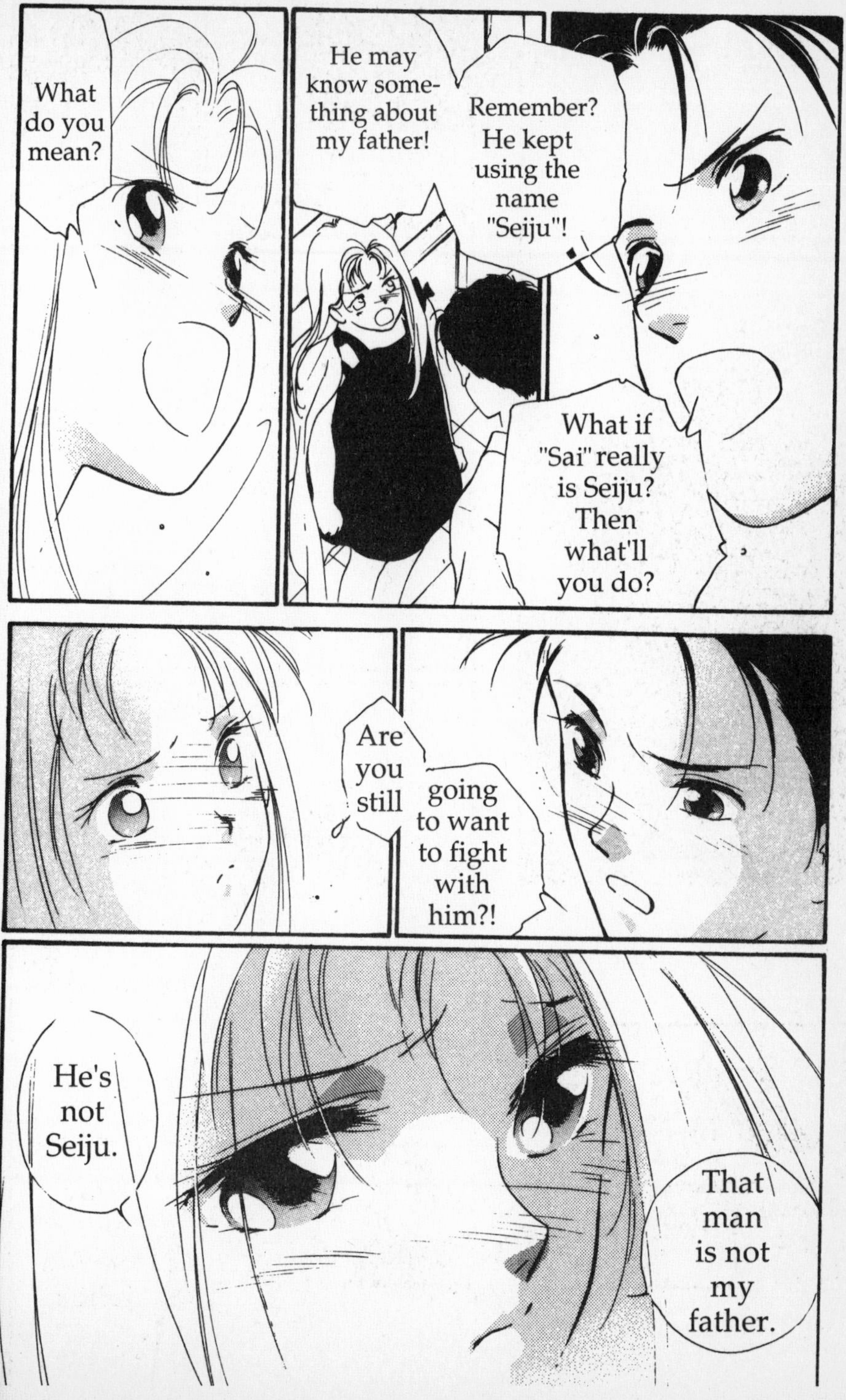

What do you mean?
He may know some-thing about my father!
Remember? He kept using the name "Seiju"!
What if "Sai" really is Seiju? Then what'll you do?
Are you still
going to want to fight with him?!
He's not Seiju.
That man is not my father.

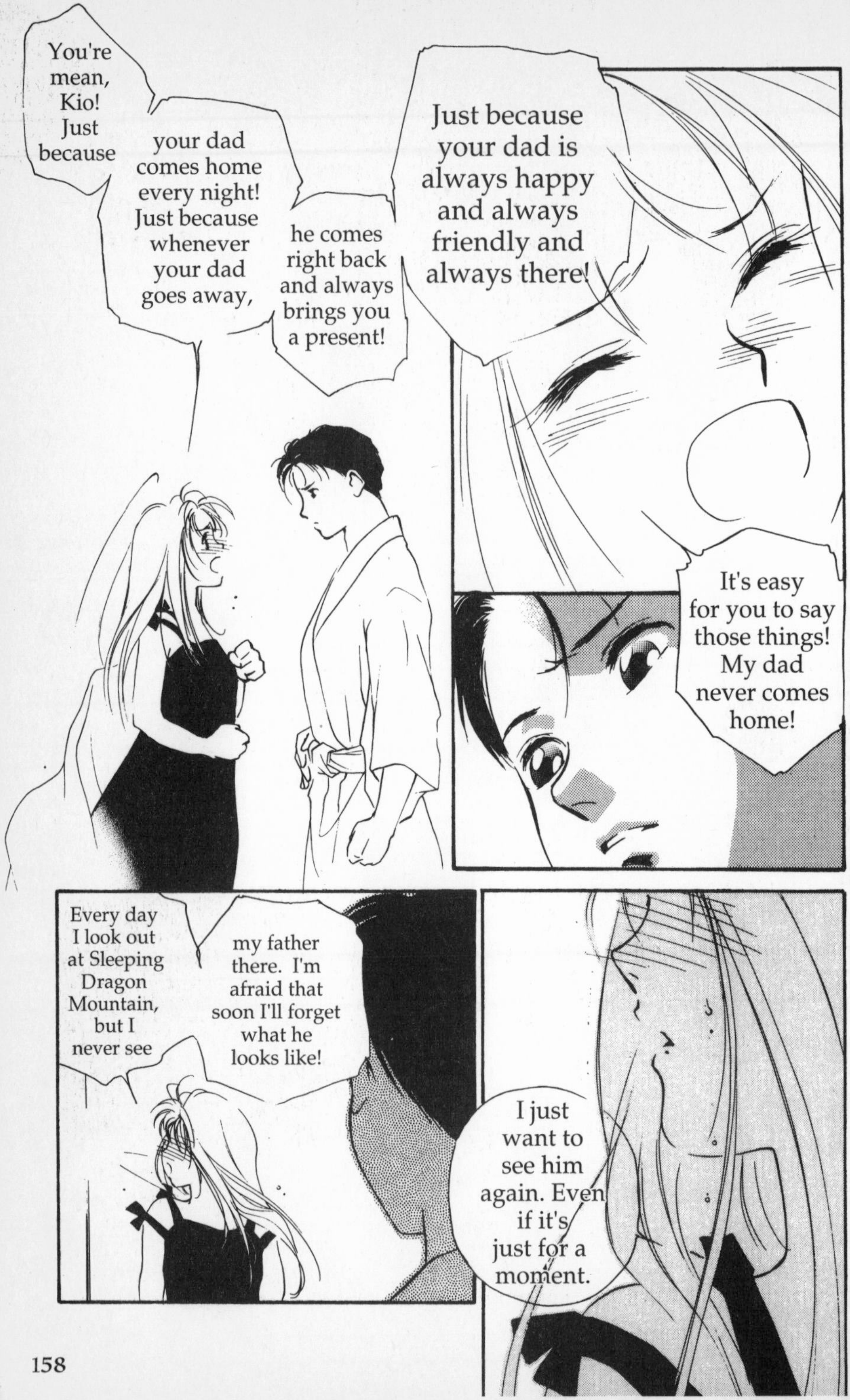

You're mean, Kio! Just because
your dad comes home every night! Just because whenever your dad goes away,
he comes right back and always brings you a present!
Just because your dad is always happy and always friendly and always there!
It's easy for you to say those things! My dad never comes home!
Every day I look out at Sleeping Dragon Mountain, but I never see
my father there. I'm afraid that soon I'll forget what he looks like!
I just want to see him again. Even if it's just for a moment.

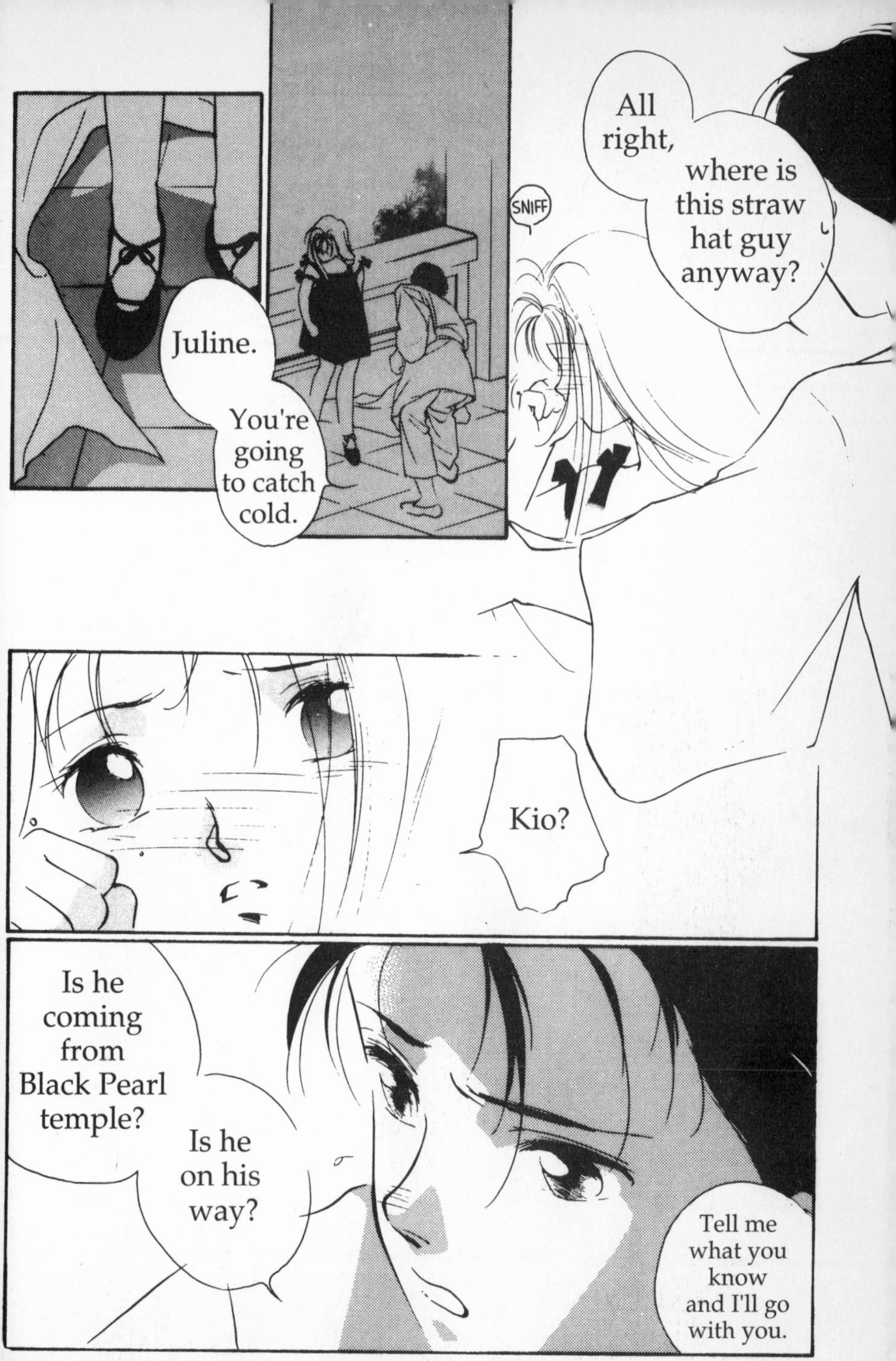
Juline.
You're going to catch cold.
SNIFF
All right, where is this straw hat guy anyway?
Kio?
Is he coming from Black Pearl temple?
Is he on his way?
Tell me what you know and I'll go with you.

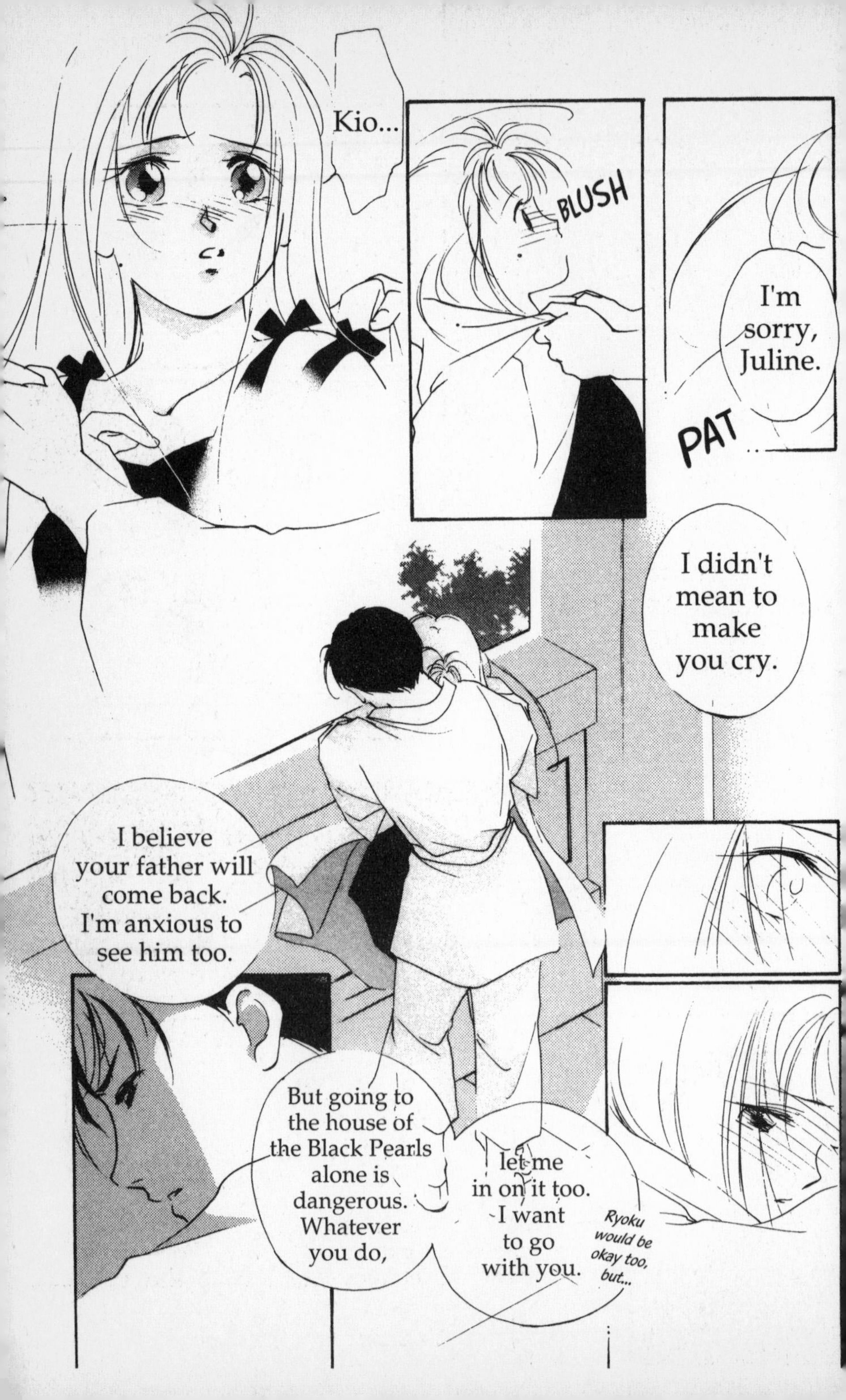
Kio...
BLUSH
I'm sorry, Juline.
PAT
...
I didn't mean to make you cry.
I believe your father will come back. I'm anxious to see him too.
But going to the house of the Black Pearls alone is dangerous. Whatever you do,
let me in on it too. I want to go with you.
Ryoku would be okay too, but...

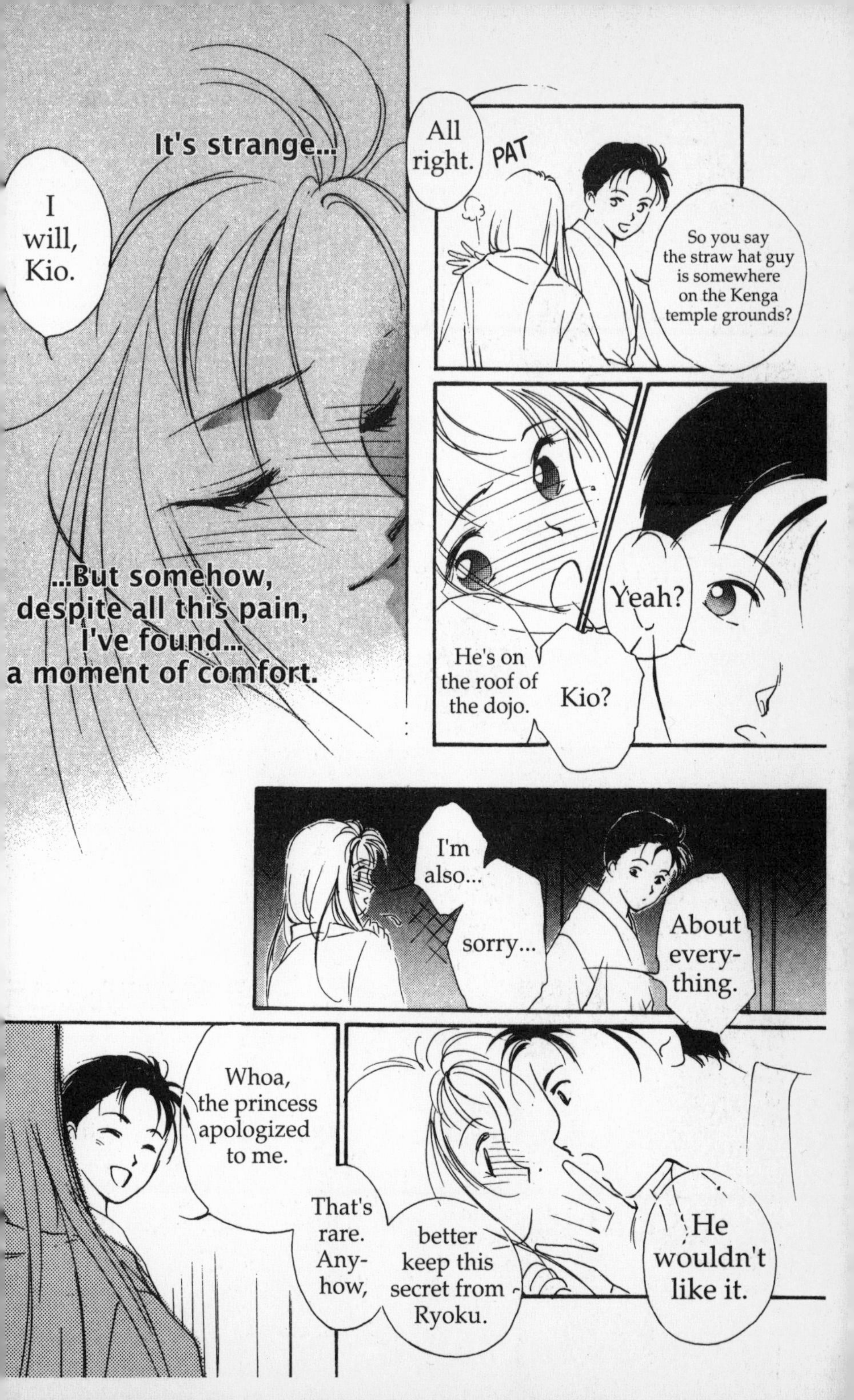
It's strange...
I will, Kio.
...But somehow, despite all this pain, I've found... a moment of comfort.
All right.
PAT
So you say the straw hat guy is somewhere on the Kenga temple grounds?
He's on the roof of the dojo.
Kio?
Yeah?
I'm also...
sorry...
About every-thing.
Whoa, the princess apologized to me.
That's rare. Any-how,
better keep this secret from Ryoku.
He wouldn't like it.

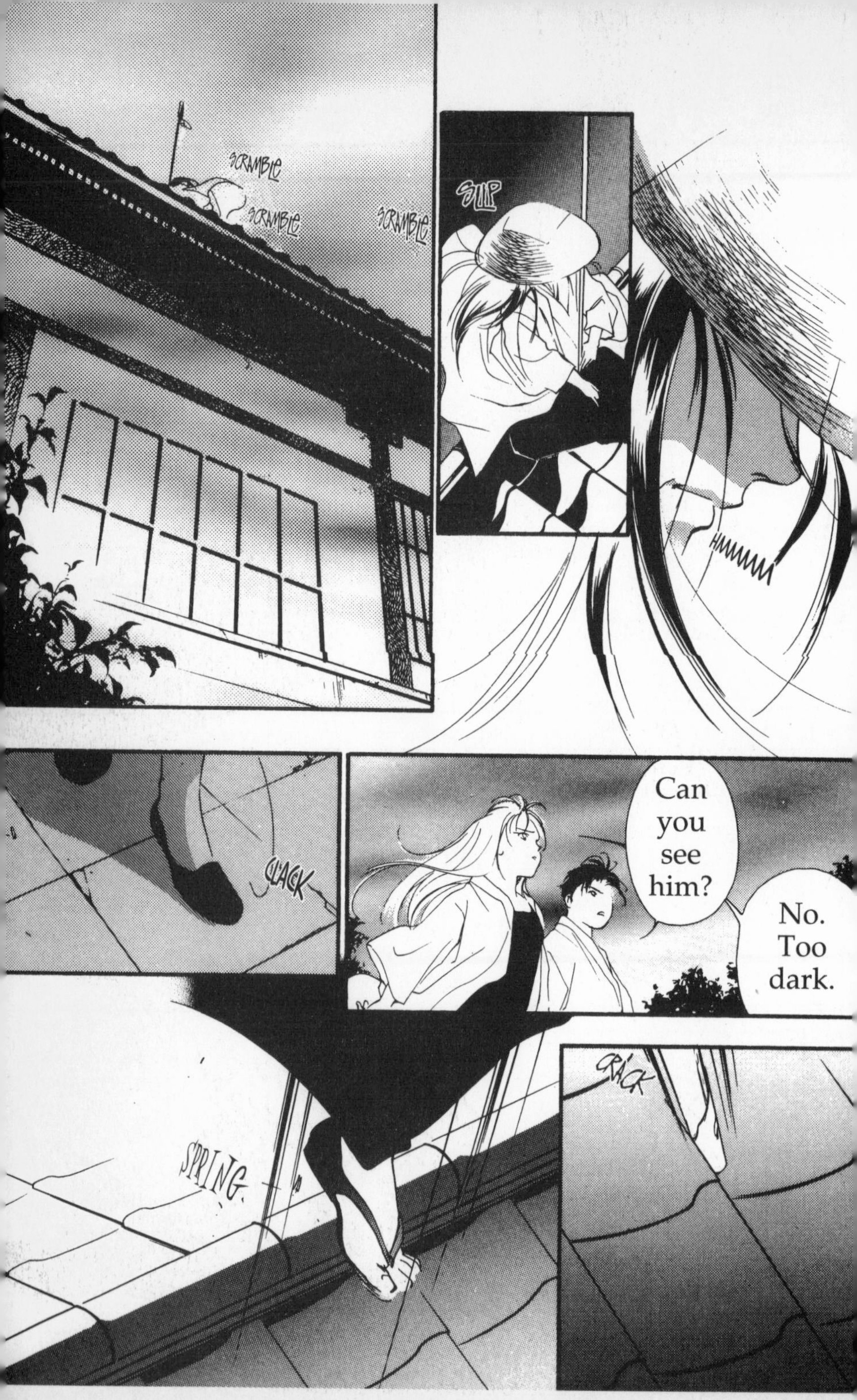
SCRAMBLE
SCRAMBLE
SCRAMBLE
SLIP
HMMMM
CLACK
Can you see him?
No. Too dark.
SPRING
CRACK

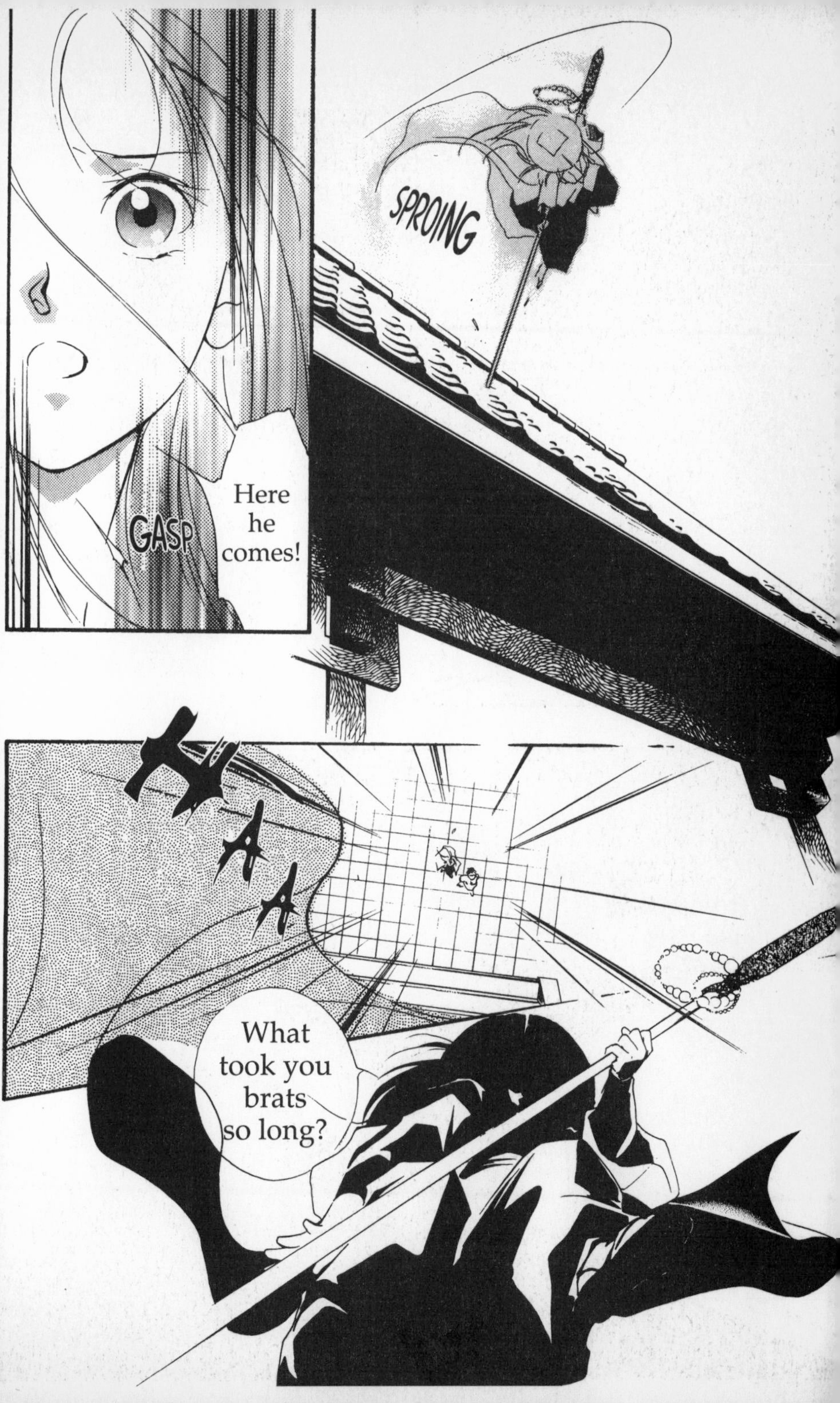
GASP
Here he comes!
SPROING
HAAA
What took you brats so long?

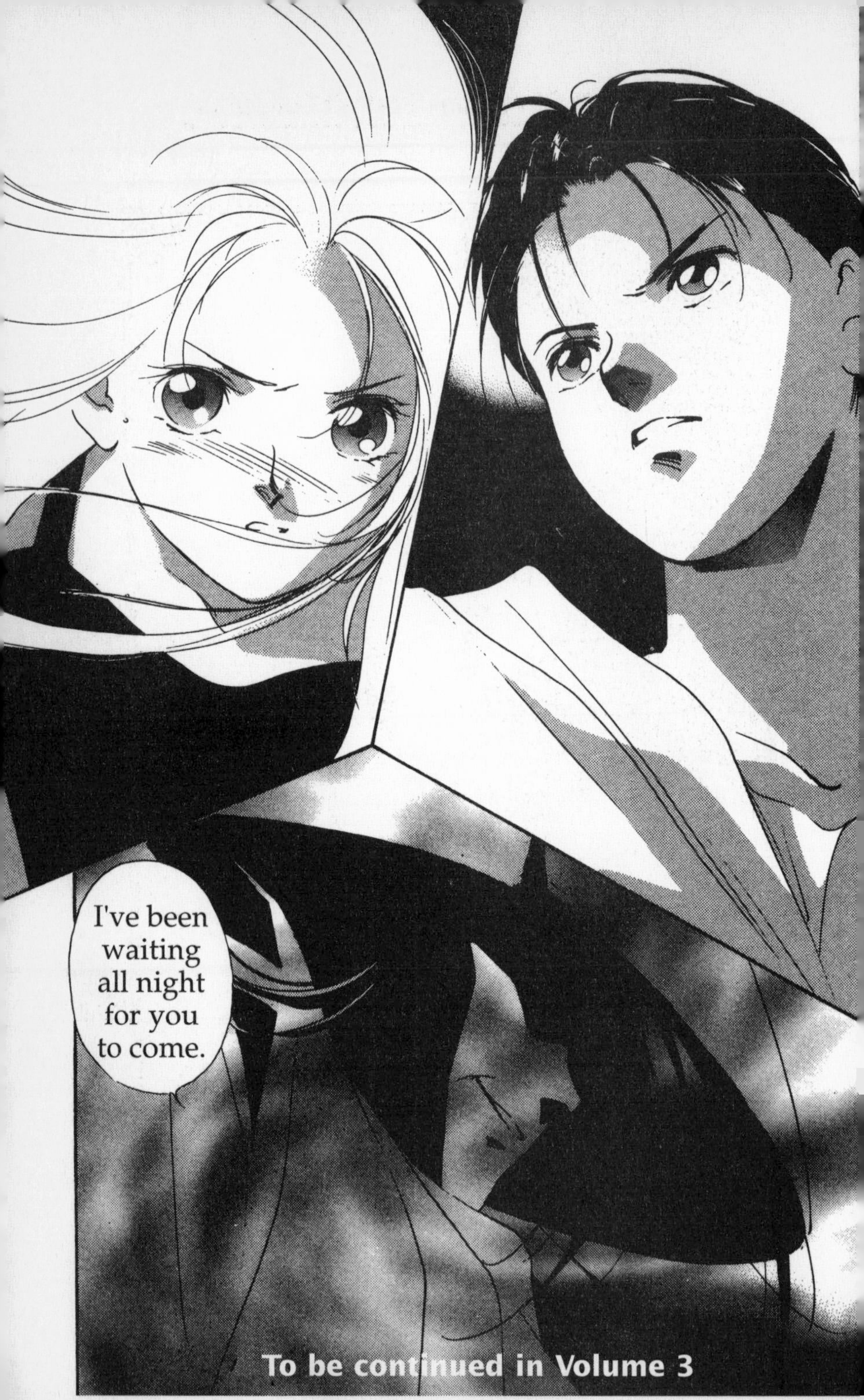
I've been waiting all night for you to come.
To be continued in Volume 3

Martial Arts Girl Juline---Portrait Collection

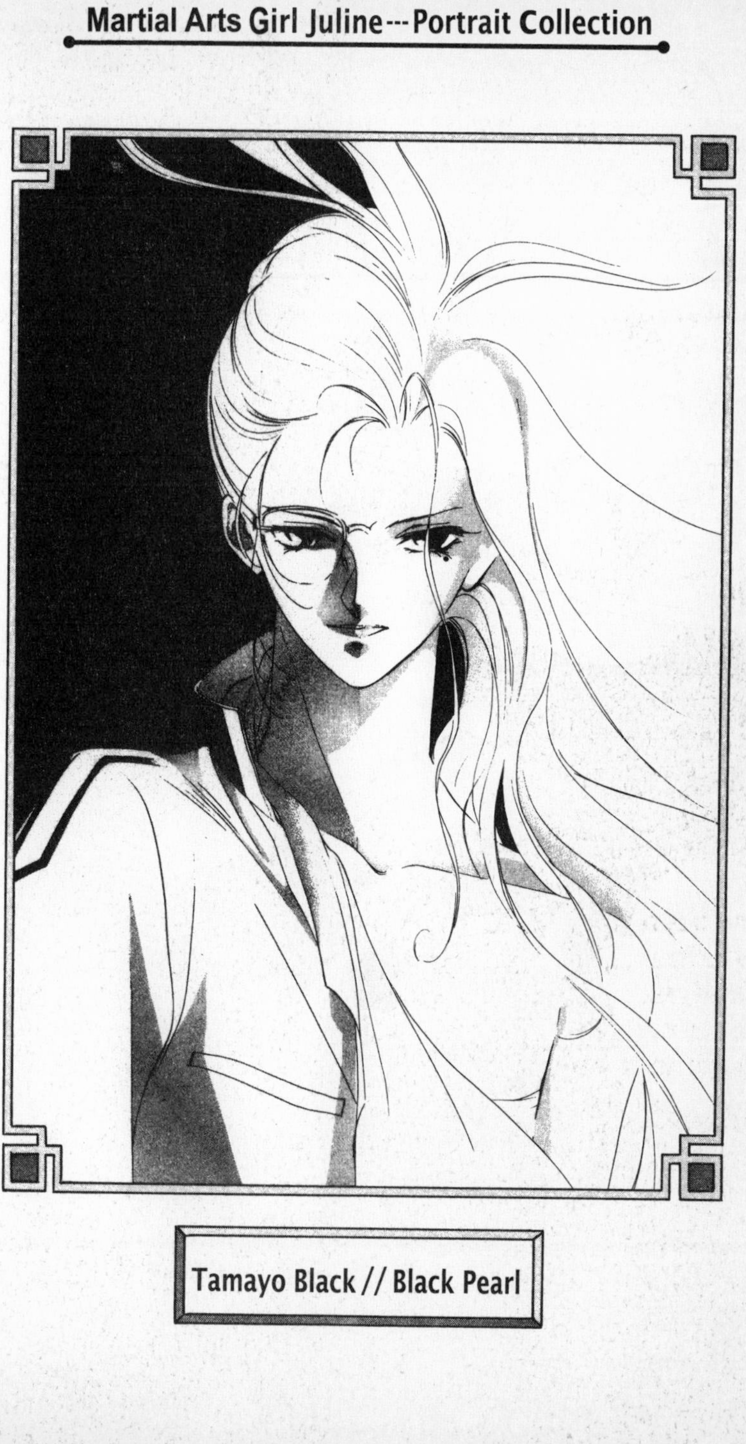

Tamayo Black // Black Pearl

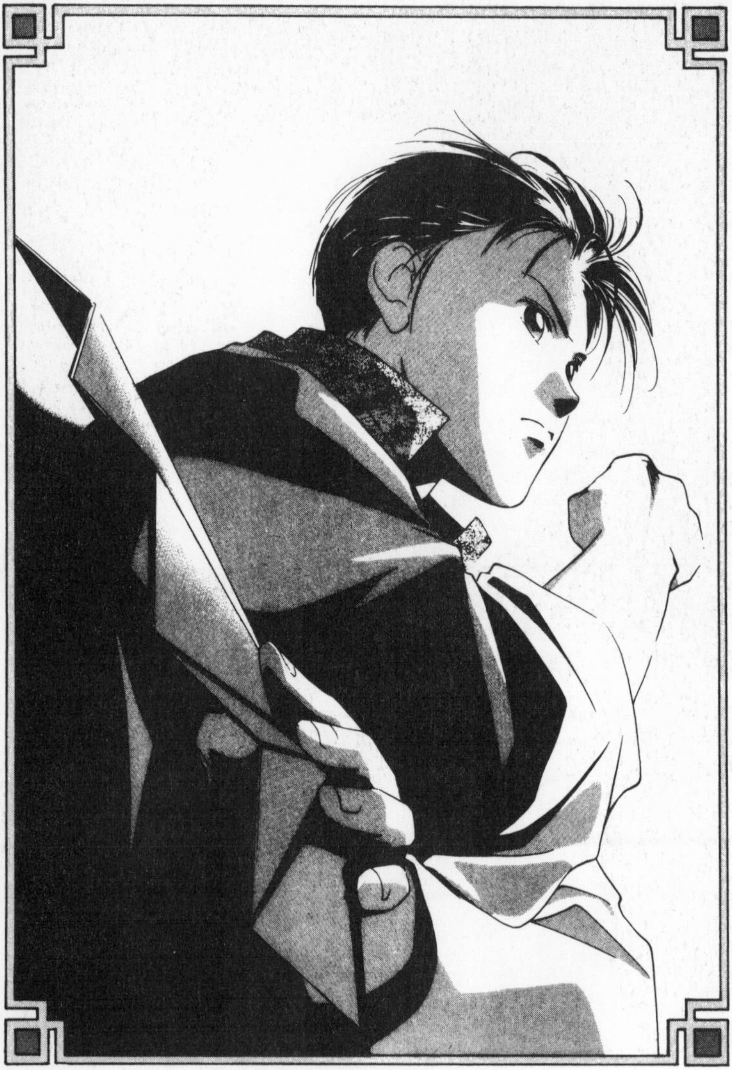

Kio

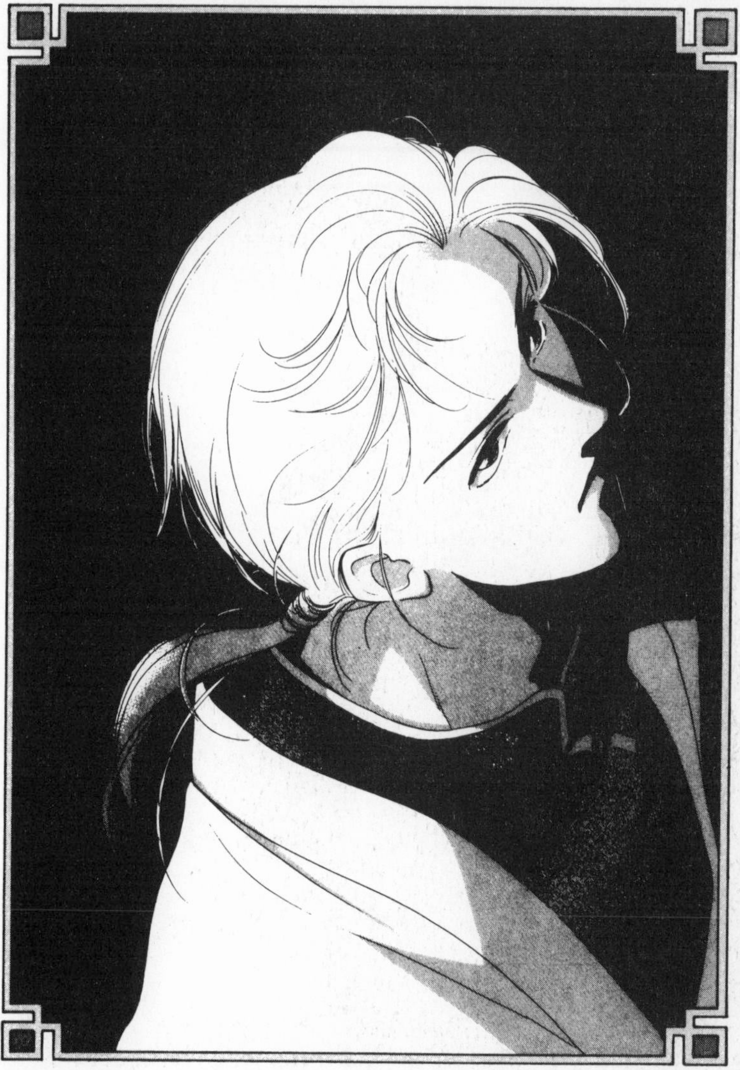

Ryoku